CW01498789

THE CONFESSIONS *of* SAMUEL PEPYS

Also by Guy de la Bédoyère

Samian Ware
Finds of Roman Britain
Buildings of Roman Britain
Towns of Roman Britain
Roman Villas and
the Countryside
The Writings of John Evelyn
The Diary of John Evelyn
Particular Friends: The
Correspondence of Samuel
Pepys and John Evelyn
Hadrian's Wall: A
History and Guide
The Golden Age of
Roman Britain
The First Polio Vaccine
The Discovery of Penicillin
The First Computers
Battles over Britain: The
Archaeology of the Air War
Voices of Imperial Rome
Pottery in Roman Britain
Aviation Archaeology in Britain
Companion to Roman Britain
Eagles over Britannia: The
Roman Army in Britain

The Home Front
Gods with Thunderbolts:
Religion in Roman Britain
Defying Rome: The Rebels
of Roman Britain
Roman Britain. A New History
The Letters of Samuel Pepys
The Romans for Dummies
Cities of Roman Italy
The Real Lives of
Roman Britain
Praetorian: The Rise and Fall
of Rome's Imperial Bodyguard
Domina: The Women who
Made Imperial Rome
Gladius: Living, Fighting, and
Dying in the Roman Army
Pharaohs of the Sun: How
Egypt's Despots and Dreamers
Drove the Rise and Fall of
Tutankhamun's Dynasty
Populus: Living and Dying
in the Wealth, Smoke, and
Din of Ancient Rome
The Fall of Egypt and
the Rise of Rome

THE CONFESSIONS *of* SAMUEL PEPYS

HIS PRIVATE REVELATIONS

Newly transcribed, selected and edited by

GUY DE LA BÉDOYÈRE

abacus
books

ABACUS

First published in Great Britain in 2025 by Abacus

1 3 5 7 9 10 8 6 4 2

A CIP catalogue record for this book is available from the British Library.

ISBN 978-0-349-14740-6

Typeset in Spectrum by M Rules
Printed and bound in Great Britain by
Clays Ltd, Elcograf S.p.A.

Papers used by Abacus are from well-managed forests and other responsible sources.

Abacus
An imprint of
Little, Brown Book Group
Carmelite House
50 Victoria Embankment
London EC4Y 0DZ

The authorised representative
in the EEA is
Hachette Ireland
8 Castlecourt Centre
Dublin 15, D15 XTP3, Ireland
(email: info@hbgi.ie)

An Hachette UK Company
www.hachette.co.uk

www.littlebrown.co.uk

In nature's infinite book of secrecy, a little I can read.

WILLIAM SHAKESPEARE, *Antony and Cleopatra*

Letters and writing . . . by these we may discourse with them that are remote from us, not only by the distance of many miles, but also of many ages.

Short-hand-writing by Characters [is] so frequent with us in *England*, and much wondered at by Foreigners; which hath a great advantage for speed and swiftness in writing; those who are expert in it being able this way to take any ordinary discourse *verbatim*.

JOHN WILKINS, *Mercury, or The Secret and Swift Messenger* (1641), and *Essay towards a real character and a philosophical language* (1668)

CONTENTS

INTRODUCTION

Music and Women I Cannot But Give Way To

The celebrated seventeenth-century English diarist and naval official Samuel Pepys (1633–1703) has been well served when it comes to biographies and editions of his diary. The principal appeal of that diary today is his relationship with his wife Elizabeth, the frustrations of managing his household and the servants, his pursuit of other women, and special observations, such as his descriptions of the plague and the Great Fire of London or being mesmerized by Charles II's mistresses. However, the true extent and implications of Pepys's self-confessed adulterous activity, including the coercion and sexual violence, and understanding his behaviour have often been glossed over in the past and sometimes evaded.

The central theme of the diary, kept from 1 January 1660 to 31 May 1669 and a masterpiece of introspection, is Pepys's marriage to a woman he loved but betrayed relentlessly with his obsessive sexual pursuits of girls and women. Among them were his own servants, his mistresses, acquaintances, and those he encountered by chance. His story is just as much their story, recorded in a way that has no equal.

Pepys outlived the diary by thirty-four years, but Elizabeth died just over five months after he ended it. His diary therefore represents only a small, though very important, part of his life, but covered about two-thirds of their marriage, which lasted from December 1655 to November 1669. The diary is consequently also a uniquely valuable portrait of the relationship between a man and a woman.

By focusing on this significant part of Pepys's remarkable life, the detail can be drawn out finally for a modern readership and seen within the context of the whole diary. He chose to record his private life in graphic and incriminating detail almost as if he was an independent witness to his own existence. He also ensured the diary survived as an integral part of his whole legacy. The habit in editions of the transcribed diary text of suppressing or sidestepping this key side to Pepys has denied us the chance to know him properly. After all, in the words of his own motto, *mens cuiusque is est quisque* ('the mind of each person is the person they are').[1]

Samuel Pepys was born near Fleet Street close to St Bride's church in London on 23 February 1633, and christened on 3 March, not far from where he conducted much of his adult professional and private life. During the diary years of 1660–69 Pepys knew some of the most exalted people in England, while dealing with official business in his capacity as an important member of the Navy Board.

The phonetic spelling of 'Peapis' in the parish birth register and in the record of an undergraduate incident at Cambridge in October 1653 as 'Peapys' preserves clues to its contemporary pronunciation. At the time 'ea' was pronounced 'ai', thus 'Paipes'. Other contemporary variant spellings expand the range of possibilities to 'Peppis'.

Pepys's forebears had once been farmers. By the seventeenth century there had been landed gentlemen, lawyers, and tradesmen, but large families and marriage settlements dispersed the Elizabethan Pepys family wealth. As a result, John Pepys (1601–80), father of the diarist and ten other children, was a modest tailor in London. His wife and their mother Margaret died in 1667. Samuel Pepys was the fifth child, but by 1664 eight of his siblings were already dead (seven of them by 1641).

Samuel Pepys began his education in Huntingdon, a reflection of his family roots but probably because it was considered safer during the Civil War. After the hostilities he was brought back to London to continue his education at St Paul's School where he won an Exhibition to Cambridge in 1650. In January 1649 he witnessed the execution of Charles I in London. He matriculated the following year, taking his degree at Magdalene College in 1654 during the Commonwealth.

Pepys took advantage of the opportunities which existed in London for men of ability and ambition with useful connections. He lived in a hierarchical, patriarchal, and deferential society and was dependent on the patronage of his cousin Edward Mountagu for his subsequent employment.[2] Pepys said he had benefited from 'chance without merit'.[3] In 1654 Mountagu, then on Cromwell's Council of State, employed Pepys as his secretary. This was a crucial step, but on 1 December 1655 Pepys made a disadvantageous marriage to the fifteen-year-old Elizabeth St Michel. Her father, Alexander Marchant de St Michel, was a Huguenot refugee, having converted from Catholicism, as well as being something of a fantasist and amateur inventor.[4] Pepys was enthralled by Elizabeth, so much so that on 27 February 1668 he compared the experience to being so overcome by music that he felt sick; Pepys lived life with an unusual intensity and self-absorption.[5] She brought him nothing but herself, and obligations to her family which Pepys observed throughout the rest of his life.

In 1656 Pepys was made clerk at the Exchequer to Sir George Downing, a ruthless diplomat and promoter of England's financial and commercial interests. Around this time and soon after their wedding, he and Elizabeth had separated temporarily, referred to later by Pepys as their 'differences' and without explanation (15 August 1663). Pepys did not like to be reminded of this unsettled period.[6]

Mountagu's appointment as General-at-Sea in 1660 and the man to bring Charles II home gave Pepys an entrée to the administration of the restored monarchy. Pepys was appointed Mountagu's secretary and invited to accompany the fleet to The Hague to fetch Charles. By June 1660, with Mountagu ennobled as the 1st Earl of Sandwich and made Vice-Admiral of the Kingdom, Pepys was promoted to Clerk of the Acts on the Navy Board. In this capacity he played an increasingly prominent role in the Restoration Navy. He sought in every way to elevate his standing through his professional contacts among Navy administrators, his financial dealings, how he dressed, and with whom he socialized.

On 23 January 1661 Pepys attended his first meeting of Gresham College, later to become the Royal Society. He was instinctively drawn to this group of like-minded men who shared his interests and his fascination with all that was new. Pepys regarded his membership as a privilege which elevated his self-esteem, but he was an appreciator and admirer of men like Christopher Wren, Robert Boyle, and Robert Hooke rather than being an innovator himself.

Pepys excelled as Clerk of the Acts. His responsibilities during the Second Anglo-Dutch War (1665–7) brought him into the heart of government. His social and professional contacts grew apace along with his personal wealth, much acquired through gratuities in return for favours. His success was founded on his ability to organize his private and business affairs. To both he applied his appetite for meticulous record-keeping and detail.

Pepys's diary ('my Journall') consists of about 1.25 million words contained in six volumes, covering the nine years and five months that he kept it. Its vitality and candid nature have served to diminish the rest of his life in the eyes of later ages ever since a bowdlerized and truncated transcription of its text was first published in 1825. He wrote it mainly in shorthand, using Thomas Shelton's Tachygraphy to do so. He must already have been competent in Shelton's system before 1660 though the diary manuscript shows evolution in his usage. Shorthand was convenient, but also facilitated secrecy which became most evident from 1664 until the end of May 1669 when he closed the diary. Pepys also enjoyed the process of composing and writing in shorthand. The pleasures of constructing shorthand words include the opportunities to be meticulous and imaginative, both of which would have appealed to Pepys. The shorthand is discussed in more detail below.

The diary's detail easily creates the impression that it represents a comprehensive account of Pepys's life during the period covered. It does not. His extant letters frequently refer to business and matters unmentioned in the diary entries for the same days. This has important implications for some of his other activities, especially his sexual pursuits. Despite this, anyone who reads the whole diary soon discovers that much of the content is repetitive. 'Up and to the office and there business until noon' or words to that effect is a familiar refrain, almost like the opening of a song from an unwritten musical based on Pepys's life. The 'business' is sometimes dismissed as an aside and on other occasions given in rambling detail. His references to naval affairs, though important to specialists because of the discussion of matters like weeding out corruption (apart from his own) and incompetence, are of little interest to most modern readers.[7]

PEPYS'S LONDON

Pepys's London crossed the City, much of which was destroyed in the Great Fire of 1666, from the Tower of London and then west down Ludgate Hill to Fleet Street and the Strand and on to Whitehall Palace and Westminster. Pepys travelled by foot or in a coach along the ramshackle streets with their medieval churches and half-timbered houses, grand new townhouses of the aristocracy, and the decaying pile of St Paul's Cathedral. He commuted along the Thames by boat with one of the countless watermen. Pepys went upriver to the villages like Chelsea and Richmond to the west, and downriver to the Navy dockyards and facilities at Deptford and Woolwich, and beyond to Gravesend, Rochester, and Chatham.

Pepys's London also included the King and Queen, the Duke of York, and court officials, their wives and mistresses, tavern keepers, rogues, servant girls, mendicant naval personnel or their wives who came to his office, obliging drapers and shopkeepers' daughters, prostitutes, artisans, watermen, and myriad others from all walks of life. London was noisy and reeked of countless odours, from the cesspits of private houses to the animal dung and human waste in the filthy streets, the smoke of numberless fires and hearths, and the smell of cooking, blacksmiths, and other trades. Relief was to be found in Hyde Park, St James's Park, the pleasure gardens of Foxhall or Gray's Inn, and London's nearby rural hinterland. The only sounds came from the weather, the clatter of carts and carriages, building and tradesmen at work, people, and animals. At night the streets were dark and dangerous, the only light coming from the moon, torches ('links'), and candles.

THE SHORTHAND ('TACHYGRAPHY')

Thomas Shelton's Tachygraphy was a popular shorthand method first published in 1626, remaining in use into the eighteenth century, and going through various editions. Despite its limitations, the essentials are not hard to master, especially the core symbols that represent the building blocks of letters, syllables, prefixes such as con- and per-, and suffixes like -ing and -tion (see colour plate section).

Medial vowels are not usually written in Shelton's system but are expressed by the positioning of the next consonant in the word. The vowel 'a' was indicated by placing the next consonant directly above the first one, 'u' by placing it directly below, 'i' by placing it to the right at three o'clock, 'e' above and to the right, and 'o' below and to the right. These subsidiary consonants are normally written on a smaller scale. Where the word ends in a vowel a dot was used to indicate which one, according to the same positioning rules.

Indicating vowels in Shelton's system. Left to right: 'water', 'hazer' (from the polyglot), 'Bag-well', 'office', 'coach', 'cosa' (from the polyglot; note indicating the terminal 'a' with a dot), 'much', 'about', and 'my wife poor wretch'. Note the dot after \, the sign for m, indicating the 'i' sound, hence 'my'. The 'e' at the end of 'wife' is not pronounced, so the word is written as 'w(i)f'. The word 'poor' is written 'p(o)r', and 'wretch' is formed phonetically as 'r(e)ch'. Thus: 'mi wif por rech'.

Pepys could and did make mistakes, sometimes correcting himself. He also adapted the system, as all shorthand users do. His earliest diary entries are written with almost naïve clarity, the signs large and well-formed with more reliance on longhand words than later. In the middle years of the diary his shorthand became smaller and more tightly packed, complicated by the incorporation of polyglot from 1664 and extra consonants from May 1667, mainly in passages referring to sexual activities (see under Polyglot below). As his eyesight deteriorated, he reverted to larger signs, but more messily executed.

Pepys primarily used the core alphabetic and syllabic symbols to form words that are the simplest and fastest to write in Shelton's shorthand. Many of Shelton's 300 or so arbitrary signs for specific words are harder to learn because they are used less frequently. The symbol 7, for example, represents 'hope'; thus · 7 means 'I hope', while ∞ is the sign for 'good'. Pepys was habitually inconsistent. For example, he variously wrote the word 'maid' as 'mayd' or 'mayde' in longhand, used Shelton's arbitrary single symbol (δ) which represented both 'maid' and 'made', or used the individual signs for 'm' and 'd' (see colour plate section) in the same configuration as for the word 'made'.

Key members of Shelton's market included people who wanted to record sermons. Many of his arbitrary signs represent words and names found in the Bible and religious texts. Pepys recorded brief notices of sermons, including how he had slept through some (for example, 14 June 1668). He often commented on the preacher's competence but was equally likely to be scrutinizing women in the congregation, helped by producing a primitive telescope ('perspective glass') from his pocket on 26 May 1667.

Pepys kept the volumes of his diary out of anyone else's sight and only once or twice mentioned its existence to anyone else. During the Dutch emergency of 1667, his family papers and the diary, or at least the first four completed volumes, were given to his cousin Sarah Giles to look after.[8] However, there was no system of 'encryption' as has sometimes been claimed, except for the extra consonants he started using in 1667 to obscure some words (see under Polyglot below).[9] Anyone who knew or knows Shelton, or had access to one of Shelton's manuals, would have been able to read it. However, any transcription is to some extent a reconstruction. Shorthand does not fully represent the spoken or longhand forms and is normally only completely comprehensible to the original writer, generally also requiring at least some knowledge of the context.

The limitations of Shelton's shorthand system contributed more to the literary style of Pepys's diary than is usually appreciated.[10] Transcribing the shorthand is one thing. Writing in that shorthand is another matter. This editor's long personal experience of using Shelton's method in everyday life demonstrates that one easily and deliberately subsides into choosing words that are simpler to write in shorthand. This results in more repetition and an almost Homeric use of stock phrases that serve as fillers and links. Pepys's famous line 'and so to bed' uses just five signs: – *S* 2 |ᵓ. It, or variants on, was used frequently to end each day's entry. His daily opener, 'up and to the office', uses six signs. Both phrases serve as if each was a single word. These helped open and close entries, while others such as 'by water' or 'by coach' linked topics and activities.

Echoes of Pepys's spoken voice appear because speech tends towards simple, familiar, and informal terms that are more quickly written in shorthand than carefully composed longhand text. They also reflected his idiosyncratic inversions where the adverb was relocated for emphasis, such as when he referred to his wife's companion Mary Mercer's breasts, 'they being the finest that ever I saw in my life' (19 June 1666). Many of the passages read more like conversations Pepys was having with himself. A good example is Pepys's agonized soul-searching of 25–26 October 1668. He produced a stream of consciousness during which he barely paused to draw a metaphorical breath.

Pepys's process of revision and writing up parts of the diary from notes, sometimes several days in arrears, helps explain various errors in the manuscript.[11] Writing in Shelton's system means ambiguities with certain words are inevitable. Similarities between certain symbols can mean mistakes are easily made when writing, causing confusion later. Reading the shorthand back can be tiresome, leading to the reader's eyes drifting between lines. Corrections have involved variant editorial intervention when trying to transcribe some passages. Inevitably, errors in transcription also occur.

The use of longhand names and words helped Pepys (and his posthumous editors) find his way around the diary text because the shorthand does not normally indicate capitalization. This practice diminished in the latter part of the diary. Pepys usually abbreviated the first name to an initial if he included it at all, and occasionally the surname. His colleague Sir William Penn was thus sometimes reduced to 'Sir W.P.'. Pepys often avoided longhand when it came to his female liaisons, but inconsistently. For example, when on 11 April 1666 his mistress Mrs Bagwell visited him, he spelled her name out phonetically in shorthand as '·bgwl wf' ('Bagwell's wife'), the preceding raised stop indicating an apostrophe or plural 's' at the end of a word. Sometimes he wrote her name in longhand.

Adult women without titles were routinely called by Pepys 'Mrs'. This did not denote marital status – in shorthand the symbol is that for 'Mr' but with the addition of a stop in front to represent the 's' of Mrs, the abbreviation of 'mistress'. It was thus a courtesy title for a woman or girl, whether married or unmarried, but was not applied to low-status individuals such as maids. Grown women were not usually referred to or addressed by their first names.[12]

Pepys never spelled out or even abbreviated his wife Elizabeth's first name in his diary or any other surviving manuscript, either in longhand or shorthand. This was probably to prevent her realizing she had been written about, should she ever have picked up one of the diary volumes. Nor do we know if he called her by one of the various diminutive forms. Elizabeth Pepys was, instead, in shorthand, the proprietorial 'my wife', 'my poor wife', or 'my wife, poor wretch'. Another possible reason was the coincidence of her given name with that of several of his mistresses, which he also usually avoided mentioning. Of the various Elizabeths he knew, Betty Howlett/Mitchell was the only one whose first name was routinely used by him, and then always as Betty. According to one study, Elizabeth was the commonest female name in the period at 13.6 per cent of the total.[13]

THE WOMEN OF PEPYS'S DIARY

The shorthand diary served as a private confessional. Pepys collected books, ballads, medals, and prints among other items. He similarly compiled a collection of his sexual activities by recording them. His relationships with women, especially his wife, form a major narrative theme, though his references to adulterous encounters or other pursuits were only occasional until the second half of 1663. From 1664 on they increased but varied in intensity until the end of the diary on 31 May 1669.

Without the diary we would know nothing about Pepys's marriage except when it began and ended and his wife's name, or anything about his adulterous activities (and much else besides). His friend Robert Hooke's sexual relations with his female servants show that Pepys was not alone (see below), but it is impossible now to know how widespread this was.[14] He made occasional hints that some other men he knew had similar inclinations to his, including his brother Tom (see his friend Peter Llewellyn's tale on 25 February 1661, for example).[15]

Pepys's interests ranged from the servant girls he molested or prostitutes he visited to Charles II's mistress Barbara Palmer, Lady Castlemaine, about whom he could only fantasize. In between were his wife, the women whose social company he enjoyed, including the actress Elizabeth Knepp and several others, and his mistresses such as Betty Martin and Elizabeth Bagwell.

Pepys delighted both in observing women and their company. He recognized this and his susceptibility. On 30 June 1661 he wandered in Gray's Inn walks 'humming to myself' while admiring the 'fine ladies' he saw promenading there. On 29 May 1666, against his better judgement, he instantly set aside important business when a party of his wife's friends arrived.

Pepys loved and was highly attracted to his wife, but also found her frustrating and embarrassing for her volatility, impulsiveness, and lack of education. If they ever celebrated her birthday (23 October) he never mentioned it. He resented Elizabeth's challenges to his authority, saying she brought him 'nothing almost (besides a comely person) but only trouble and discontent' (4 February 1665). He dismissed her as a fool in his notes for 17 June 1668. Pepys rowed with her frequently about what he considered was her profligacy and disorganization. He was easily angered, as was Elizabeth. He once struck her so badly in the face that he wounded her close to an eye (18/19 December 1664). She was forced to wear a dressing, the bruising being visible to the whole household. Pepys recounted this with a mixture of regret, contrition, and a sense that he had been entitled to be annoyed.

That was not the only time Pepys attacked Elizabeth. On 20 May 1663 he implied he was accustomed to hitting her more often than he recorded. At the time husbands were 'legally entitled to correct their wives with condign and moderate physical punishment'. Elizabeth, having dared to challenge her husband's authority, was 'overstepping the boundaries of orderly behaviour'.[16] Pepys was therefore asserting himself over his wife as an expression of his status and entitlement, as much to himself as anyone else. For the same reason he believed he was entitled to beat his servants for any infractions of what he considered acceptable conduct.

Despite Pepys's assiduous record keeping, no letter or note written by him to Elizabeth, or vice versa, exists now. He destroyed some of her papers on 9 January 1663 following a vicious row between the couple. She had read out to him a document written in English describing her unhappiness and loneliness. Appalled that it might be read by someone else, Pepys grabbed it along with her other papers that he believed would cause him 'disgrace' and tore most of them up in front of her. He then burned them, preserving only a very few (none of which survive). The incident, which Pepys characteristically recorded in detail, illustrated how concerned he was to curate his image in the eyes of others.

Elizabeth Pepys's occasional absences, mainly with or to visit relatives, often led to her husband seeking sexual relief elsewhere within a few days of her departure. This suggests Pepys was accustomed to, or at least wanted, relatively frequent marital sex and struggled soon after his wife became unavailable. Her serious period pains were another obstacle to conjugal relations, as was her recurrent abscess on her labia.

In his youth, Pepys regarded himself as a Puritan. In some respects, he tried to remain one. He thought Elizabeth's taste in clothes was frivolous and sometimes unacceptably risqué but was also attracted by some of her indulgences (he was no stranger to expensive clothing himself, as well as accumulating a collection of fashion prints).[17] On several occasions he mentioned being repelled by women who used cosmetics. Given the extent of his philandering, and the disgust he expressed for prostitution, this was a ludicrous attempt at maintaining a moral framework in an adult lifestyle that otherwise bore little trace of Puritan standards.

The hiring of his wife's new companion Deborah ('Deb') Willet in late 1667 led to a crisis. Pepys was confronted with a girl aged sixteen by whom he rapidly became sexually obsessed and, in another life, might have married. Although he did not explicitly compare Deb with Elizabeth, he clearly believed Deb had personal qualities that Elizabeth lacked.

BEHAVIOUR AND CONCEALMENT

Pepys's references to seeing the 'great tall woman' in Holborn on 4 January and 8 February 1669 who was 6 ft 5 in (1.96 m) tall, observing 'I do easily stand under her arms', indicates that Pepys was only a little over 5 ft (1.53 m) in height. Despite cutting such an unprepossessing figure (Charles II was over 6 ft), Pepys was strong enough to overcome women, most of whom were probably even smaller than him.

Although Pepys made very occasional references to the pleasure that he claimed his sexual partners experienced, his attitude was usually solipsistic. 'I did what I would *con ella* [with her]', or variants on, was as self-centred as his thinking about what he would like to do or had done *to* a woman. He was pursuing his own 'great pleasure', indifferent to or at the expense of the women's sensibilities. Having finished, Pepys normally carried on with the rest of the day's plans, returned home to his unsuspecting wife, or even collected her from somewhere nearby where he had dropped her off earlier. He sometimes described having sex with Elizabeth and how they both enjoyed it (for example, 25 May 1668), so he was clearly aware of the difference.

The specifics of Pepys's sexual encounters were usually described in oblique or euphemistic ways and often fell short of intercourse because of the fear of pregnancy. His interests included grooming young girls, usually maids, whether they were in his employment or not. By the time they were fifteen or sixteen he was coercing some into sexual activity. Pepys, however, avoided intercourse with girls of this age. He generally preferred his mistresses to be older, usually in their twenties, and married as an obvious cover. He was unaware that his bladder stone operation in 1658 had almost certainly left him sterile. He encouraged his most enduring and compliant mistress, Betty Lane (later Martin), to marry for that reason, but despaired at her choice of husband.

Pepys was therefore clearly interested in being able safely to progress beyond petting and masturbation to having intercourse with his mistresses, and undoubtedly did so when he could. He met varying degrees of resistance, for example from Elizabeth Bagwell, but he was also persistent and aggressive in his pursuits. Married mistresses meant the relationship could then carry on safely for several years, even if it was punctuated when the women became pregnant, as Betty Martin did (presumably by her husband). Pepys certainly found pregnancy an attractive feature. Fear of venereal disease probably also played a part in Pepys's preference for consorting with the same women.[18]

Pepys was sometimes attracted to other women who already had children, such as the vulnerable naval widow Mrs Elizabeth Burrows whom he also managed to inveigle into sexual compliance. Of a similar age to Betty Martin who was born in 1636, she was probably born in 1637 (see 20 July 1665, and Glossary of People and Places). Pepys made a point of describing her as remarkably pretty for a woman with a large family, implying that he normally regarded mothers in their late twenties or older diminished beyond his interest.

Pepys's extra-marital sexual activities took place at any time during the day or evening, and often on a Sunday afternoon. He proactively sought sex but also seized unexpected opportunities. On 29 June 1663 Pepys admitted how he habitually indulged in 'a bad use of my fancy with whatever woman I have a mind to' when his wife was away. On 24 September 1663 he simply lied, telling Elizabeth he was off to Deptford dockyard but heading instead to Westminster to find Betty Lane (later Mrs Martin). During the latter years of the diary he became less able to restrain himself whether his wife was away or not.

Pepys's meetings with girls and women were so frequent that he sometimes had to jog his memory when writing up the diary, jumbling the order of the day's events (20 May 1667 is a particularly good example). It would be naïve to believe the diary is either complete or also invariably truthful, especially about sexual activity. Some of Pepys's comments hint that his habit of frequent and secretive sexual relations with other women had begun before 1660. Perhaps this was why he and Elizabeth had briefly separated in about 1656. On 4 September 1660 he consorted with a neighbour's willing daughter, quoting the Roman poet Martial's phrase *nulla puella negat* ('no girl refuses') in his diary entry. On 6 August 1661 Pepys abandoned propositioning the landlady of an inn because her husband was on the premises. This suggests that only the failure made the occasion worth recording.

On 6 July 1667 Pepys described having had sexual relations with his mistress Doll Lane, Betty's younger sister, '100 times'. Although that was obviously metaphorical, his recorded visits to Doll are a small fraction of that number and must have been far more frequent than the diary entries bear out.[19] His reference to pleasuring his wife with his finger on 7 February 1669 explains that he was practised at the technique (never otherwise mentioned). He was worried that Elizabeth might wonder where he had learned it. We cannot make a reliable judgement about what he omitted, among which may have been occasions he could not bear to admit, even to himself. However, it is demonstrably the case that Pepys's record of his sexual activity is incomplete and possibly significantly so.

Pepys referred often to how he freely 'played with' the breasts of his maids and of other women, as if they were provided for his personal gratification. This reflected contemporary acceptance of a degree of physical familiarity that blurred boundaries. Some, such as the maids, had no choice. Pepys mentioned touching the breasts of his maid Susan on 6 August 1665 and said he had been doing so for some time but had never previously referred to accosting her. There were other examples.

There is no allusion to Pepys's sexual conduct in his other papers or in the extant writings of his friends and associates such as his fellow Royal Society members John Evelyn (1620–1706) and the experimental scientist Robert Hooke (1635–1703), all of whom held him in high esteem. This is scarcely surprising but London, especially the circles in which Pepys moved, and Deptford were too small for his behaviour to have been kept entirely secret. On 29 June 1663 he was seen from the street by an outraged passer-by through the window in a wine-house in Westminster *in flagrante delicto* with Betty Lane.

Moreover, since Hooke was accustomed to sleeping with his

servants, he was unlikely to pass judgement on Pepys. Hooke took the practice for granted, using the symbol ¥ for Pisces in his perfunctory diary to indicate that he had achieved orgasm(?) in the company of one or other of the women who worked for him. There is no evidence Hooke sought liaisons outside his household or that he exacted sex in return for patronage. He recorded an instance when a woman 'solicited' him for a position, but he refused her. Hooke supplied no graphic detail, his references to sex being restricted to two or three words. However, he frequently gave small cash gifts to some of his female servants in the manner of a gratuity for unspecified services rendered.[20] The most controversial aspect of Hooke's private life was the possibility of a sexual relationship with his niece Grace who came to live with him as his ward when still a child. By the time she was sixteen he was apparently recording having had sexual relations with her, once with the words *perfecte intime omne*, 'everything perfectly intimate'.[21] Unlike Pepys though, Hooke never married. When Grace died in 1687 Hooke was devastated.

Pepys's activities were far more wide-ranging. He immersed himself in the deception and thrill his philandering involved, enhanced by the fear of being caught. It is too glib to dismiss him as a 'sex pest' or 'sex offender' as he has been called in recent times. The distasteful and abusive aspects of his sexual conduct were real and are attested in his own words (the sole source of evidence), but in their extent and nature they were also consistent with the neuropsychological disorder of addiction.

Pepys undoubtedly became addicted to the excitement of the pursuit, the risk involved, and his forceful and dominant role. After the sex, he normally removed himself, frequently experiencing self-disgust or even loathing which he sometimes directed at the women concerned. He used the diary to help expiate his guilt by confessing what he had done, and to create a titillating record of the subterfuge and fleeting pleasure. His conduct resembled that of a substance abuser. Pepys also made frequent references to his excessive alcohol consumption and its embarrassing consequences, though he appears to have found this problem easier to gain some control over.

Pepys feared being spotted. He never referred to discussing his exploits with male friends. He did not, so far as we know, conspire with other men to seduce or coerce a woman. Nor did he ever co-opt anyone into assisting him in deceiving Elizabeth or bunking off work, except when he involved his clerk Will Hewer in trying to placate Elizabeth after she had discovered him with Deb Willet in October 1668. It is possible there had been other occasions involving Will, but these go unmentioned. The only other attested help came from male or even female relatives of some of the women concerned (see below), but that proves there were people apart from Pepys and his partners who knew what was going on.

On 1 August 1662 he avoided assaulting Sir William Penn's maid Betty precisely because he was scared that she might 'refuse' him and tell Elizabeth. When Betty Mitchell's mother Mrs Howlett arranged to see him on 14 October 1667 Pepys worried that she was about to confront him about his 'freedom with her daughter'. As it happened, she was only concerned about her son-in-law, to Pepys's relief. Pepys relied on a conspiracy of silence but on 18 June 1668 Elizabeth told him that she 'had heard' he had been regularly visiting the theatre and 'carrying people abroad' during her recent absence.

Before she caught her husband touching Deb Willet's genitals on 25 October 1668, Elizabeth was quite aware that he was interested in other women: 'my wife was angry with me for not coming home, and for gadding abroad to look after beauties' (2 October 1664). On 29 May 1666 Elizabeth interrupted Pepys's work to say that if he wanted to see the 'handsomest woman in England' he should come home to see their visitor.

The dysfunctional relationships Elizabeth had with several of their maids, some of whom she sacked, were probably linked to her jealousy of the attention Pepys paid them. Whether she realized how far he was habitually going is unknown, even if she perhaps turned a blind eye to casual physical contact between him and their female staff.

Pepys's predatory inclinations appeared in various contexts. Riding in his coach up Ludgate Hill, Pepys witnessed what appears to have been the initiation of a rape. He was titillated and envied the culprits (3 February 1664). Although some of the women he knew were willing, or at least acquiescent, partners (see below), Pepys referred to using coercion and physical force himself several times. For example, on 20 February 1665 he hurt himself with the exertion of raping Mrs Bagwell, whom he had also raped on the preceding 20 December ('against her resistance I did it'). On 13 November 1668 he confided in himself that he was still set on having Deb Willet's 'maidenhead'. His frequent references to 'towsing' and 'tumbling' his mistresses were euphemisms designed to play down the aggression he displayed during forceful sex, which he clearly found exciting in an era when it was almost impossible for a woman to make and sustain an allegation of rape.[22] Towsing had violent connotations. Shakespeare used the word once and only in connection with torture by the rack.[23]

Pepys benefited from the preparedness of some women to consort with him, whatever their motives. His money and influence were factors. On 23 July 1664, a meeting with the worldly-wise Betty Martin (by then aged twenty-eight and just married) took place: 'So spending 5s or 6s upon her, I could do what I would.' The money was in part spent on paying for a meal and drinks for her first (the amount was equivalent to a day's pay for a skilled London artisan). On 20 February 1666 Betty asked him for a substantial loan after the sex. He paid a shilling (about £9 today) to a prostitute for touching his 'thing' on 1 September 1668. Earlier that year, on 6 May, after assaulting his maid Nell, he rewarded her with the same sum, evidently equating the two scenarios in terms of their value to him.

Elizabeth Bagwell acted with the connivance of her naval carpenter husband William and his parents for the benefit of his career advancement. She was not alone. Once she was married Betty Martin had similar plans for her husband's future. On 12 August 1665 Mrs Bagwell's father-in-law, the Deptford dockyard foreman Owen Bagwell, facilitated a meeting between her and Pepys in the interests of his son's preferment, her mother-in-law Alice playing a similar role a few days later. On 11 August a waterman called Delkes had brought his married daughter to Pepys for the same reason, this time for his son-in-law's release from naval service. There were also women desperate to have their husbands' naval promissory notes ('tickets') paid, such as the widow Elizabeth Burrows. Many other such naval wives, whether widowed or not, were drawn directly into prostitution as the only means of supporting themselves.[24] Mrs Burrows may therefore have resigned herself to Pepys as a lesser evil.

Mrs Bagwell and Delkes's daughter were effectively being prostituted by their relatives. Elizabeth Bagwell resisted some of Pepys's advances to begin with, but she eventually acquiesced, probably feeling obligated to accede to the demands her husband and his family made of her. Key members of their families had spotted Pepys's power, and that he was susceptible to temptation. If so, his reputation had probably preceded him. It appears from the diary that the Bagwells had been working on Pepys for some time before any sexual activity occurred. If so, then once revealed, his nature was exploited. Elizabeth Bagwell was still soliciting his help for her husband over twenty years later (see Epilogue) though after the diary was closed on 31 May 1669, we know nothing about what she had conceded, if anything, in return in the intervening years.

Aspects of Pepys's personality and appearance probably helped some women find him attractive, at least initially. We can only speculate, for example, about the effect of his speaking voice but we know he could sing. The actress Elizabeth Knepp seems to have found him engaging company, despite his wandering hands. One woman appeared actively to seduce him, though of course we only have Pepys's version of events. Judith Penington, the unmarried sister of the Quaker leader Isaac Penington, was approaching forty when Pepys encountered her socially in late 1665. She was thus far older than any other woman he is known to have had physical relations with, and apparently sought nothing else from him either. Pepys was astonished by her uninhibited flirting, given her background and class. Her brother was concerned about her irreligious behaviour (see Glossary of People and Places).

Pepys was fascinated by the blatant decadence of Charles II's court, which he often described with prurient and hypocritical disapproval. His origins were betrayed by his bourgeois attempts to conceal his activities and preserve his professional standing. He often made oaths to show restraint and congratulated himself for his self-control. He soon broke the oaths, usually to his shame, and gradually abandoned the practice. There is little doubt that Elizabeth Pepys soon spotted the real threat to her marriage that her husband's infatuation with Deb Willet posed. After Elizabeth caught him with her on 25 October 1668, Pepys was wracked with remorse but remained unable to control his inclinations (see Chapter 10 and Epilogue).

Pepys owned and read a copy of Thomas Ridley's 1607 *A View of the Civil and Ecclesiastical Law*. Ridley classified adultery as a form of 'filthyness' and a cause of divorce, so Pepys was fully aware of the risk of public disgrace and opprobrium.[25] Yet he habitually succumbed to temptation and then tormented himself.

Thomas Edgar, the probable author of a book on women's rights published in 1632, bemoaned in a section on rape the futility of women making marital vows 'when men have so many millions of ways to make them break them'.[26] He described how if 'sweet words, fair promises, tempting, flattering, swearing, lying' failed to 'beguile the poor soul', then 'rough handling, violence and plain strength of arms' would be employed 'to make them prisoners of lust's thieves . . . so drunken are men with their own lusts'. Edgar believed that were it not for the law, women aged from twelve years upwards would be unable to escape 'ravishing' at all. However, the law was relatively ineffectual when it came to protecting women. Edgar's comments reflected a contemporary culture in which Pepys, despite his guilt and subterfuge, operated with relative impunity, even though he feared being exposed.

POLYGLOT

Pepys's guilt and love of secrecy led to his use of foreign words, usually written in shorthand, in his diary accounts of sexual activities. This began in January 1664, initially only with French and developing into a polyglot. He normally limited himself to individual words and short phrases used in sentences that were otherwise English. This occluded his activities while simultaneously recording them in a daring and suggestive way.

Pepys was competent in French, Spanish (his surviving library contains 185 Spanish works), Latin, and some Greek. He understood Portuguese and followed a Portuguese sermon on 17 March 1667. There are occasional instances of possible Portuguese words, but there were more similarities then between Spanish and Portuguese than today. The shorthand's limitations mean it is not always possible to be sure which form he intended. He sometimes included words in Italian as well as Latin and Greek. Cotgrave's 1611 French–English and Percivale's 1623 Spanish–English dictionaries, both of which Pepys knew, have been used to help with transcriptions and identify suitable translations.[27]

Pepys never explained why he started using the polyglot, though by his time there was already a developed interest in polyglot dictionaries.[28] A clue lies in the diary for 2 August 1660 when Pepys used the French *chose* ('thing') while referring to the painful conditions Elizabeth suffered from. It is likely that was how the half-French Elizabeth referred to her genitals when speaking to her husband. Unfortunately, we have virtually no reported speech of hers, but Elizabeth was probably given to using French in her conversation, especially for delicate matters. She was not alone.[29] On 9 January 1663 Pepys recorded that she had written to him in English, implying she would not normally have done so. It is easy to see then why Pepys might have been accustomed when talking with her to substituting certain English words with French ones, adapting this later in his diary by utilizing a wider range of languages, especially Spanish. The polyglot of course did not of itself conceal what he had written, but by writing it in shorthand he achieved a modest additional layer of security.

The polyglot may reflect a real increase in Pepys's sexual escapades, especially during the Plague Year of 1665 when the fragility of life became painfully apparent. After his bladder stone operation in 1658 he already knew how lucky he was to be alive, compounded by the death of his younger brother Thomas in March 1664 (and the deaths of several other siblings). As his records of sexual behaviour became more frequent, so did the polyglot.

By May 1667, surely inspired by the work of the mathematician, savant, and clergyman John Wilkins (1614–72), Pepys had started inserting additional consonants into certain English words in the shorthand to obscure these passages, in addition to the polyglot. Pepys greatly admired the polymath Wilkins, as he recorded after walking to Redriffe in his company on 1 May 1665; by 16 March 1669 he referred to him as 'my friend'. Wilkins was a founding Fellow of the Royal Society and was made Bishop of Chester in 1668.

Pepys owned at least six of Wilkins's books, including a 1641 edition of *Mercury, or The Secret and Swift Messenger* which discussed various techniques for the encryption of text and its speedy transmission. Wilkins explained how among other ways 'augmenting words with the addition of other letters . . . and interposing G and K, P, T, R etc' could be used to obscure the meaning.[30] Pepys applied the method by using the symbols for l, m, n, and r in selected shorthand English words, for which the consonant-based Tachygraphy made this a suitable adaptation. This way, for example, 'girl' became 'gimerl', and 'maidenhead' became 'maladimen hered'.

Thereafter Pepys fluctuated between this method of disguising his text and using polyglot in passages referring to his sexual and related activities. Wilkins also recommended 'doubling the Vowels that make the Syllables'. This refinement, however, was obviously impossible in a shorthand system that does not normally show the vowels. With only a very few exceptions such as 6 August 1668, Pepys did not apply extra consonants to polyglot words. Fortunately, he did not adopt some of the other encryption techniques described by Wilkins, which included the inversion of words or letter substitutions.

This highly likely explanation for Pepys's new habit appears to have gone unnoticed until now. On 11 January 1666 Pepys visited Wilkins at his home and was overwhelmed by the 'sober' and 'ingenious' company he was welcomed into. This included news of Wilkins's forthcoming new book on creating a universal written language which excited Pepys.[31] He may well have already possessed Wilkins's *Mercury, or The Secret and Swift Messenger*, but might have been given a copy on 11 January or bought it afterwards.

The polyglot words and phrases usually served as exact substitutes for their English equivalents. They represented continuations of the surrounding English text. The shorthand was designed for English; Pepys had to think more carefully about how to construct foreign words and phrases phonetically.[32] The diary manuscript for 15 December 1664 shows that when Pepys included a French phrase, the shorthand signs became larger and more spaced as he tried to form words that he never normally wrote.

Pepys faced problems with writing shorthand French because of the language's diphthongs and digraphs, such as *ou* or the ending -*ais*. Spanish is easier to represent in Shelton's system (a statement of fact) than French because it only has five vowel phonemes and this may partly explain Pepys's increasing use of it. *Tocar* ('touch') is much simpler and less ambiguous to write in shorthand than *toucher*, for example. It is also occasionally not possible to distinguish shorthand English from non-English forms.

Transcribing and then translating the polyglot is often challenging because of the phonetic spellings and Pepys's intentional or accidental imprecision. Lateral thought is often required to work out the meaning because variant readings are possible. The polyglot in his entry for 23 August 1665 is one of the most complicated to understand because, exceptionally, it included his botched attempt at two pairs of Greek words, one in shorthand and one in longhand.

Pepys used the polyglot erratically. Some words or phrases were used repeatedly, others occasionally or even only once (see Glossary of Polyglot). He applied the usefully vague English 'thing' to sexual acts, orgasms, or genitals, substituting this in the polyglot variously with the French *chose*, the Spanish *cosa*, or, on a couple of occasions, the Greek *pragma*. The phrase *hazer me hazer*, in the contemporary Spanish spelling, appears often. Pepys employed the second *hazer* as a euphemism for ejaculate or orgasm. Since on some occasions, for example 9 April 1668, he used the English wording 'make myself do', that is how *hazer me hazer* and equivalents have normally been translated here. French and Latin words for 'make' or 'do' were sometimes substituted. These polysemous terms helped disguise the details of the sexual acts concerned. He was unusually explicit on 21 December 1666 with 'so as to make *mi mismo espender*' ('so as to make me spend myself').

The evasive phrase 'do almost what I would with her' was a variant on 'I did what I would *con ella*'. Both have a rhythmic alliterative, even metrical, tone as does *hazer me hazer*. They had joined the other stock phrases that Pepys utilized in the diary. They also reflect how habituated Pepys became to his adulterous episodes. Reduced to a few shorthand signs, these passages were squeezed in between his other business of the day.

EDITIONS OF THE DIARY[33]

Despite some mistakes and other minor issues like smudges and omissions, Pepys's shorthand is generally legible and clearly written. His cursive hand and faintness caused by his pen running dry or the passage of time can make some shorthand signs hard to read. Transcriptions of Pepys's diary are not direct copying because they involve a great deal of work expanding the shorthand. However, they lack the independent creativity of composition or translations. In Pepys's case that only applies to the polyglot, but until very recently no translations of any of those passages have appeared in print.

The catalyst for publication was the appearance of John Evelyn's diary. Evelyn had an enduring posthumous reputation thanks mainly to his book *Sylva*, a Royal Society publication on arboriculture. His longhand diary was published from a bowdlerized selection made by the antiquarian William Bray in 1818 to great acclaim and appeared in many further editions. However, the original had no contentious passages. Bray's unsatisfactory text was not superseded until 1955 by Esmond S. de Beer's definitive edition.

By 1818 in Cambridge a plan was also forming to publish Pepys's diary. A student called John Smith was given the challenging task to transcribe the text. It is usually believed that Smith, later the Reverend, was unaware that the diary was written in Shelton's system even though a copy of Shelton was still in the Pepysian Library. Whether or not that was true, Smith transcribed much of the text with surprising accuracy by 1822. This version was used by Richard Griffin, later ennobled as Lord Braybrooke, for the first published edition of Pepys in 1825, called the *Memoirs of Samuel Pepys Esq. MA FRS*. Braybrooke, like most editors of the time, had no qualms about silently modifying the text with reckless and haphazard zeal as he saw fit, whether with additions or cuts, though some of the latter were restored in an 1848–9 edition. Passages with any content regarded as obscene or distasteful were omitted and their existence usually concealed by merging the preceding and following text.

A new transcription of the complete text was made by the Reverend Mynors Bright (1818–83), president and proctor of Magdalene College, using Pepys's copies of Shelton's works. He then published about 80 per cent between 1875 and 1879. Bright made occasional transcription errors or silent modifications, and misunderstood some names, places, and terms. Bright found the polyglot passages challenging and made some mistakes when transcribing them. He often transcribed French words where Pepys had clearly intended Spanish, such as *chose* instead of *cosa*, or *mains* instead of *manos*.[34] Bright was initially confounded by the additional consonants Pepys had introduced in May 1667. Apparently unaware of John Wilkins's ideas (see above under Polyglot), he despairingly called them 'dummy letters' and regretted eventually unravelling the passages concerned, because they were 'quite unfit for publication'.[35]

Henry Wheatley (1838–1917) produced during the 1890s what became the standard diary edition until the Latham and Matthews transcription was published in the 1970s. Wheatley used Bright's transcription, restoring some of the omitted passages, among them parts of the more controversial sections and thereby unwittingly perpetuating some of Bright's polyglot transcription errors. Wheatley also left the polyglot untranslated and imported other corrections made by a Fellow of Trinity College called Hugh Callendar. Wheatley was unable to read the shorthand but also introduced additions and omissions of his own, sometimes without explanation or rationale. Nonetheless, his edition was considerably more complete than Braybrooke's version of Smith's work, or Bright's published version.

The scholars Robert Latham and William Matthews began work in the 1960s to produce a definitive edition of the complete diary. Their transcription noted most of the difficulties caused by the shorthand, introduced a new level of accuracy, and was accompanied by far more sophisticated and extensive editorial matter.

Latham and Matthews's achievement was titanic. Their comprehensive notes throughout the text and their *Companion* volume have no precedent or equal in studies of Samuel Pepys. They made no excisions and no changes to the substantive text apart from what they believed were legitimate corrections. Some archaic spellings were incorporated to retain a flavour of the original where they found precedents in Pepys's longhand manuscripts, and they normally retained his diary spellings in longhand words. Otherwise, they transcribed the text into modern British spelling but did not translate or analyze the polyglot passages, most of which had never been published previously. This was in marked contrast to their exemplary detailed annotation of the rest of the text.[36] They mysteriously used the term *lingua franca* to refer to Pepys's polyglot passages. Pepys's sporadic polyglot was anything but a lingua franca, not least because he never used it to communicate with anyone else, let alone a non-English speaker.

The background to this editorial policy was the first publication of the unexpurgated text of D. H. Lawrence's novel *Lady Chatterley's Lover* in 1960. The publisher Penguin was prosecuted in England under the Obscene Publications Act of 1959 but a verdict of not guilty was returned on 2 November 1960. By that year a decision had already been made to publish the entire Pepys diary text, including all previously excised passages. Thanks to the new law, the legal advice already given to Latham and Matthews was only to publish with caution. The polyglot could thus be included but should not be translated, and nor should those individual passages or words even be identified as being published for the first time.[37]

Given the furore that then erupted soon afterwards over *Lady Chatterley*, this advice was adhered to thereafter throughout the appearance of the Latham and Matthews transcription and editorial matter in eleven volumes published during the 1970s and early 1980s. The offending sections were there but without translation or further comment. This bypassing also resulted in some transcription errors going unnoticed. Consequently, anyone trying to translate the passages was liable to be confused.[38] However, transcribing the shorthand in any significant quantity is extremely strenuous visually and physically. The polyglot passages are without question the most difficult of the whole diary text.[39]

If they had attempted translations, Latham and Matthews would have undoubtedly realized that some of their transcribed polyglot words were improbable readings and a few impossible.[40] Some interesting meanings, and Pepys's use of metre, alliteration, and rhymes in the polyglot, were also overlooked (see 23 August 1665 and Christmas Eve 1667, for example).

They sensibly removed what they called Pepys's 'extraneous consonants' from certain English words which he also used in passages concerned with incriminating sexual activity in the later part of the diary. However, like Mynors Bright they did not connect this to the work of John Wilkins (see above, under Polyglot), and instead referred to it as 'garbled shorthand'.[41] In a few instances they mistook polyglot words for this so-called 'garbled shorthand', for example, the Latin *foras* on 31 March 1668.

There are consequently some instances where Latham and Matthews's readings should now be reconsidered, particularly in the polyglot.[42] Beyond these, the scale of the differences between their text and earlier editions, although often important when it came to rectifying some significant earlier misunderstandings and mistranscriptions, has been exaggerated. Their readings were for the most part inevitably very similar to Bright's (as any transcriber's efforts would be since they are all derived from the same shorthand text) and many of Bright's errors are inconsequential. Variations mainly involve editorial decisions about spelling, expansions of abbreviations, paragraphing and punctuation, and in the pre-Latham and Matthews's editions (see below), excisions of certain passages, including those of a sexual or compromising nature, and others. The result is that the various diary editions are quite different in tone.

A NOTE ABOUT THE TEXT

Most published selections from Pepys's diary use a wide range of passages to give a flavour of the whole. They have introductions and glossaries but otherwise eschew a running commentary in favour of Pepys's words. These serve as invaluable introductions to Pepys, but an unintended consequence is to disrupt or even obscure the detail and implications of some of the long-running themes.

The purpose of this book is not to create a gratuitously distorted or scurrilous account of Pepys's private life. Instead, the intention is finally to complete Pepys's own story, because for one reason or another, all the previous transcribers of his diary in some way sought either to omit or occlude an important component of his testimony. The revelations here of the content and the methods Pepys used to compose the passages concerned should now take their proper place as key parts of the diary and evidence for Pepys's personality and mind, alongside the rest of the text. They may serve to stimulate further study of this fascinating aspect of the diary, especially the light thrown on the way he used the shorthand.

Focusing on the theme of Pepys's sexual relationships with women has made it possible to include the most relevant passages, which are otherwise buried in longer entries. Extracted like this and in order, the evolving patterns of his behaviour become clearer. Most of Pepys's numerous casual references to other girls and women are omitted, such as the tavern keeper's 'very pretty daughter' at the Ship in Billiter Lane.[43] The chapter headings are all quotes from the diary.

Few of those who have written about Pepys have studied the original diary text. All the diary passages quoted here have been taken by the editor from his fresh transcriptions of Pepys's original shorthand text made during 2024, the first for half a century. The polyglot in them has all been translated and dissected during unprecedented intensive and forensic study, a challenging task thanks to the various languages Pepys used, his variant spellings, archaisms, grammatical mistakes, and ambiguities in the shorthand.

Recent years have brought dramatic technological improvements unavailable to Latham and Matthews, and unimaginable to earlier editors. It is now possible to study the diary through digital scans of microfilm images and digital colour photographs, both of which can be enhanced and enlarged at will. There is, however, no claim here that these new transcriptions constitute definitive readings. That is impossible for all the reasons that have been explained. However, every transcriber of Pepys's diary owes a debt to all previous transcribers. Reading Pepys accurately is a cumulative process that has now lasted two centuries.

Revised readings, which were not anticipated when the work for this book began, have been introduced where they fulfil one or more of the following criteria: they are more plausible and accurate transcriptions of the shorthand, better match contemporary spellings and usages, and in the case of the polyglot correspond more convincingly to the context by generating translations that make sense as opposed to not doing so.[44] It is hoped that the transcribed passages included here are now closer to Pepys's original meaning than previously published versions.

The availability of online genealogical resources, digitized wills, and other sources has made it possible to make significant advances in tracing more details and ages of some of the girls and women Pepys had relations with. This is particularly true of the sisters Betty Martin and Doll Lane, as well as Elizabeth Bagwell and Deb Willet, but also applies to some others. This new information has been added to the text, notes, and Glossary of People and Places.[45]

The spelling policy has been to modernize most words for a contemporary readership and make them consistent, but with occasional concessions to Pepys's forms, such as 'musique' for 'music'. Longhand names and abbreviations have also been made consistent but Pepys's preferred spelling for the names has normally been used, though in the Glossary and commentary the more correct forms are supplied. Absolute consistency is impossible because of the nature of Pepys's text. The polyglot's spelling is more problematic, because Pepys had to construct it phonetically in shorthand and used contemporary forms.

Abbreviations have been expanded or modified. Pepys's use of *l.* after digits to indicate a sum in pounds has been replaced with the £ sign to avoid confusion for a modern readership. To obtain a modern equivalent of the sums of money or prices Pepys cited, his figure should be multiplied by about 173 at the time of writing.[46] Thus £5 provided to Elizabeth for a petticoat was the equivalent today of about £865.

Pepys's use of paragraphs was careless. This can make some lengthy passages tiresome to read. Therefore, some additional paragraphing has been introduced where it is sensible to do so.

Pepys's punctuation was limited mainly to a triangle of dots (∴) or later in the diary a tick (√) to mark the start of a new sentence, brackets, dashes, and occasionally commas. He only occasionally used apostrophes. Consequently, it has always been necessary for editors to introduce some punctuation for clarification. The new transcriptions here have usually involved limiting this intervention and restoring Pepys's stops, which were occasionally replaced by other editors with commas, dashes, or semi-colons. The editorial removal of Pepys's sometimes curiously placed stops has a significant effect on the style and rhythm of the diary. However, in a few instances Pepys's stops appear in the middle of sentences and those have been omitted to avoid confusion. Conversely, on 7 February 1669 Pepys was writing feverishly in a continuous stream. To preserve something of that pace and to show his mind working, the new transcription of that passage here does not include modern punctuation and reflects the original.

Dates: Pepys used 'Old Style' (Julian) calendar dates in accordance with Britain at the time. The dates given were therefore ten days behind those in Europe where the Gregorian calendar was followed. Britain did not switch over until 1752. New Year's Day was legally 25 March, meaning that Pepys conventionally used dual dates for 1 January to 24 March as, for example, 1659/60 and 1660/61. Today 1 January 1659/60 is treated as 1660 and so on.

Throughout this book, other references to dates in Pepys's diary appear. Some of these refer to diary entries not included in the present selection. In those cases, the reader should turn to the Latham and Matthews printed edition of the diary text or consult the most easily accessible online version (based on Wheatley's edition but with amendments), available at the time of writing at https://www.pepysdiary.com/

It has been this editor's good fortune to write many books, mainly on the ancient world. However, the opportunity to produce several concerning Samuel Pepys has been a particular privilege, especially this one. Learning to read Pepys's diary in the original shorthand and to use that shorthand for over two decades routinely in everyday life has been an unmatched experience. During a lifetime spent in the pursuit of historical research no other figure has emerged from the past with such unnerving and compelling vividness, leaving this practitioner of Thomas Shelton's Tachygraphy with the memorable fancy that Pepys is alive and well and sitting only inches away.

Guy de la Bédoyère
Welby, Lincolnshire, and Augusta, Western Australia, where this book began in 2024 and was completed in February 2025

Transcription conventions

Non-English words are italicized; where Greek words were represented in shorthand they have been transcribed here into Roman lettering, but if in longhand the Greek letters are retained; modern translations are indicated thus, [ ]; modifications or additions are indicated thus, < >; where Pepys used numerals these are normally retained; contracted names are silently expanded (but not forenames reduced to an initial only); additional or modified punctuation is silent but generally punctuation is as close as possible to Pepys's original; Pepys's variant longhand spellings of names are retained in the diary extracts but the individuals concerned are otherwise referred to with correct spellings.

1

1660

Nulla Puella Negat

In 1660 England was on the cusp of change. The Rump Parliament was collapsing, soon followed by the Restoration of Charles II. Pepys began the year in Axe Yard at Whitehall, where he lived with his wife Elizabeth and their servant Jane.

On 13 January 1660, after Pepys and his wife had dined at a neighbour's house, there is a hint that Elizabeth was already unsettled by what her husband was up to (she was nineteen years old).

> From thence home again, and my wife was very unwilling to let me go forth but with some discontent would go out if I did, and I going forth towards White hall I saw she fallowed me, and so I stayed and took her round through White hall,[1] and so carried her home angry.

The domestic lives of women, including mistresses and their servants, compared to those of men were highlighted on 16 January. Pepys had been out to dine with friends:

> Thence we went to the Greene Dragon on Lambeth hill, both the Mr Pinkneys, Smith, Harrison, Morrice that sang the bass, Sheply and I, and there we sang of all sorts of things and I ventured with good success upon things at first sight, and after that I played on my flagilette* and stayed there till 9 a-clock very merry and drawn on with one song after another till it came to be so late.
>
> After that Sheply, Harrison and myself, we went towards Westminster on foot, and at the Golden Lion near Charing cross, we went in and drank a pint of wine, and so parted and thence home, where I found my wife and maid a-washing.

A few days later on 20 January, Pepys mentioned Betty Lane for the first time (and see 4 August below). He clearly already knew her. She was to become his mistress and remained so for much of the diary period, her married name being Mrs Martin. She was christened in East Retford, Nottinghamshire, on 2 May 1636. By 1660 she was old enough to have had some sexual experience (on 29 June 1663 Betty implied to Pepys that she had 'been abroad' often with men in the past), and had moved away from home to London to work:[2]

> Thence to Westminster hall where Mrs Lane and the rest of the maids have their white scarfs, having all been at the burial of a young bookseller in the hall.

As tension mounted, public contempt for the Rump Parliament and its supporters increased and became more overt. Pepys continued to indulge himself, going to bed 'with my head not too well' after drinking too much on 8 February. On 21 October 1653 he had been disciplined at Magdalene in front of all the Fellows 'for having bene scandalously overseene in drink'.[3]

On 12 February Pepys fell out with Elizabeth:

---

* Flageolet, a type of wind instrument resembling a recorder.

So to bed, where my wife and I had some high words upon my telling her that I would fling the dog which her brother gave her out at the window if he pist the house any more.

On Shrove Tuesday (6 March) Pepys visited Mountagu's lodgings. He was told by his patron to accompany him as his secretary on a visit to the exiled King; the prospect of Charles II returning was now imminent. Later the same day:

> . . . I went to see Mrs Jem* at whose chamber door I found a couple of ladies, but she not being there we hunted her out and found that she and another had hid themselfs behind a door. Well, they all went down into the dining room, where it was full of tag, rag, and bobtail, dancing, singing, and drinking, of which I was ashamed and so after I had stayed a dance or 2, I went away.

Although he was only about to cross to Holland, Pepys knew he might die in a shipwreck. On 17 March he wrote out his will, leaving Elizabeth everything except his books, which would go to his brother John. He gave her money and his most important papers before they parted, she travelling by coach to a family friend's house at Huntsmoor in Buckinghamshire. The night before (16th) he had recorded that he was 'very sad to part with my wife'. On 19 March he mused to himself:

> My mind is still much troubled for my poor wife but I hope that this undertaking will be worth my pains.

Pepys's rising importance was beginning to attract attention. On 23 March two men came to see him, one bringing his wife with whom to entice Pepys, but who on this occasion seemed able to resist:

---

* 'Mrs Jem' was Mountagu's thirteen- or fourteen-year-old daughter Jemima, whom P was supposed to keep an eye on.

> Hither come Gill. Holland, and brought me a Stick-rapier and Shelston a sugar-loaf and had brought his wife who he said was a very pretty woman, to the Ship tavern hard by for me to see but I would[4] not go.

Shelston was back to see Pepys on 10 September 1660, described by him as a 'simple fellow that looks after an imployment' (i.e. looking for a job). Mr Shelston was obviously not too simple if he had calculated that offering his wife's favours was likely to be to his advantage, the only plausible reason for him bringing her along to be scrutinized. Either he had learned that Pepys was susceptible, or this was an early episode in which Pepys started to become familiar with the potential perks of his position. Pepys often sneered at those husbands he had cuckolded, oblivious to the possibility that he was being mocked behind his back for the ease with which he could be bought.

Later the same day Pepys had boarded Mountagu's ship, the 60-gun third-rate *Swiftsure*, at Long Reach, a stretch of the Thames between Purfleet and Dartford. Once they set sail, an accident the next day (24 March) led to the first report of Pepys beating a servant:

> . . . the boy Eliez[r]. flung down a can of beer upon my papers which made me give him a box of the eare, it having all spoiled my papers and cost me a great deal of work. So to bed.

While waiting for the fleet to sail, on 26 March Pepys commemorated his operation in 1658 at his cousin Jane Turner's house to remove the bladder stone that had caused him so much agony. He was unaware that the procedure, which he was lucky to survive, probably sterilized him. The psychological effects of this brush with death perhaps contributed to some of his later recklessness:

> This day it is 2 years since it pleased God that I was cut of the stone at Mrs Turner's in Salisbury-court. And did resolve while I live to

> keep it a festival as I did the last year at my house, and for ever to have Mrs Turner and her company with me. But now it pleases God that I am where I am and so am prevented to do it openly, only within my soul I can and do rejoice and bless God, being at this time blessed be his holy name, in as good health as ever I was in my life.

On 28 March Pepys talked with a 'well bred' man called Banes. Pepys was impressed and 'went up sat and talked with him in Latin and French', skills he would later deploy as part of his polyglot to write about his sexual activities with other women.

On 2 April Pepys transferred to the 80-gun first-rate ship *Naseby* (soon to be renamed the *Royal Charles*) to which Mountagu had moved. Pepys ruminated in his new cabin on 3 April about missing Elizabeth:

> My heart exceeding heavy for not hearing of my dear wife and indeed[5] I do not remember that ever my heart was so apprehensive of her absence as at this very time.

On 11 April, during a late-night conversation in his cabin, Pepys showed an officer his 'manner of keeping a Journall'. It was one of only two occasions (the other being 9 March 1669) when Pepys mentioned telling anyone else that he kept a diary.

The fleet set sail for Holland on 11 May. On the 17th in The Hague he met the King, 'a very sober man', and the Duke of York. On 18 May, Pepys wondered about trying his hand with a local woman:

> Back by water, where a pretty sober Duch lass sat reading all the way and I would[6] not fasten any discourse upon her.

On 19 May, Pepys was taken to a brothel, which he referred to as a 'Duch house', by friends who included Charles Anderson, Pepys's roommate at Magdalene:

> where there was an exceeding pretty lass and right for the sport, but it being Saturday we would[7] not have much of her company, but however I stayed with them . . . till 12 at night. By that time Charles was almost drunk, and then broke up, he resolving to go thither again (after he had seen me at my lodging) and lie with the girl which he told me he had done in the morning.

Pepys's wording reflects his personal familiarity with brothels, which is unsurprising given the time, his company, and his inclinations. On another occasion he described a notorious madam he had known at Cambridge.[8]

The next day (20 May) in Scheveningen, a short distance from The Hague, Pepys grew bolder. It was normal for strangers of both sexes to be given beds in the same room in inns:

> Up early . . . by wagon[9] to Schiveling where it not being yet fit to go off, I went to lie down in a chamber in the house, where in another bed there was a pretty Duch woman in bed alone, but though I had a month's-mind to her I had not the boldness to go to her. So there I slept an hour or 2. At last she rose, and then I rose and walked up and down the chamber and saw her dress herself after the Duch dress, and talked to her as much as I could, and took occasion from her ring which she wore on her first finger, to kiss her hand, but had not the face to offer anything more. So at last I left her there and went to my company.

On 25 May the English fleet had arrived off Dover and preparations were made to disembark. The King set off immediately, Pepys and others returning to the ships. On 28 May the day ended strangely:

> This night I had a strange dream of bepissing myself which I really did, and having kicked the *clos*[10] off I got cold and found myself all muck wet in the morning and had a great deal of pain in making water which made me very melancholy.

The curious condition troubled him for several days. Pepys landed at Deal on 29 May but continued to commute back and forth to the ship, now anchored with the others in the Downs. By 8 June he was feeling the lack of female company on his journey to London by road:

> Come to Gravesend. A good handsome wench I kissed, the first that I have seen a great while.

By 10 June Pepys had been reunited with Elizabeth. On 17 June he was admiring the celebrated beauty Frances Butler, and the 'many beauties' he saw promenading in the Gray's Inn walks, but the next day he was 'very lonely all night' for his wife who had gone to collect her luggage from where she had been staying in Buckinghamshire.

By 4 July 1660 Pepys was inspecting the houses in Seething Lane that formed part of and belonged to the Navy Office complex. Before too long he and Elizabeth would move into one and remain there for the rest of the diary period.

On 13 July Pepys caught sight of a woman who would come to fascinate him but be forever beyond his reach, except in his dreams. The King and his brothers were 'with Madam Palmer, a pretty woman that they have a fancy to, to make her husband a cuckold'. She was Barbara Palmer, née Villiers, who had married Roger Palmer in April 1659. Now, a year later and still only nineteen, she was the King's mistress and became a dominant presence in the early Restoration court. Her husband was ennobled as the Earl of Castlemaine in 1661, making her the Countess of Castlemaine.

Elizabeth Pepys appears to have suffered badly from dysmenorrhea (a symptom of endometriosis causing severe abdominal cramps). She also had an enduring abscess on her labia. On 2 August:

> When I came home I found my wife not very well of her old pain in the lip of her *chose* ['thing'] which she had when we were first married.[11]

Pepys probably used *chose* here because, given her French origins, Elizabeth is likely to have referred to herself that way. He also used it in his polyglot from 1664 but came to prefer the Spanish *cosa* when referring to genitals and sex acts.

On 4 August Pepys mentioned a private meeting with Betty Lane (later Mrs Martin) for the first time, and, exceptionally, used the diminutive of her first name. She was twenty-four years old, unmarried, and ran an established drapery business:

> . . . I went and bespoke some linen of Betty Lane[12] in the hall and after that to the Trumpett where I set and talked with her &c.

The '&c' may have been harmless but given what happened a few days later it is clear Pepys was not only interested in the linen (12 August).

On 5 August Pepys sent home an ointment he had obtained from a doctor in Holborn. Elizabeth had a bad night which 'troubled' Pepys who felt himself becoming 'not a little impatient'. He may have become irritated by her mood, or more likely the enforced abstinence from sex caused by her painful menstruation and the abscess on her labia which flared up repeatedly. She had recovered two days later (7 August). So had Pepys who by 8 August was:

> . . . at ease, I taking my pleasure with my wife in the morning, being the first time after her being eased of her pain.

This was one of the first references Pepys made to his sex life with Elizabeth. He equated his ease (i.e. relief) from sexual tension with her being eased of her pain.

On 12 August Pepys picked up Betty Lane for their first recorded sexual encounter. He made sure she was in the right state of mind by plying her with alcohol:

> . . . I went to walk, and meeting Mrs Lane of Westminster hall I took her to my Lord's and did give her a bottle of wine in the garden where Mr Fairbrother of Cambrige* did come and find us and drank with us.
>
> After that I took her to my house where I was exceeding free with dallying with her and she not unfree to take it.

The venue was Pepys's vacated house in Axe Yard, close to Sandwich's London home. The affair with Betty Lane went unmentioned again until 1663 (during which time her mother Anne died in East Retford) but this does not preclude the possibility that it continued sporadically in the interim. On 18 August Pepys struggled to keep his temper when his father encouraged Elizabeth to splash out on clothes:

> This morning I took my wife towards Westminster by water, and landed her at White friars with 5£[13] to buy her a petticoat. And I to the Privy Seale. By and by comes my wife to tell me that my father hath persuaded her to buy a most fine cloth of 26s a yard, and a rich lace, that the petticoat will come to 5£ at which I was somewhat troubled, but she doing it very innocently I could not be angry. I did give her more money and sent her away . . .

Pepys was impressed the next day (19 August) by his wife's new clothes, but not by how she looked after herself:

> Home to dinner where my wife had on her new petticoat that she bought yesterday which endeed is a very fine cloth and a fine lace but that being of a light colour, and the lace all silver, it makes no

* Sic for Cambridge. Fairbrother was a lawyer friend of P's.

> great show . . . I went up to put my papers in order and finding my wife's clothes lie carelessly laid up I was angry with her, which I was troubled for.

Pepys soon afterwards made more of his first explicit references to infidelity. The tone and content suggest Pepys was already primed to seize opportunities. The woman concerned was called Diana, probably the daughter of a Mrs Crisp, a former neighbour at their old house in Axe Yard and with whom he had lodged earlier in the year, a safe distance from Elizabeth in their new house.[14] On 2 September:

> I drank till the daughter began to be very loving to me and kind and I fear is not so good as she should be.

Whether he feared it or not, Pepys took advantage of Diana being 'not so good'. After leaving Sandwich's house (on 12 July 1660 Edward Mountagu had been made 1st Earl of Sandwich) on 4 September:

> . . . to Axe yard to my house where standing at the door Mrs Diana comes by, whom I took into my house upstairs and there did dally with her a great while and find that in Latin *nulla puella negat* ['no girl refuses'].[15] So home by water and there sat up late setting my papers in order, and my money also, and teaching my wife her Musique lesson in which I take great pleasure.

The phrase 'did dally with her' was deliberately oblique because Pepys had not yet devised ways of being more explicit while still disguising what he had written. However, there is no doubt about what he meant as the Latin (from the Roman poet Martial) made clear.

Pepys bumped into Diana Crisp again on 16 September, this time calling her Dinah:

> So home and in my way met with Dinah who spoke to me and told me she had a desire to speak to <me> about some business when

> I come to Westminster again. Which she spoke in such a manner that I was afeared she might tell me something that I would not hear of our last meeting at my house at Westminster.

Pepys was probably worried that Diana was going to tell him she was pregnant; if so, the 'dally a great while' of 4 September (and with Betty Lane on 12 September) is revealed as a euphemism for sexual intercourse.

On 22 September he passed the time at Mountagu's chamber:

> . . . and upon the leads* gazing upon Diana who looked out at a window upon me. At last I went out to Mr Harper's and she standing over the way at the gate, I went over to her and appointed to meet tomorrow in the afternoon at my Lord's.

Overnight (23 September) Diana thought better of the assignation:

> . . . Diana did not come according to our agreement.

Diana's non-appearance could simply have been due to unavoidable circumstances. Another possibility is that she had agreed to meet Pepys to get rid of him and had no intention of turning up. Fear of pregnancy was a significant disincentive. She never appeared in the diary again.

On 13 October Pepys and Elizabeth had another row, illustrating how an angry Pepys was inclined to violence on such occasions:

> . . . I went by water home where I was angry with my wife for her things lying about, and in my passion kicked the little fine Baskett which I bought her in Holland and broke it, which troubled me after I had done it.

---

* A lead-covered section of flat roof.

Tuesday 23 October 1660 was Elizabeth's twentieth birthday. Although Pepys wrote down a full diary entry the occasion went unmentioned. Indeed, although Pepys almost invariably recorded his own birthday annually on 23 February, he never referred to hers. The next day (24th) he and Elizabeth quarrelled about a lost half-crown (2s 6d, or today 12.5p, the equivalent of about £22):

> I took occasion to be angry with my wife before I rise about her putting up of ½ a crowne of mine in a pepper box, which she hath forgot where she hath lain it. But we were friends again as we are always.

One of the reasons that Pepys was easily enraged this time was probably because by 31 October he was struggling with enforced abstinence from sex, and more concerned about the discomfort that caused him:

> My wife hath been so ill of late of her old pain that I have not known her this fortnight almost, which is a pain to me.

Another row followed on 6 November:

> At night to bed, and my wife and I did fall out about the dog's being put down into the Sellar* which I had a mind to have done because of his fouling the house and I would have my will. And so we went to bed and lay all night in a Quarrell. This night I was troubled all night with a dream that my wife was dead which made me that I slept ill all night.

On 22 November Pepys took Elizabeth to an audience with Charles II's widowed mother, the dowager Queen Henrietta Maria, and her daughters Mary, Princess of Orange (and mother herself of the future William III), and Henrietta. This gave Pepys the opportunity to pass

* = 'cellar'.

judgement on their looks, comparing them unfavourably with Elizabeth who had recently adopted the fashion of wearing black face spots:

> The Queen a very little plain old woman, and nothing more in her presence in any respect nor garbe then any ordinary woman. The Princess of Orange I have often seen before. The Princess Henriettee[16] is very pretty but much below my expectation. And her dressing of herself with her hair frized short up to her eares did make her seem so much the less to me.
>
> But my wife standing near her with 2 or 3 black paches on and well dressed, did seem to me much handsomer then she.

On 1 December Pepys's temper was aimed at the maid Jane Birch, then aged about sixteen, whom he beat with a broom:

> This morning, observing some things to be laid up not as they should be by the girl, I took a broom and basted* her till she cried extremely which made me vexed but before I went out, I left her appeased and so to White hall . . .

An evening's heavy drinking followed, 'my brains somewhat troubled with so much wine', leading to the inevitable consequences the next morning (2 December):

> My head not very well and my body out of order by last night's drinking. Which is my great folly.

Another drinking bout occurred on 27 December. The maid concerned was Jane Birch again, Pepys revealing now that he was beginning to find her physically interesting, a subject he returned to on 1 and 6 August 1662. On 16 September 1668, by which time she

---

* To scold vigorously.

was approaching her mid-twenties and shortly to be married, he assaulted her, but even then made it clear he had already been doing so for a while:

> About the middle of the night I was very ill, I think with eating and drinking too much, and so I was forced to call the mayde (who pleased my wife and I in her running up and down so innocently in her smock) and vomited in the Bason, and so to sleep, and in the morning was pretty well. Only got cold, and so had pain in pissing as I used to have.

2

1661

I Did Please Myself By Strength Of Fancy

By 1661 Samuel and Elizabeth Pepys were living in Seething Lane, next to the Navy Office and the church of St Olave's. He was now Clerk of the Acts. Elizabeth was often marginalized by his activities, both private and professional.

Pepys was easily roused to jealousy when it came to Elizabeth. On 10 January:

So to Mrs Hunt's where I found a Frenchman, a lodger of hers, at dinner, and just as I came in was kissing my wife, which I did not like, though there could not be any hurt in it.

On 18 January Pepys returned home from Woolwich to find the pet monkey had escaped:

At home found all well but the Monkey loose which did anger me and so I did strike her till she was almost dead that

> they might make her faste* again. Which did still trouble me more.

It was a mark of the man that he was capable of such spontaneous cruelty.

On 4 February Pepys and his wife were due to go to dinner at the Dolphin tavern with the shipbuilder Captain John Taylor. However, Pepys's parents arrived at their house en route to a cousin at Blackwall and had promised to take them. Pepys declined but 'at last I let my wife go with them'. Pepys, thus freed of Elizabeth, went off to the tavern on his own:

> . . . where Sir William Pen and the Comptroller† and several others were, men and women, and we had a very great and merry dinner. And after dinner the Comptroller begun some sports, among others the Nameing of people round and afterwards demanding Questions of them that they are forced to answer their names to, which do make very good sport. And here I took pleasure to take the forfeits of the ladies who could not do their duty, by kissing of them. Among others a pretty lady who I found afterwards to be wife to Sir W. Batten's son.

On 18 February Pepys showed that he could be generous to his wife, but noted the cost:

> In the afternoon my wife and I and Mrs Martha Batten, my Valentine, to the Exchange, and there upon a payre of embroydered and 6 payre of plain white gloves I laid out 40s upon her. Then we went to a mercer's at the end of Lombard-streete, and there she bought a suit of Lutestring‡ for herself. And so home.

---

* To secure or restrain.

† Colonel Robert Slingsby, Comptroller of the Navy.

‡ Lustring, a glossy silk fabric.

Pepys enjoyed a story he was told by two friends, who included a work crony called Peter Llewellyn ('Luellin'),[1] on 25 February. The story is a rare instance of evidence for how certain other men of his acquaintance had their own ruses for assaulting women:

> Luellin and I to my Lord's and there dined. He told me one of the prettiest* stories, how Mr Blurton, his friend that was with him at my house 3 or 4 days ago, did go with him the same day from my house to the Fleece taverne by Guildhall[2] and there (by some pretence) got the mistress of the house, a very pretty woman, into their company. And by and by Luellin calling him Doctor she thought that he really was so and did privately discover her disease to him. Which was only some ordinary infirmity belonging to women. And he proffering her physic. She desired him to come some day and bring it, which he did and withal hath the sight of her thing below and did handle it. And he swears the next time that he will do more.

On 26 February Pepys took a shine to an unnamed woman whom he met at his cousin Mrs Turner's:

> Then Mrs The† and I, and a Gentleman that dined there and his daughter, a perfect handsome young and very tall lady that lately came out of the country (and Mr Thatcher the Virginall maister) to Bishopsgate street, and there see the new Harpsicon made for Mrs The. We offered 12£. They demand 14£. The maister not being at home, we could make no bargain so parted for tonight. So all by coach to my house, where I found my Valentine with my wife, and here they drank and then went away. Then I sat and talked with my Valentine and my wife a good while and then saw her home, and went to Sir W. Batten to the Dolphin, where Mr Newborne

---

* In the old sense of 'craftiest' or 'most cunning'.

† John and Jane Turner's daughter Theophila (b. 1652), then aged about nine.

> &c were and there after a quart or 2 of wine we home, and I to bed where (God forgive me) I did please myself by strength of fancy with the young country *Segnora* that was at dinner with us today.

This is one of several oblique references in the diary to masturbation at the sight or thought of a woman.

One of Pepys's many drinking sessions occurred on 2 April. Elizabeth had gone to her father-in-law's house, along with Pepys's sister Pall now employed by them as a servant, while Pepys's building work to improve their house was underway:

> . . . to the Dolphin to Sir W. Batten and Pen and other company, among others Mr Delabar. Where strange how these men, who at other times are all wise men, do now in their drink betwitt[3] and reproach one another with their former conditions, and their actions as to public concernments, till I was ashamed to see it.

Pepys woke up the next morning:

> . . . my head akeing all day from last night's debauch. To the office all the morning, and at noon dined with Sir W. Batten and Pen, who would needs have me drink 2 drafts of Sack today to cure me of last night's disease. Which I thought strange but I think find it true.

With Elizabeth away, other opportunities arose on 6 April:

> Then with Mr Creed and Moore to the Leg* in the Palace to dinner. Which I gave them. And after dinner I saw the girl of the house, being very pretty, go into a chamber, and I went in after her and kissed her.

---

* The Leg tavern, King St, Westminster.

Although Pepys referred only to having kissed the girl, this may be a euphemism for more intrusive physical contact which he had not yet found more secretive ways of recording.

On 8 April, Pepys made a trip downriver to Gravesend, Rochester, and Chatham in the company of Sir William and Lady Batten and others. The following morning (9 April), Pepys mused on his standing now in such esteemed company:

> . . . in generall it was a great pleasure all the time I stayed here to see how I am respected and honoured by all people and I find that I begin to know now how to receive so much reverence, which at the beginning I could not tell how to do.

Later the same day, Pepys was impressed by Rebecca Allen, then aged about eighteen, younger daughter of Captain John Allen, Clerk of the Ropeyard at Chatham dockyard:

> Sir William and I by coach to the Dock and there viewed all the store-houses and the old goods that are this day to be sold, which was great pleasure to me, and so back again by coach home where we had a good dinner. And among other strangers that come, there was Mr Hempson and his wife a pretty woman and speaks Latin. Mr Allen and 2 daughters of his, both very tall* and the youngest very handsome, so much as I could not forbear to love her exceedingly, having among other things the best hand that ever I saw.
>
> After dinner, we went to fit books and things . . . for the Sale by an inch of candle,† and very good sport we and the ladies that stood by had to see the people bid . . . The sale being done, the

---

* P was about 5 ft 1 in (1.55 m) tall (see Introduction), so this was a relative judgement.

† An auction in which an inch-long section of candle was cut out and lit for each lot. The winner was the one who bid just before the light burned out.

> ladies and I and Captain Pett and Mr Castle took barge and down we went to see the *Sovereigne*, which we did, taking great pleasure therein. Singing all the way, and among other pleasures, I put my Lady, Mrs Turner, Mrs Hempson, and the 2 Mrs Allen's into the lantern* and I went in and kissed them, demanding it as a fee due to a Principall officer. With all which we were exceeding merry and drunk some bottles of wine and neat's tongue &c. Then back again home and so supped, and after much mirth to bed.

More entertainment (despite a disappointing pair of violinists) followed on 10 April, Elizabeth being safely away with Pepys's father:

> We had a fine collacion but I took little pleasure in that for the illnesse of the Musique and for the intentnesse of my mind upon Mrs Rebecca Allen.
>
> After we had done eating the ladies went to dance, and among the men we had, I was forced to dance too. And did make an ugly shift. Mrs R. Allen danced very well and seems the best humourd woman that ever I saw. About 9 a-clock Sir William and my Lady went home, and we continued dancing an houre or 2, and so broke up very pleasant and merry and so walked home, I leading Mrs Rebecca. Who seemed I know not why, in that and other things, to be desirous of my favours and would in all things show me respects.
>
> Going home, she would needs have me sing, and I did pretty well and was highly esteemed by them.
>
> So to Captain Allen's (where we were last night, and heard him play of the Harpsicon and I find him to be a perfect good Musician) and there having no mind to leave Mrs Rebecca, I did what with talk and singing (her father and I), Mrs Turner and I stayed there till 2 a-clock in the morning and was most exceeding merry and I had the opportunity of kissing Mrs Reb. very often.

---

* A large candlelit lantern, one of several at the stern of a ship, in this case the *Sovereign*.

Pepys was sorry about leaving the following day (11 April) and was bothered by his motives:

> At 2 a-clock, with very great mirth, we went to our lodging and to bed. And lay till 7, and then called up by Sir W. Batten. So I rise. And we did some business and then came Captain Allen, and he and I withdraw and sung a song or 2 . . .
>
> The young ladies come too, and so I did again please myself with Mrs Rebecca. And about 9 a-clock, after we had breakfasted, we Sett forth for London, and endeed I was a little troubled to part with Mrs Rebecca. For which God forgive me.

Rebecca Allen was the first woman Pepys described himself having a serious romantic interest in outside his marriage. On 24 March 1669 he finally managed to lay his hands on her (see Chapter 10), by then Mrs Jowles.

On 14 April London was filled with people and excitement as the coronation of Charles II approached. Pepys visited Elizabeth, who was staying at his father's house near St Bride's church during the disruptive building work at their Seething Lane home. Pepys feigned wanting to go home in the hope he would be asked to stay but initially Elizabeth, to his dismay, decided to leave too. Pepys provided another reference to the frequency of his sexual relations with Elizabeth:

> Then to my father's, and after supper seemed willing to go home, and my wife seeming to be so too I went away in a discontent but she, poor wretch, Fallowed me as far in the rain and dark as Fleete bri<d>ge to fetch me back again, and so I did, and lay with her tonight. Which I have not done these 8 or 10 days before.

Two days later Pepys slept with Elizabeth at his father's house again (16 April), and probably on the 19th.

On 23 April Pepys witnessed the glory of the coronation but ended the day with more excessive drinking:

> At last I sent my wife and her bedfellow to bed and Mr Hunt and I went in with Mr Thornbury (who did give the company all their wines, he being yeoman of the wine-cellar to the King) to his house and there, with his wife and 2 of his sisters, and some gallant sparks that were there, we drank the King's health, and nothing else, till one of the gen<t>lemen fell down stark drunk and there lay speweing. And I went to my Lord's pretty well. But no sooner a-bed with Mr Shepley but my head began to turn and I to vomitt, and if ever I was foxed it was now. Which I cannot say yet, because I fell asleep and sleep till morning. Only when I waked I found myself wet with my spewing . . .[4]

On Sunday 5 May Pepys and Elizabeth fell out over whether Mrs Pearse ('Pierce') was a beauty or not:

> Then to supper in the banquet house* and there my wife and I did talk high, she against and I for Mrs Pierce (that she was a beauty) till we were both angry.

On 24 May, Pepys appears to have tried to take an opportunity to accost one of Sandwich's maids, but mistook her for one called Susan whom he had probably assaulted on a previous occasion:

> Then down to the Kitchin to eat a bit of bread and butter which I did. And there I took one of the maids by the chin thinking her to be[5] Susan but it proved to be her sister which is very like her.

The lace Elizabeth had bought was soon on display on Sunday 9 June when she went to the Countess of Sandwich's at the Wardrobe in Blackfriars (Sandwich was Master of the Wardrobe):

---

* A garden or summer house.

> This day my wife put on her black silk gown which is now laced all over with black gimp lace as the fashion is. In which she is very pretty.
>
> She and I walked to my Lady's at the Wardrobe and there dined and was exceeding much made of.

On 6 August Pepys had to travel to Huntingdon. On the way back he stopped at Baldock ('Baldwick') in Hertfordshire to overnight at an inn. He took a shine to the landlady:

> . . . the ways being very bad, got to Baldwick, and there lay and had a good supper by myself. The landlady being a pretty woman but I darst not take notice of her, her husband being there.

Pepys only desisted because of the landlady's husband's presence, though in other respects he would have considered her being married as an advantage. This suggests that had her husband not been around, he would have tried his luck.

On 10 August Pepys was unimpressed by a new maid his wife had hired. Her looks so put him off he was not going to try and force himself on her. That may have been the reason Elizabeth employed her:

> This morning came the mayde that my wife hath lately hired for a Chamber mayd. She is very ugly so that I cannot care for her but otherwise she seems very good.

The maid was called Doll (Dorothy) but she only lasted until 27 November 1661 (see below), largely due to her tongue.

In about 1656 Pepys and Elizabeth had been temporarily separated. She moved to lodgings in Charing Cross. Pepys said later (4 July 1664) how much he disliked being reminded of this unfortunate episode. Meanwhile, on 13 August 1661 at his father's house, he 'took some old papers of difference between me and my wife and took them away'. He evidently did not want anyone else to have access to them. They may have been among those that he destroyed later (see 31 December 1664). They do not exist now.

On 30 August Pepys was a little perturbed on a visit to the theatre in Drury Lane when Elizabeth met a male friend she had known in France:

> Then my wife and I to Drury lane to the French Comedy, which was so ill done and the Scenes and company and everything else so nasty and out of order and poor, that I was sick all the while in my mind to be there. Here my wife met with a son of my Lord Somersett whom she knew in France, a pretty <man> but I showed him no great countenance to avoyd further acquaintance. That done, there being nothing pleasant but the foolery of the Farce, we went home.

The man Pepys was so worried about was Thomas Somerset, grandson of the 1st Marquess of Worcester (see 2 September below).

On 31 August Pepys was out again with Peter Llewellyn ('Luellin') when they were propositioned by prostitutes at Bartholomew Fair, held annually in August at West Smithfield. Pepys did not wish to be spotted in the women's company:

> At home and the office all the morning and at noon comes Luellin to me, and he and I to the taverne and after that to Bartholomew faire and there upon his motion to a pitiful alehouse, where we had a dirty slut or 2 come up that were whores but my very heart went against them, so that I took no pleasure but a great deal of trouble in being there and getting from thence for fear of being seen.

Pepys was also becoming troubled by conduct in the Restoration court, despite his own predilection for heavy drinking and pursuing other women:

> ... at Court things are in very ill condition, there being so much æmulacion,* poverty, and the vices of swearing, drinking, and whoring, that I know not what will be the end of it but confusion. And the Clergy so high, that all people that I meet with do protest against their practice. In short, I saw no content or satisfaccōn anywhere, in any one sort of people.

On 2 September Pepys was worried about some of the company Elizabeth was keeping:

> ... my wife hath been busy all the day making of pies, and hath been abroad and bought things for herself, and tells that she met at the change with my young ladies of the Wardrobe and there helped them to buy things, and also with Mr Somersett, who did give her a bracelet of rings which did a little trouble me, though I know there is no hurt yet in it but only for fear of further acquaintance.

However, on 5 September Pepys had more cause for concern when he and Elizabeth visited his uncle Thomas Fenner, who had married Pepys's maternal aunt Katherine (by chance she died a few days later and was buried on the 15th):

> ... to my uncle Fenners to dinner (in the way meeting a French footman with feathers who was in quest of my wife, and spoke with her privately, but I could not tell what it was, only my wife promised to go to some place tomorrow morning, which do trouble my mind how to know whither it was) where both his sons and daughters were, and there we were merry and dined.

Elizabeth met with the French footman, to Pepys's great disquiet (6 September). When she finally came home, he made her pay:

---

* Competition for status.

> I home to dinner all alone, and thence my mind being for my wife's going abroad much troubled and unfit for business, I went to the Theatre . . . I home. Where my wife had been long come home, but I seemed very angry, as endeed I am, and did not all night show her any countenance, neither before nor in bed, and so slept and rise discontented.

On 17 September, Pepys and Elizabeth set out on family business at Impington in Cambridgeshire. The following day (18 September), the journey continued from Ware (Herts). Pepys made a rare observation of the pleasures of Elizabeth's company:

> The next morning up early and begun our march. The way about Puckrige very bad and my wife in the very last dirty place of all got a fall but no hurt though some dirt. At last she begun, poor wretch,[6] to be tired and I to be angry at it, but I was to blame for she is a very good companion as long as she is well.

On 29 September, Pepys's excessive drinking was having increasingly serious consequences. Concealing his shortcomings was an occupational hazard and his attempts to do so became progressively more complicated:

> . . . to Sir W. Pens and there supped where his Brother, a traveller, and one that speaks Spanish very well, and a merry man, supped with us, and what at dinner and supper I drank I know not how of my owne accord, so much wine, that I was even almost foxed, and my head aked all night. So home and to bed without prayers, which I never did yet since I came to the house, of a Sonday night, I being now so out of order that I durst not read prayers for fear of being perceived by my servants in what case I was.

On 1 October, Elizabeth sought permission from her husband to learn music alongside him from his tutor, the royal musician John Goodgroome:

> This morning my wife and I lay long in bed, and among other things fell into talk of Musique, and desired that I would let her learn to sing. Which I did consider and promised her she should, so before I rose, word was brought me that my singing master Mr GoodGroome was come to teach me and so she rose and this morning began to learn also.

Elizabeth was not enjoying her bad-tempered new maid, causing Pepys more problems on 30 October:

> At my coming home I am sorry to find my wife displeased with her maid Doll whose fault is that she cannot keep her peace but will always be talking in an angry manner, though it be without any reason and to no purpose. Which I am sorry for. And do see the inconvenience that doth attend the increase of a man's fortune by being forced to keep more servants, which brings trouble.

Doll left the Pepys household on 27 November after another falling-out with Elizabeth, being replaced on 28 November by Sarah, 'a tall and very well favoured wench'. Meanwhile, more irritations followed, exposing Pepys's inclination to violence towards those unable to fight back. The victim on 2 November was his current servant boy Wayneman Birch, brother of their maid Jane:

> This night my boy Wainman, as I was in my chamber overheard him let off some Gunpouder, and hearing my wife chide him below for it, and a noise made, I call him up, and find that it was powder that he had put in his pocket, and a mach carelessly with it, thinking that it was out, and so the mach did give fire to the powder, and had burned his side and his hand that he put into his

> pocket to put out the fire. But upon examination and finding him in a lie about the time and place that he bought it, I did extremely beat him. And though it did trouble me to do it yet I thought it necessary to do it.

On 9 November, the Countess of Sandwich, whom Pepys revered, urged him to spend more on Elizabeth. Pepys pretended to be delighted with such encouragement:

> After dinner I to the Wardrobe* and there stayed talking with my Lady all the afternoon till late at night. Among other things my Lady did mightily urge me to lay out money upon my wife, which I perceived was a little more earnest then ordinary, and so I seemed to be pleased with it, and do resolve to bestow a lace upon her. And what with this and other talk, we were exceeding merry.

Meanwhile, on 10 November Pepys came home drunk and disorderly from the Rose tavern, disgracing himself in front of Elizabeth and the servants:

> I to Sir W. Batten's, where Captain Cocke was, and we sent for 2 bottles of Canary to the Rose which did do me a great deal of hurt, and did trouble me all night, and endeed came home so out of order that I was loath to say prayers tonight as I am used ever to do on Sundays which my wife took notice of and people of the house which I was sorry for.

Captain George Cocke was a colourful figure who appears in the diary on several occasions (see below, 15 August 1665).

Lady Sandwich helped Elizabeth choose the lace on the 11th. This caused the parsimonious Pepys some anxiety:

---

* Sandwich was Master of the Wardrobe, a royal department that dealt with ceremonial costumes and fabric furnishings of the palace.

> So to the Wardrobe where I found my Lady hath agreed upon a lace for my wife of 6£, which I seemed much glad of that it was no more, though in my mind I think it too much, and I pray God keep me so to order myself and my wife's expenses that no inconvenience in purse or honour fallow this my prodigality.

The lace was not cheap. £6 was equivalent to over £1000 today. He was still ruminating on the expense of a wife two days later (13th):

> . . . it raining very hard I went home by Coach with my mind very heavy for this my expenseful life, which will undo me I fear, after all my hopes, if I do not take up.* For now I am coming to lay out a great deal of money in clothes upon my wife, I must forbear other expenses.

Pepys had arranged for the artist Daniel Saville to produce portraits of himself and his wife. The work had started in late November. On 13 December he went with Elizabeth for her turn:

> Dined at home and then with my wife to the painter's, and there she sat the first time to be drawn while I all the while stood looking on a pretty lady's picture, whose face did please me extremely. At last, he having done, I find that the dead colour† of my wife is good, above what I expected, which pleases me exceedingly.

Further visits to Saville followed. Pepys, however, made the mistake of criticizing his wife's choice of ribbons on the way home on 19 December:

---

* 'take up' = 'agree on'.

† The monochrome underpainting layer that established the composition onto which the full colour image was then executed.

> This morning my wife dressed herself fine to go to the christening of Mrs Hunts child, and so she and I in the way in the morning went to the painter's and there she sat till noon, and I all the while looking over great variety of good prints which he hath. And by and by comes my boy to tell us that Mr Hunt hath been at our house to tell us that the christening is not till Saturday next. So after the painter had done I did like the picture pretty well. And my <wife> and I went by coach home. But in the way I took occasion to fall out with my wife very highly about her ribbands being ill mached and of 2 Colours, and to very high words, so that I (like a passionate fool) did call her whore, for which I was afterward sorry. But I set her down at home, and went myself by appointment to the Dolphin, where Sir Wm. Warren did give us all a good dinner. And that being done, to the office and there sat late, and so home.

Pepys had overlooked Elizabeth's determination to fight her corner. The result was a vexatious showdown, but he still went out to dinner by himself.

On 22 December a fleeting reference helps explain Pepys's jealous anger about anything involving his wife. A Captain Robert Holmes had in the past made an advance towards her, another clue that Pepys's own behaviour towards women was not necessarily unusual. Pepys never mentioned this previously. He also feared that Holmes would try his luck again (see 29 December, and 6 January 1662, below):

> To church in the morning where the Reader made a boyish young sermon. Home to dinner, and there I took occasion from the blackness of the meat as it came out of the pot, to fall out with my wife and my maid for their sluttery* and so left the table, and went up to read in Mr Selden[7] till church time, and then my wife and I to church, and there in the pew with the rest of the company was Captain Holmes in his gold-laced suit, at which I was troubled

* Slovenliness and untidiness.

> because of the old business which he attempted upon my wife. So with my mind troubled I sat still, but by and by I took occasion from the rain now holding up (it raining when we came into the church) to put my wife in mind of going to the christening (which she was invited to) of N. Osbornes child. Which she did, and so went out of the pew, and my mind was eased.

Part of the reason for Pepys's anger was how he usually chose women of lesser status when he wanted sexual services. By approaching Elizabeth, Holmes was implicitly treating her, and by extension Pepys, as of lesser status.

On the 29th Pepys had to make plans to avoid Captain Holmes:

> Long in bed with my wife. And though I had determined to go to dine with my wife at my Lady's, (chiefly to put off dining with Sir W. Penn today because Holmes dined there) yet I could not get a coach time enough to go thither, and so I dined at home, and my brother Tom with me. And then a coach came and I carried my wife to Westminster, and she went to see Mrs Hunt, and I to the Abby . . .

Pepys ended the year determined, he thought, to stay away from the theatre and drinking (31 December):

> I have newly taken a solemne oath about abstaining from plays and wine, which I am resolved to keep according to the letter of the oath which I keepe by me.

3

1662

I Glutted Myself With Looking On Her

During 1662 Pepys became concerned about the expense of his lifestyle and Elizabeth's needs. Pepys's domestic problems mounted as Elizabeth became lonely, and increasingly frustrated.

Pepys began 1662 concerned about living costs and still trying to clean up his act. On 5 January he explained how he wanted to avoid being thought ill of:

> After church to Sir W. Batten's (where on purpose I have not been this fortnight, and I am resolved to keep myself more reserved to avoyd the contempt which otherwise I must fall into) and so home and sat and talked and supped with my wife and so up to prayers and to bed . . .

On 6 January Pepys was up against Captain (erroneously given as Major on this occasion) Holmes who had designs on Elizabeth. Luckily, she was not interested either:

> ... to dinner to Sir W. Pens (it being a solemn feast day with him, his wedding day, and we had, besides a good chine of beef and other good cheer, 18 mince pies in a dish, the number of the years that he hath been married) where Sir W. Batten and his Lady, and daughter was, and Colonel Treswell and Major Holmes, who I perceive would fain get to be free and friends with my wife but I shall prevent it, and she herself hath also a defyance* against him.

On 24 January Pepys tried to show off the new pictures of himself and Elizabeth which he was pleased with. The Countess of Sandwich was not impressed with Elizabeth's portrait and Pepys immediately and obsequiously revised his opinion:

> Thence to my painter's and there I saw our pictures in the frames which please me well. Thence to the Wardrobe, where very merry with my Lady, and after dinner I sent for the pictures thither, and mine is well liked but she is much offended with my wife's, and I am of her opinion that it do much wrong her. But I will have it altered.

Meanwhile, by 26 January Pepys was able to record that cleaner living made him feel better:

> But thanks be to God, since my leaving drinking of wine I do find myself much better and do mind my business better and do spend less money and less time lost in idle company.

On 22 February Saville's paintings of Pepys and Elizabeth arrived. Their display in the dining room which 'comes now to appear very handsome with all my pictures' was an important part of the couple's status.

---

* A mistrust of him.

Pepys felt obliged on 28 February to use corporal punishment on Wayneman Birch again. The plan backfired:

> The boy failing to call us up as I commanded, I was angry and resolved to whip him for that and many other faults, today . . .
>
> Home, and to be as good as my word I bade Will[1] get me a rod, and he and I called the boy up to one of the upper rooms of the Controllers house toward the garden, and there I reckoned all his faults and whipped him soundly, but the rods were so small that I fear they did not much hurt to him, but only to my arme, which I am already, within a Quarter of an houre not able to stir almost.

On 21 March, Pepys went to Sandwich's lodgings. This included meeting up with Sandwich's housekeeper Sarah:

> With Sir W. Batten by water to White hall and he to Westminster. I went to see Sarah and my Lord's Lodgeings, which are now all in dirt, to be repaired against my Lord's coming from sea with the Queene . . .

Sarah was probably the housekeeper who had been in trouble with Sandwich for misbehaviour and was sacked but rehired on 15 June 1660. Pepys refers to her again on 7 September and 7 November 1662 and both times it is evident he was accustomed to her favours. Given his standing with the Sandwich family, Pepys was taking a risk except that on this occasion he knew Sandwich was away. Given the fleeting nature of this mention on 21 March, Pepys probably omitted to mention other visits to her.

On 6 April Pepys heard a sermon in the chapel at Whitehall about a subject close to his heart, but ignored its relevance to his own life:

> Thence to the Chappell and there though crowded heard a very honest sermon before the King by a Canon of Christ Church. Upon these words, 'Having a form of godliness but denying' &c.

> Among other things, did much insist upon the sin of adultery. Which methought might touch the King, and the more because he forced it into his sermon methought, besides his text.

Pepys set off for Portsmouth on 22 April, the day after news had arrived that the Queen had landed (the news was false: she did not arrive until 15 May), much to Elizabeth's annoyance. She had wanted to go with him. Pepys tried to persuade her to go to the Pepys family house at Brampton, 60 miles (96 km) north of London, rather than stay at home but she had refused. Given what ensued, it becomes easier to see why Pepys did not want Elizabeth along:

> After taking leave of my wife which we could hardly do kindly because of her mind to go along with me, Sir W. Penn and I took coach and so over the bridge to Lambeth. W. Bodham and Tom Hewet going as clerks to Sir W. Penn, and my Will for me. Here we got a dish of buttered eggs, and there stayed till Sir G. Carteret came to us from White hall who brought Dr Clerke with him at which I was very glad, and so we set out. And I was very much pleased with his company and were very merry all the way. He among good[2] Storys telling us a story of the monkey that got hold of the young lady's cunt[3] as she went to stool to shit and run from under her coats and got upon the table which was ready laid for supper after dancing was done. Another about a Hectors crying 'God damn you rascall'. We came to Gilford* and there passed our time in the garden cutting of Sparagus for supper, the best that ever I eat in my life but in that house last year.[4] Supped well, and the Doctor and I to bed together.

Once in Portsmouth, which they reached on the 23rd, Pepys and his friends spent several days in anticipation, waiting for news of the Queen's arrival. He caught sight of Mrs Pearse but was unable

---

* Guildford.

to ascertain where she was staying. Nonetheless there were other opportunities, as he reported on 29 April:

> ... after our work was done, Sir G. Carteret, Sir W. Penn and I walked forth, and I spied Mrs Pierce and another lady passing by. So I left them and went to the ladies, and walked with them up and down, and took them to Mrs Stephens's, and there gave them wine and sweetmeats, and were very merry and then comes the Dr, and we carried them by coach to their lodging, which was very poor but the best they could get, and such as made much mirth among us. So I appointed one to watch when the gates of the towne were ready to be shut and to give us notice, and so the Dr and I stayed with them playing and laughing, and at last were forced to bid good night for fear of being locked into the towne all night. So we walked to the yard, designing how to prevent our going to London tomorrow that we might be merry with these ladies, which I did. So to supper, and merrily to bed.

After putting off the trip home by a day, the jolly was over. With the Queen still nowhere in sight, Pepys and his cronies gave up and set off back to London on 1 May.

Pepys found himself conveniently having to ogle women on his wife's behalf on 4 May:

> ... my wife and I walked to Grayes Inne to observe fashions of the ladies, because of my wife's making some clothes.

Pepys was given to worry about his moral standards and lack of restraint, and troubled by his indulgences. On 20 May, he justified this paradox:

> But though I am much against too much spending yet I do think it best to enjoy some degree of pleasure now that we have health,

money, and opportunities, rather then to leave pleasures to old age or poverty when we cannot have them so properly.

On 31 May Pepys described how his maid Sarah helped prepare him for bed. He was accustomed to his female servants doing this. These circumstances on other occasions afforded opportunities for his hands to stray. Although Pepys makes no mention of assaulting Sarah, the fact that Elizabeth fell out with Sarah soon afterwards and pushed her into leaving suggests she suspected something had been going on:

> . . . so home. And had Sarah to comb my head clean, which I find so foul with poudering and other troubles, that I am resolved to try how I can keep my head dry without pouder. And I did also in a sudden fit cut off all my beard which I had been a great while bringing up, only that I may with my pumice stone do my whole face as I now do my chin, and to save time. Which I find a very easy way and gentile. So she also washed my feet in a bath of hearbes, and so to bed.

Pepys was quick with his fists when it came to almost anyone in his household. Among his targets was Will Hewer, his clerk. On 8 June:

> Home, and observe my man Will to walk with his cloak flung over his shoulder like a Ruffian which, whether it was that he might not be seen to walk along with the footboy I know not but I was vexed at it, and coming home, and after prayers, I did ask him where he learned that immodest garb, and he answered me that it was not immodest, or some such slight answer, at which I did give him 2 boxes on the ears which I never did before, and so was after a little troubled at it.

On Sunday 15 June Pepys was angered by Elizabeth's chosen outfit for church:

> . . . my wife not being dressed as I would have her, I was angry, and she, when she was out of doors in her way to church, returned home again vexed. But I to church, Mr Mills, an ordinary sermon. So home, and found my wife and Sarah gone to a neighbour church. At which I was not much displeased. By and by she comes again, and, after a word or 2, good friends.

On 21 June Pepys punished the diminutive Wayneman Birch again. He was astonished at the violence the boy withstood while sticking to his story. Pepys beat him until his own arm was hurt:

> I having from my wife and the maids' complaints made of the boy, I called him up, and with my whip did whip him till I was not able to stir, and yet I could not make him confess any of the lies that they tax him with. At last, not willing to let him go away a conqueror, I took him in task again, and pulled off his frock to his shirt, and whipped him till he did confess that he did drink the Whay,* which he hath denied. And pulled a pinke† and above all did lay the candlesticke upon the ground in his chamber, which he had denied this Quarter of this year. I confess it is one of the greatest wonders that ever I met with, that such a little boy as he could possibly be able to suffer ½ so much as he did to maintain a lie. I think I must be forced to put him away. So to bed with my arme very weary.

William Griffith ('Griffen') was the doorkeeper at the Navy Office. He had a maid whom it is inconceivable Pepys had not noticed before, but 30 June 1662 is the first time she was mentioned:

> Up betimes and to my office, where I find Griffen's girl making it clean but, God forgive me, what a mind I had to her, but did not meddle with her. She being gone, I fell upon boring holes for me

---

* Whey.

† A small pointed weapon.

> to see from my closet into the great office without going forth, wherein I please myself much.

The reference is characteristically vague. Pepys probably meant that he was pleased at having created the opportunity to spy on proceedings in the office. He undoubtedly enjoyed secrecy and being privy to knowledge others lacked. This helped him in other contexts to manipulate his mistresses.

By 22 July preparations for Elizabeth to move out to Brampton for the duration of major building works in their house were still being made. The couple had suffered badly from heavy rain pouring in through the roof:

> All day at the office, only at home at dinner. Where I was highly angry with my wife for her keys being out of the way, but they were found at last, and so friends again . . .

With Elizabeth safely in Brampton, Pepys's mind began to wander on 1 August:

> . . . at the office all the afternoon till evening to my chamber where, God forgive me, I was sorry to hear that Sir W. Pens maid Betty was gone away yesterday, for I was in hopes to have had a bout with her before she had gone, she being very pretty. I had also a mind to my own wench but I dare not for fear she should prove honest* and refuse and then tell my wife.

Pepys thereby admitted that he had been tempted to try his luck with Sir William Penn's maid Betty and one of his own, meaning Jane Birch (by now about eighteen years old), and that he could not rely on his victims keeping their mouths shut. In Jane's case, given how long she had been in the Pepys household (since at least 1658), that

* Virtuous.

was a risk. He had therefore probably not assaulted her before. On 6 August Pepys was still struggling with temptation:

> Thence home and at my office all the morning and dined at home and can hardly keep myself from having a mind to my wench, but I hope I shall not fall to such a shame to myself.

Pepys persistently resorted to his vows to mend his ways and tried to remind himself of them, as he did on 17 August:

> . . . I went and walked an hour in the Temple garden reading my vows, which it is a great content to me to see how I am a changed man in all respects for the better since I took them. Which the God of Heaven continue to me and make me thankful for.

And then on 20 August, he wavered when it came to drink:

> . . . I went to Westminster hall with Mr Moore, and there meeting Mr Townsend, he would needs take me to Fleetestreete to one Mr Barwell, Squire Sadler to the King, and there we and several other Wardrobe men dined. We had a venison pasty and other good plain and handsome dishes. The mistress of the house a pretty, well-carriaged woman, and a fine hand she hath, and her maid a pretty brown lass. But I do find my nature ready to run back to my old course of drinking wine and staying from my business and yet, thank God, I was not fully contented with it, but did stay at little ease.

On 23 August Pepys watched the King and Queen land in a barge at Whitehall, but was transfixed by the Countess of Castlemaine:

> But that which pleased me best was that my lady Castlemayne stood over against us upon a piece of White hall. Where I glutted myself with looking on her.

The hapless clerk Will Hewer received another beating and a lecture on his conduct. After writing up his diary at the office on 27 August, Pepys went home and invested a ludicrous amount of time inflicting his views on Will for the sake of asserting his primacy:

> . . . and Will having been making up books at Deptford with other clerks all day, I did not think he was come home, but was in fear for him, it being very late, what was become of him. But when I came home I found him there at his ease in his study, which vexed me cruelly that he should no more mind me, but to let me be all alone at the office waiting for him. Whereupon I struck him, and did stay up till 12 a-clock at night chiding him for it, and did in plain terms tell him that I would not be served so and that I am resolved to look out some boy that I may have the bringing up of after my own mind, and which I do entend to do, for I do find that he hath got a taste of liberty since he came to me that he will not leave. Having discharged my mind, I went to bed.

The following day, Pepys was pleased to discover that Will now got himself up without having to be called several times. It did not last. By 7 April the following year (1663) Pepys was annoyed to find Will had reverted to loafing in bed after he had been called.

On 7 September Pepys had an eventful Sunday afternoon while Elizabeth was still away in the country (she did not return until the 27th):

> Thence to my Lord's where nobody at home but a woman that let me in and Sarah above, whither I went up to her and played and talked with her and, God forgive me, did feel her, which I am much ashamed of but I did no more, though I had so much a mind to it that I spent in my breeches.

Sarah married around this time but gained a reputation for being a drunkard. Sandwich wanted to keep her on, but subsequently asked

Pepys to give her some advice about being sober. Pepys obliged on 25 December.

On 14 September came another example of contemporary male behaviour:

> Among other things Sir W. Penn did tell me of one of my servants looking into Sir J. Minnes's window when my Lady Batten lay there, which doth much trouble them, and me also, and I fear will wholly occasion my losing the leads.* One thing more he told me of my Jane's cutting off a carpenter's long Mustacho and how the fellow cried, and his wife would not come near him a great while, believing that he had been among some of his wenches. At which I was merry though I perceive they discourse of it as a crime of hers, which I understand not.

Sir George Carteret had useful advice for Pepys on 23 September, which he recorded but without acknowledging how it might apply to him:

> In our coming home Sir G. Carteret told me how in most *Cabaretts*† in France they have writ upon the walls in fair letters to be read *Dieu te regarde* ['God is watching you'] as a good lesson to be in every man's mind . . .

Perhaps one of the reasons was that the next day (24 September) Pepys was pleased to record:

> It is my content that by several hands today I hear that I have the name of a good-natured man among the poor people that come to the office.

---

* P's right to use a lead-covered section of flat roof.

† Taverns.

Pepys was greatly pleased by what he regarded as improvements in Elizabeth's behaviour, crediting himself for keeping her that way, as he recounted on Sunday 2 November:

> Lay long with pleasure talking with my wife. In whom I never had greater content, blessed be God, then now, she continuing with the same care and thrift and innocence (so long as I keep her from occasions of being otherwise) as ever she was in her life, and keeps the house as well.

Pepys was soon disappointed with Elizabeth again. On 12 November:

> So home and to supper and to bed. And a little before and after we were in bed we had much talk and difference between us about my wife's having a woman, which I seemed much angry at, that she should go so far in it without consideration and my being consulted with.

The row continued overnight (13 November):

> Up and began our discontent again and sorely angered my wife, who endeed do live very lonely. But I do perceive that it is want of work that doth make her and all other people think of ways of spending their time worse, and this I owe to my building, that doth not admit of her undertaking anything of work, because the house hath been and is still so dirty . . .
>
> And this afternoon, my wife in her discontent sent me a letter which I am in a quandary what to do whether to read it or not, but I purpose not but to burn it before her face that I may put a stop to more of this nature. But I must think of some way either to find her somebody to keep her company or to set her to work and by and imployment to take up her thoughts and time. After having done what I had to do I went home to supper. And there

> was very sullen to my wife and so went to bed and to sleep (though with much ado, my mind being troubled) without speaking one word to her.

The next day (14th) began well when Pepys seemed to be reconciled to the inevitable, but soon deteriorated because it was apparent that Elizabeth wanted to get rid of her maid Sarah, and had written him a letter:

> She begun to talk in the morning and to be friends, believing all this while that I had read her letter, which I perceive by her discourse was full of good counsel, and relating the reason of her desiring a woman, and how little charge she did entend it to be to me. So I begun and argued it as full and plain to her, and she to reason it highly to me, to put her away, and take one of the Bowyers[5] if I did dislike her, that I did resolve when the house is ready she shall try her for a while. The truth is, I having a mind to have her come for her Musique and dancing.
>
> So up and about my painters all the morning and her brother coming I did tell him my mind plain, who did assure me that they were both of the sisters very humble and very poor, and that she that we are to have, would carry herself so. So I was well contented and spent part of the morning at my office, and so home and to dinner and after dinner, finding Sarah to be discontented at the news of this Woman, I did begin in my wife's chamber to talk to her and tell her that it was not out of unkindness to her but my wife came up, and I perceive she is not too reconciled to her whatever the matter is, that I perceive I shall not be able to keep her, though she is as good a servant (only a little pettish) that ever I desire to have, and a creditable servant. So she desired leave to go out to look <for> a service, and did, for which I am troubled and fell out highly afterwards with my wife about it.

By 18 November Pepys and Elizabeth had come temporarily to an accommodation regarding the prospect of a companion for her. On 22 November the question of Elizabeth's putative new companion at the expense of getting rid of Sarah exploded:

> This morning, from some difference between my wife and Sarah her maid, my wife and I fell out cruelly to my great discontent. But I do see her set so against the wench, whom I take to be a most extraordinary good servant, that I was forced for the wench's sake to bid her get her another place. Which shall cost some trouble to my wife, however, before I suffer to be.

They made up the following day, but more tension followed over a variety of matters, always linked to Elizabeth's boredom and frustration. The ever thrifty (when it came to other people spending his money rather than himself) Pepys worked out that Elizabeth having a companion might save him money (30 November):

> I am also somewhat uncertain what to think of my going about to take a woman servant into my house, in the Quality of a Woman for my wife. My wife promises it shall cost me nothing but her meat and wages, and that it shall not be attended with any other expenses, upon which terms I admit of it, for that it will, I hope, save me money in having my wife go abroad on visits and other delights. So that I hope the best, but am resolved to alter it, if matters prove otherwise then I would have them.

They fell out again over the maid Sarah, whom Elizabeth had 'a deadly hate' for and Pepys wanted to keep, on 2 December. She was paid off on 5 December, greatly distressed, as was Pepys. Winifred Gosnell arrived later the same day to be Elizabeth's companion. Pepys liked Winifred, who could sing and dance, and how it looked that his wife had a woman to accompany her to church. However, it soon transpired that Winifred's uncle, a justice, wanted her home three times a week, and if that was not possible, she would not be allowed to take any position (8 December):

> For which we are both troubled but there is <no>[6] help for it, and believing it to be a good providence of God to prevent my running behind hand in the world, I am somewhat contented therewith and shall make my wife so, who poor wretch, I know will consider of things, though in good earnest the privacy of her life must needs be irkesome to her. So I made Gosnell <sing?>* and we sat up looking over the book of Dances till 12 at night, not observing how the time went, and so to prayers and to bed.

Winifred left the next day. On 10 December a new cookmaid called Susan arrived.

On 16 December Pepys encountered the sacked maid Sarah who told him worrying news about Elizabeth's wayward brother Balty:

> . . . I went by coach to my brother's, where I met Sarah, my late mayd (who had a desire to speak with me, and I with her to know what it was) who told me out of good will to me, for she loves me dearly, that I would beware of my wife's brother, for he is begging or borrowing of her and often, and told me of her Scallop whisk and her borrowing of 50s for Will, which she believes was for him and her father. I do observe so much goodness and seriousness in the maid, that I am again and again sorry that I have parted with her, though it was full against my will then. And if she had anything in the world I would commend her for a wife for my brother Tom. After much discourse and her professions of love to me and all my relations, I bade her good night and did kiss her, and endeed she seemed very well-favoured to me tonight, as she is always.

---

* Space in the manuscript here.

Pepys went to bed on 19 December:

> . . . a little displeased with my wife who, poor wretch, is troubled with her lonely life, which I know not how without great charge to help as yet, but I will study how to do it.

Ructions with the servants, present and past, rumbled on. On 26 December:

> Thence home and find my wife busy among her pies, but angry for some sawcy words that her maid Jane hath given her which I will not allow of, and therefore will give her warning to be gone. As also we are both displeased for some slight words that Sarah, now at Sir W. Penn's, hath spoke of us, but it is no matter. We shall endeavour to joyne the Lyon's skin to the Foxes tail.*

Pepys was concerned that his money had dropped to £630 from £680 recently, though it turned out to be more like £650 (about £113,000 today). Doubtless this lay behind being unable to resolve how to deal with Elizabeth being out of fashion in the winter on 29 December:

> . . . sat late talking with my wife about our entertaining Dr Clarkes lady and Mrs Pierce shortly, being in great pain that my wife hath never a winter gowne, being almost ashamed of it that she should be seen in a taffata one when all the world wears Moyre.[7] So to prayers and to bed. But we could not come to any resolution what to do therein, other then to appear as she is.

---

* In other words, combine the impression of a lion's strength with a fox's cunning.

4

1663

So Deadly Full Of Jealousy

In 1663 Pepys became increasingly obsessed with jealousy about Elizabeth. He angrily destroyed Elizabeth's papers rather than risk anyone else finding out what she had written about her unhappiness. His diary references to sexual escapades became more frequent in the second half of 1663.

On 6 January Elizabeth was in trouble for leaving some of her things in a coach. Pepys carefully explained that it was really her fault, even though she had given them to him to look after:

> Thence Mr Battersby (the apothecary), his wife and I and mine by coach together, and setting him down at his house, he paying his share, my wife and I home and find all well. Only myself somewhat vexed at my wife's neglect in leaving of her scarfe, waistcoat, and night dressings in the coach today that brought us from Westminster, though I confess, she did give them to me to look after. Yet it was her fault not to see that I did take

> them out of the coach. I believe it might be as good as 25s loss or thereabouts.

Pepys also recorded (7 January) his disquiet that the maid Sarah who had gone to William Penn's household had told them so much that Pepys family affairs were being gossiped about. The next day (8 January), Wayneman was in trouble again too:

> Up pretty earely and sent my boy to the Carriers with some wine for my father for to make his feast among his Brampton friends this Christmas. And my muffe to my mother, sent as from my wife. But before I sent my boy out with them, I beat him for a lie he told me. At which his sister (with whom we have of late been highly displeased, and warned her to be gone) was angry, which vexed me to see the girl I loved so well, and my wife, should at last turn so much a fool and unthankful to us.

On 9 January the whole matter of Elizabeth and her desperate desire for companionship erupted in one of the most melodramatic incidents that Pepys ever recorded:

> Waking in the morning, my wife I found also awake and begun to speak to me with great trouble and tears, and by degrees from one discourse to another at last it appears that Sarah hath told somebody that hath told my wife of my meeting her at my brother's and making her sit down by me while she told me stories of my wife, about her giving her Scallop to her brother and other things. Which I am much vexed at, for I am sure I never spoke anything of it, nor could anybody tell her but by Sarahs own words. I endeavoured to excuse my silence herein hitherto by not believing anything she told me, only that of the Scallop which she herself told me of.
>
> At last we pretty good friends, and my wife begun to speak again of the necessity of her keeping somebody to bear her

company, for her familiarity with her other servants is it that spoils them all, and other company she hath none (which is too true) and called for Jane to reach her out of her trunk, giving her the keys to that purpose, a bundle of papers, and pulls out a paper, a copy of what, a pretty while since, she had wrote in a discontent to me, which I could[1] not read, but burnt. She now read it and was so picquant, and wrote in English, and most of it true, of the retirednesse of her life and how unpleasant it was, that being wrote in English, and so in danger of being met with and read by others, I was vexed at it and desired her and then commanded her to teare it. When[2] she desired to be excused it, I forced it from her and tore it, and withal took her other bundle of papers from her, and leapt out of the bed and in my shirt clapped them into the pocket of my breeches, that she might not get them from me, and having got on my stockings and breeches and gown, I pulled them out one by one and tore them all before her face, though it went against my heart to do it, she crying and desiring me not to do it. But such was my passion and trouble to see the letters of my love to her, and my Will wherein I had given her all I have in the world, when I went to sea with my Lord Sandwich, to be joyned with a paper of so much disgrace to me and dishonour if it should have been found by anybody. Having torn them all, saving a bond of my uncle Rob[ts], which she hath long had in her hands, and our Marriage-licence, and the first letter that ever I sent her when I was her servant,* I took up the pieces and carried them into my chamber, and there, after many disputes with myself whether I should burn them or no, and having picked up the pieces of the paper she read today, and of my Will which I tore, I burnt all the rest. And so went out to my office. Troubled in mind.

The destruction even of his own letters to her showed the extent to which Pepys had lost control over himself when confronted

---

* = 'lover'.

with his fears of being exposed as a husband with a miserable wife. Pepys was appalled and ashamed by her spelling (see 31 January below).

By the end of the day Pepys believed he had soft-soaped Elizabeth, albeit at great expense to save his own face:

> I went to my wife and agreed upon matters, and at last for my honour am forced to make her presently a new Moyre* gown to be seen by Mrs Clerke, which troubles me to part with so much money but however, it sets my wife and I to friends again, though I and she never were so heartily angry in our lives as today almost, and I doubt the heartburning will not soon <be> over. And the truth is I am sorry for the tearing of so many poor loving letters of mine from Sea and elsewhere to her.

Nonetheless, Elizabeth continued to raise the question of her having a companion again (for example on 16 January). On 12 January, Pepys gave Wayneman another beating (on 6 March Pepys told Wayneman's brother he would have to go):

> After dinner to the Change to buy some linen for my wife, and going back met our 2 boys. Mine had struck down Creed's boy in the dirt with his new suit on in the dirt all over dirty, and the boy taken by a gentlewoman into a house to make clean, but the poor boy was in a pitiful taking and pickle but I basted my rogue soundly.

On 21 January Elizabeth was very badly affected by period pains:

> Up early leaving my wife very ill in bed *de ses Mois* ['of her monthlies']. . . . I home, where I find my wife ill in bed all day, and her face swelled with pain.

---

* Mohair, silk.

By the 23rd Elizabeth had recovered from the worst. On the 28th she was robbed:

> So home and there find my wife come home, and seeming to cry for bringing home in a coach her new Ferrandin* waistcoat, in Cheapside, a man asked her whether that was the way to the tower and while she was answering him, another on the other side, snatched away her bundle out of her lap, and could not be recovered. But ran away with it, which vexes me cruelly, but it cannot be helped.

Pepys agreed to pay for another one the following day. On 31 January Pepys found more fault with his wife:

> So to dinner late and not very good, only a rabbit not ½ roasted, which made me angry with my wife. So to my office, and there till late, busy all the while. In the evening examining my wife's letter entended to my Lady and another to Madamoiselle,† they were so false spelt that I was ashamed of them and took occasion to fall out about them with my wife, and so she writ none at which however, I was sorry, because it was in answer to a letter of Madam<oiselle> about business.

Jane Birch was finally let go in early February. Pepys found she had left by the time he returned home on 2 February:

> . . . for which my wife and I are very much troubled, and myself could hardly forbear shedding tears. For fear the poor wench should come to any ill condition after her being so long with me.

After much agonizing over who the candidate should be, Elizabeth's new companion arrived on 12 March. Mary Ashwell was the daughter of a former colleague of Pepys:

---

* A fabric made of silk and other material.

† The French governess employed by the Sandwiches.

> . . . I went home where I found Mary Ashwell come to live with us, of whom I hope well, and pray God she may please us. Which though it cost me something yet will give me much content.

Pepys was pleased with Mary and impressed by her musical accomplishments.

Elizabeth's period pains started again on 20 March. Unperturbed, Pepys went off to spend money on himself while worrying about whether Thomas Pepys would molest a new servant girl, regardless of his own inclinations. Evidently Thomas, like his brother, regarded servants as fair game:

> . . . I find my wife in great pain abed of her months. I stayed and dined by her. And after dinner walked forth, and by water to the Temple and in Fleet Street bought me a little sword with gilt handle, cost 23s. And silk stockings to the colour of my riding cloth suit, cost 15s. And bought me a belt there too, cost 15s. And so calling at my Brothers I find he hath got a new maid, very likely* girl, I wish he do not play the fool with her.

Pepys faced more problems on 9 April with the household staff:

> At noon dined at home and am vexed to hear my wife tell me how our mayd Mary doth endeavour to corrupt our cookmaid, which did please me very well. But I am resolved to rid the house of her soon as I can.[3]

On 10 April Pepys spent more money to keep Elizabeth in fashion:

> . . . walked to the new Exchange, there laid out 10s on pendents and painted leather gloves, very pretty and all the mode.

---

* In the archaic sense of 'attractive'.

On 23 April Pepys was angry with Wayneman again:

> At Cards till late and being at supper, my boy being sent for some mustard to a neat's tongue, the rogue stayed ½ an hour in the streets it seems at a Bonfire, at which I was very angry, and resolve to beat him tomorrow.

Pepys was true to his word the next day (24 April), this time so exerting himself with the corporal punishment that he lost his breath. The punishment of course was for Wayneman's benefit:

> Up betimes, and with my salt eele* went down in the paler† and there got my boy and did beat him till I was fain to take breath 2 or 3 times, yet for all I am afeared it will make the boy never the better, he is grown so hardened in his tricks, which I am sorry for, he being capable of making a brave man, and is a boy that I and my wife love very well.

On Sunday 26 April Pepys recorded a vignette of his household leisure time:

> In the evening . . . my wife, Ashwell, and the boy and I, and the dog, over the water and walked to Halfway[4] house and beyond into the fields gathering of Cowslipps, and so to Halfway house with some cold lamb we carried with us, and there supped, and had a most pleasant walk back again. Ashwell all along telling us some parts of their maske‡ at Chelsy School, which was very pretty, and I find she hath a most prodigious memory, remembering so much of things acted 6 or 7 years ago.

---

* A knotted rope end.

† Parlour.

‡ Masque.

However, by 27 April Elizabeth's new accomplishments, encouraged by Mary Ashwell's influence, were starting to bother Pepys, especially the dancing:

> At home with my wife and Ashwell talking of her* going into the country this year, wherein we had like to have fallen out, she thinking that I have a design to have her go, which I have not, and to let her stay here I perceive will not be convenient, for she expects more pleasure then I can give her here, and I fear I have done very ill in letting her begin to learn to dance.

Anything Elizabeth did had to be in Pepys's gift. The next day (28 April) he decided she was better at the dancing than he had thought:

> Up betimes and to my office and there all the morning. Only stepped up to see my wife and her dancing maister at it, and I think after all she will do pretty well at it.

Pepys constantly fretted about Elizabeth's household management. On 2 May he decided to confront her. She responded in kind, the pair hurling insults that referred to Elizabeth's impoverished origins and Pepys being the son of a tailor:

> So up and to my office (being come to some angry words with my wife about neglecting the keeping of the house clean, I calling her 'beggar' and she me 'pricklouse', which vexed me)[5] and there all the morning. So to the Exchange and then home to dinner, and very merry and well pleased with my wife . . .

However, Elizabeth started to wonder if Mary Ashwell might be more of a threat than an asset. On 3 May:

---

* Elizabeth.

> Home to dinner with my wife, who not being very well did not dress herself but stayed at home all day, and so I to church in the afternoon and so home again, and up to teach Ashwell the grounds of time and other things on the Tryangle,* and made her take out a psalm very well, she having a good eare and hand. And so a while to my office, and then home to supper. And prayers to bed. My wife and I having a little falling out because I would not leave my discourse below with her and Ashwell to go up and talk with her alone upon something she hath to say. She reproached me but I had rather talk with anybody then her, by which I find I think she is jealous of my freedom with Ashwell. Which I must avoid giving occasion of.

Although Pepys had been co-opted by Elizabeth into taking part in her dancing lessons (4 May), he was alarmed to discover on 12 May that dancing was starting to take over her life:

> Up between 4 and 5 and after dressing myself then to my office to prepare business against the afternoon. Where all the morning, and dined at noon at home, where a little angry with my wife for minding nothing now but the dancing maister,[6] having him come twice a day, which is a folly.

The dancing master was a Mr Pembleton. Pepys became increasingly perturbed by him and on 15 May was greatly displeased by what he found when he went home after the day's work and activities:

> ... where I found it almost night, and my wife and the Dancing Maister alone above, not dancing but talking. Now so deadly full of jealousy I am that my heart and head did so cast about and fret that I could not do any business possibly, but went out to my office, and anon late home again and ready to chide at everything,

* Triangular-shaped keyboard instrument.

> and then suddenly to bed and could hardly sleep, yet durst not say anything, but was forced to say that I had bad news from the Duke concerning Tom Hater as an excuse to my wife. Who by my folly hath too much opportunity given her with the man, who is a pretty neat black* man, but married. But it is a deadly folly and plague that I bring upon myself to be so jealous and by giving myself such an occasion more then my wife desired of giving her another month's dancing. Which however shall be ended as soon as I can possibly. But I am ashamed to think what a course I did take by lying to see whether my wife did wear drawers today as she used to do, and other things to raise my suspicion of her, but I found no true cause of doing it.[7]

One biographer suspected that Pepys had reasonable grounds for concern but was never to establish the truth. Elizabeth perhaps took the opportunity to drive her husband half-mad with jealous frustration.[8] On 19 May:

> Thence to the office till the evening, we sat and then by water (taking Pembleton with us) over the water to the Halfway house, where we played at 9 pins, and there my damned jealousy took fire, he and my wife being of a side and I seeing of him take her by the hand in play though I now believe he did only in passing and sport.

On 20 May Pepys came home to find Pembleton had dined with Elizabeth. The next day (21 May), Pepys admitted he was worried about losing his 'command over' Elizabeth:

> I home and danced with Pembleton, and then the barber trimmed me, and so to dinner. My wife and I having high words about her dancing to that degree that I did retire and make a vowe to

---

* Dark-haired, dark-complexioned.

myself not to oppose her or say anything to dispraise or correct her therein as long as her month lasts,* in pain of 2s 6d for every time which, if God pleases, I will observe, for this roguish business hath brought us more disquiet then anything hath happened a great while.

After dinner to my office where late and then home and Pembleton being there again, we fell to dance a country dance or 2, and so to supper and bed. But being at supper my wife did say something that caused me to oppose her in, she used the word 'Devil', which vexed me, and among other things I said I would not have her to use that word, upon which she took me up most scornefully which, before Ashwell and the rest of the world, I know not nowadays how to check as I would heretofore, for less then that would have made me strike her.† So that I fear without great discretion I shall go near to lose too my command over her, and nothing doth it more then giving her this occasion of dancing and other pleasures, whereby her mind is taken up from her business and finds other sweets besides pleasing of me, and so makes her that she begins not at all to take pleasure in me or study to please me as heretofore. But if this month of her dancing were but out (as my first was this night, and I paid off Pembleton for myself) I shall hope with a little pains to bring her to her old wont.

Pembleton even proved to be a problem at church. Pepys had hoped to go and ogle a friend of Peg Penn's on 24 May, whom Elizabeth had even told her husband about, but then he spotted the dancing master in the congregation:

... so at noon dined and my wife telling me that there was a pretty lady come to church with Pegg Pen today, I against my

* Her month of dancing lessons.

† P implied here that he may have struck Elizabeth more often than he mentions doing so in the diary.

> intention had a mind to go to church to see her and did so. And she is pretty handsome. But over against our gallery I espied Pembleton, and saw him leer upon my wife all the sermon, I taking no notice of him, and my wife upon him, and I observed she made a curtsey to him at coming out without taking notice to me at all of it, which with the consideration of her being desirous these 2 last Lord's days to go to church both forenoon and afternoon doth really make me suspect something more then ordinary, though I am loath to think the worst, but yet it put and do still keep me at a great loss in my mind, and makes me curse the time that I consented to her dancing, and more my continuing it a 2nd month, which was more then she desired, even after I had seen too much of her carriage with him. But I must have patience and get her into the country, or at least to make an end of her learning to dance as soon as I can.

Pepys was confronted by Pembleton again on 26 May, after an amorous start to the day with Elizabeth:

> Lay long in bed talking and pleasing myself with my wife. So up and to my office a while and then home, where I find Pembleton, and by many circumstances I am led to conclude that there is something more then ordinary between my wife and him, which doth so trouble me that I know not at this very minute that I now write this almost what either I write or am doing, nor how to carry myself to my wife in it, being unwilling to speak of it to her for making of any breach and other inconveniences, nor let it pass for fear of her continuing to offend me and the matter grow worse thereby. So that I am grieved at the very heart, but I am very unwise in being so.

Pepys had to go out on business but returned later. His suspicions were aroused:

> . . . I went home to see how things were, and there I find as I doubted Mr Pembleton with my wife, and nobody else in the house, which made me almost mad, and going up to my chamber after a turn or 2 I went out again and called somebody on pretence of business and left him in my little room at the door . . . telling him I would come again to him to speak with him about his business, so in great trouble and doubt to the office, and Mr Coventry nor Sir G. Carteret being there I made a quick end of our business and desired leave to be gone, pretending to go to the Temple, but it was home and so up to my chamber, and as I think if they had any intention of hurt I did prevent doing anything at that time, but I continued in my chamber vexed and angry till he went away, pretending aloud, that I might hear, that he could not stay, and Mrs Ashwell not being within they could not dance. And, Lord, to see how my jealousy wrought so far that I went softly up to see whether any of the beds were out of order or no, which I found not, but that did not content me, but I stayed all the evening walking, and though anon my wife came up to me and would have spoke of business to me, yet I construed it to be but impudence, and though my heart full yet I did say nothing, being in a great doubt what to do. So at night, suffered them to go all to bed, and late put myself to bed in great discontent, and so to sleep.

In the middle of the night following, Pepys rose to relieve himself, waking Elizabeth:

> . . . she took hold of me and would know what ayled me, and after many kind and some cross words I began to tax her discretion in yesterday's business, but she quickly told me my owne, knowing well enough that it was my old disease of Jealousy which I disowned but to no purpose. After an hour's discourse, sometimes high and sometimes kind, I found very good reason to think that her freedom with him is very great and more then

was convenient, but with no evil intent. And so after awhile I caressed her and parted seeming friends, but she crying in a great discontent.

After business elsewhere in London on 27 May, Pepys returned:

. . . so home. Where I find my wife in a musty* humour, and tells me before Ashwell that Pembleton had been there, and she would not have him come in unless I was there, which I was ashamed of but however, I had rather it should be so then the other way.

So to my office to put things in order there. And by and by comes Pembleton, and word is brought me from my wife thereof that I might come home so I sent word that I would have her go dance, and I would come presently. So being at a great loss whether I should appear to Pembleton or no, and what would most proclaim my jealousy to him, I at last resolved to go home . . . and then went up, and there we danced country dances and single, my wife and I, and my wife paid him off for this month also and so he is cleared.

The following day, despite his jealousy, on the anniversary of Charles II's coronation (29 May), Pepys had been to the theatre and drinking, and then on to his brother's:

. . . so home and in my way did take 2 turns forward and backward through the Fleete ally to see a couple of pretty whores that stood of the doors there and God forgive me I could scarce stay myself from going into their houses with them, so apt is my nature to evil after once as I have these 2 days set upon pleasure again.

That he found it necessary to walk to and fro shows how hard Pepys found it to resist the temptation.

---

* Sulking, resentful.

Pembleton remained in the neighbourhood. Another complication had emerged. Elizabeth was jealous of Pepys and the attention he was paying to her companion Mary Ashwell. On Sunday 31 May:

> Lay long in bed talking with my wife. And do plainly see that her distaste (which is beginning now in her again) against Ashwell arises from her jealousy of me and her, and my neglect of herself, which indeed is true, and I to blame, but for the time to come I will take care to remedy all.
>
> So up and to church, where I think I did see Pembleton, whatever the reason is I did not perceive him to look up towards my wife, nor she much towards him, however, I could hardly keep myself from being troubled that he was there. Which is a madness not to be excused now that his coming to my house is past, and I hope all likelihood of her having occasion to converse with him again.

On 3 June Pepys suspected that Wayneman had been sent away to Pembleton's. Pepys was immediately on the alert again the following day (4th) because Elizabeth and Mary Ashwell were about to go away for a while:

> Up betimes and my wife and Ashwell and I whiled away the morning up and down while they got themselves ready, and I did so watch to see my wife put on drawers, which poor soul she did, and yet I could not get off my suspicion, she having a mind to go into Fanchurch street before she went out for good and all with me, which I must needs construe to be to meet Pembleton, when she afterwards told me it was to buy a fan that she had not a mind that I should know of, and I believe it is so. Especially I did by a wile get out of my boy that he did not yesterday go to Pembleton's or thereabouts, but only was sent all that time for some starch, and I did see him bringing home some. And yet all this cannot make my mind quiet.

The women set off and returned later the same day. Pepys carried on with the day's business, but could not settle his mind:

> So I to dinner alone and so to my chamber, and then to the office alone, my head akeing and my mind in trouble for my wife, being jealous of her spending the day, though God knows I have no great reason. Yet my mind is troubled.

Elizabeth would not let Pepys see where her father Alexander de St Michel lived in comparative poverty, conscious of her husband's obsession with status. Pepys took her near to where he lived the next day (5 June):

> About 10 a-clock my wife and I not without some discontent abroad by coach, and I set her at her father's but their condition is such that she will not let me see where they live. But goes by herself when I am out of sight.

More rowing followed on 8 June:

> After dinner my wife and I had a little jangling* in which she did give me the lie, which vexed me, so that finding my talking did but make her worse, and that her spirit is lately come to be other then it used to be and now depends upon her having Ashwell by her, before whom she thinks I shall not say nor do anything of force to her, which vexes me and makes me wish that I had better considered all that I have of late done concerning my bringing my wife to this condition of heat. I went up vexed to my chamber . . .

However, Pepys managed to work out that part of the problem with Elizabeth was the attention he was paying to Mary Ashwell (11 June):

---

* Squabble.

> ... spent the evening with my wife, and she and I did jangle mightily about her cushions that she wrought with worsteds the last year, which are too little for any use, but were good friends by and by again. But one thing I must confess I do observe, which I did not before, which is, that I cannot blame my wife to be now in a worse humour then she used to be for I am taken up in my talk with Ashwell, who is a very witty girle, that I am not so fond of her as I used and ought to be, which now I do perceive I will remedy. But I would to the Lord I had never taken any, though I cannot have a better then her.

On 14 June Pepys's brother Tom told him he was 'a very thriving man'. Pepys was more concerned about saving money:

> ... my wife and I did even our reckonings, and had a great deal of serious talk, wherein I took occasion to give her hints of the necessity of our saving all we can. I do see great cause every day to curse the time that ever I did give way to the taking of a woman for her, though I could never have had a better, and also the letting of her learn to dance, by both which her mind is so devilishly taken off her business and minding her occasions, and besides hath got such an opinion in her of my being jealous, that it is never to be removed I fear, nor hardly my trouble that attends it, but I must have patience.
>
> I did give her 40s to carry into the country tomorrow with her, whereof 15s is to go for the coach hire for her and Ashwell, there being 20s paid here already in earnest.
>
> In the evening our discourse turned to great content and love, and I hope that after a little forgetting our late differences, and being a while absent one from another, we shall come to agree as well as ever.

Pepys was delighted when Sandwich commented on Elizabeth (15 June) in the company of various others, but this reflected the need for a man like him to believe his wife was an embellishment to himself:

> Sometimes they talked of handsome women, and Sir J. Mennes saying that there was no beauty like what he sees in the country markets and specially at Bury, in which I will agree with him that there is a prettiest woman I ever saw. My Lord replied thus, 'Why Sir John, what do you think of your neighbour's wife?' looking upon me. 'Do you not think that he hath a great beauty to his wife? Upon my word he hath.' Which I was not a little proud of.

With Elizabeth away, Pepys's attention characteristically wandered. On 29 June he met up with Betty Lane in Westminster. Pepys was seen, causing him great concern:

> . . . to the hall and fell in talk with Mrs Lane and after great talk that she never went abroad with any man as she used heretofore to do, I with one word got her to go with me and to meet me at the further Rhenish wine-house. Where I did give her a Lobster and do so towse her and feel her all over, making her believe how fair and good a skin she has, and endeed she hath a very white thigh and leg but monstrous fat.[9] When weary I did give over and somebody, having seen some of our dalliance, called aloud in the street, 'Sir, why do you kiss the gentlewoman so?' and flung a stone at the window. Which vexed me. But I believe they could not see my towsing her, and so we broke up and went out the back way without being observed I think, and so she towards the hall and I to White hall . . .

Pepys thus implied he was already practised at such seductions, flattering Betty while also being disgusted by her. 'I with one word got her to go with me' suggested he normally expected to have to take more time and trouble:

> So home and up to my lute long, and then after a little Latin chapter with Will, to bed. But I have used of late, since my wife went, to make a bad use of my fancy with whatever woman I have a mind to. Which I am ashamed of and shall endeavour to do so no more.

Up to this point, Pepys had rarely mentioned in the diary consorting with other women. But with this single statement he made it clear he was accustomed to seeking them out.

While at Deptford on 9 July, Pepys tracked down a naval carpenter called William Bagwell. He had an ulterior motive in the form of Mrs Bagwell. Pepys revealed his coercive determination to have his way with her. The entry marks an important development in his predatory behaviour and was a portent for more to come. This was his first mention of the Bagwells but he clearly already knew them, and had done for several years:

> . . . I by water to Deptford and there mustered the Yard, purposely (God forgive me) to find out Bagwell, a carpenter, whose wife is a pretty woman that I might have some occasion of knowing him and forcing her to come to the office again. Which I did so luckily that going thence he and his wife did of themselfs meet me in the way to thank me for my old kindness, but I spoke little to her but shall give occasion for her coming to me.

The 'old kindness' referred to a position Pepys had found William Bagwell, probably as ship's carpenter on the *Dolphin* soon after the Restoration (see 23 December 1665 below).

On 13 July Pepys watched the King and Queen and their entourage promenading in St James's Park. This afforded an opportunity to see how Lady Castlemaine was faring, and to admire Frances Stuart ('Steward'):

> Here was also my Lady Castlemayne rode among the rest of the ladies, but the King took methought no notice of her nor

> when they light did anybody press (as she seemed to expect and stayed for it) to take her down but was taken down by her own gentleman. She looked mighty out of humour and had a Yellow plume in her hat (which all took notice of) and yet is very handsome but very melancholy, nor did anybody speak to her or she so much as smile or speak to anybody. I fallowed them up into White hall and into the Queenes presence, where all the ladies walked, talking and fidling with their hats and feathers, and changing and trying one another's but on another's heads and laughing. But it was the finest sight to me, considering their great beautys and dress, that ever I did see in all my life. But, above all, Mrs Steward in this dress with her hat cocked and a red plume, with her sweet eye, little Roman nose, and excellent *Taille* ['figure'][10] is now the greatest beauty I ever see I think in my life and, if ever woman can, doth exceed my Lady Castlemayne, at least in this dresse nor do I wonder if the King changes, which I verily believe is the reason of his coldness to my Lady Castlemayne.

Frances Stuart was still unmarried. On 22 July Pepys heard one theory that Charles II was seeking out a husband for her as a cover so that she could become his mistress. She was to marry in 1667, but never did comply with the King's wishes.

Meanwhile, on 15 July Pepys had designs on Betty Lane, or any other available woman:

> And God forgive me, had a mind to have got Mrs Lane abroad or fallen in with any woman else in that hot[11] humour. But it so happened she could not go out nor I met with anybody else and so I walked homeward . . .

The entry is further evidence of the behaviour Pepys was habituated to but did not usually mention in the diary. Two days later (17 July) Pepys was willingly enticed into the Bagwells' home:

> ... coming home I was saluted by Bagwell and his wife (the woman I have a kindness for) and they would have me into their little house which I was willing enough to, and did salute his wife. They had got wine for me, and I perceive live prettily and I believe the woman a virtuous modest woman.

By 'kindness' Pepys meant he was attracted to her. Paradoxically he was keen to describe Mrs Bagwell as virtuous and modest, although giving in to him would require her not to be either (see Glossary of People and Places for what is known about her).

On 18 July Betty Lane was available but while Pepys waited for her, he admired Betty Howlett, who was then about seventeen. The entry needs reading with care. 'Mrs Lane' meant Betty Lane and not her mother (who had died in 1662). 'Mrs Howletts' meant Mrs Howlett senior, Betty Howlett's mother. The second paragraph here includes phrasing Pepys substituted his polyglot for from mid-1664 on, this being one of his explicit records of a sexual encounter. He made a point of noting that the encounter fell short of sexual intercourse ('doing what I would, but the last thing of all'):

> ... to Westminster hall where I expected some bands made by Mrs Lane and while she went to the starchers for them I stayed at Mrs Howletts who with her husband were abroad and only their daughter (which I call my wife) was in the shop and I took occasion to buy a pair of gloves to talk to her and I find her a pretty-spoken girl and will prove a mighty handsome wench. I could love her very well.
>
> By and by Mrs Lane comes and my bands not being done she and I parted and met at the Crowne in the palace yard where we eat (a chicken I sent for) and drank and were mighty merry and I had my full liberty of towsing[12] her and doing what I would, but the last thing of all for I felt as much as I would and made her feel my thing also, and put the end of it to her breast and by and by to her very belly. Of which I am heartily ashamed. But I doth resolve never to do more so.

> But Lord to see what a mind she hath to a husband and how she showed me her hands to tell her her fortune and everything that she asked ended always whom and when she was to marry. And I pleased her so well, saying as I know she would have me, and then she would say that she had been with all the Artists[13] in town and they always told her the same things. As that she should live long and rich, and have a good husband, but few children, and a great fit of sickness, and 20 other things which she says she hath always been told by others.
>
> Here I stayed late before my bands were done and then they came, and so I by water to the Temple and thence walked home, all in a sweat with my tumbling of her and walking . . .

At twenty-seven Betty Lane was still unmarried. Denying Pepys intercourse ('the last thing of all') was an obvious precaution. In 1664 she married and became Mrs Martin, subsequently having children. Pepys's resolution 'never to do more so' of course came to nothing. Betty Lane/Martin was his most enduring mistress in the diary years, but he was much more beguiled by the thought of Betty Howlett (later Mitchell), as he explained on 24 July when he visited the shop of her future mother-in-law, Mrs Mitchell, at Westminster Hall:

> . . . sent for beer and sugar and drank and made great cheer among it with her and Mrs Howlett, her neighbour, and their daughters, especially Mrs Howlett's daughter Betty, which is a pretty girl and one I have long called wife being, I formerly thought, like my own wife.

On 26 July Elizabeth still being away, Pepys visited Epsom spa's famous wells.[14] He was able to reflect on his first experience of a relationship with a woman:

> . . . so up and down by Minnes's wood, with great pleasure viewing my old walks, and where Mrs Hely[15] and I did use to walk and

talk, with whom I had the first sentiments of love and pleasure in woman's company, discourse, and taking her by the hand. She being a pretty woman.

On 4 August, Pepys was disappointed once again that he could not find Betty Lane. Instead, he took his barber Richard Jervas and Jervas's wife out to visit her ventriloquist mother, but had an ulterior motive:

> So over the water to Westminster hall and not finding Mrs Lane, with whom I purposed to be merry, I went to Jervas's and took him and his wife over the water to their mother Palmers (the woman that speaks in the belly, and with whom I have 2 or 3 years ago made good sport with Mr Mallard)[16] thinking because I had heard that she is a woman of that sort that I might there have light upon some lady of pleasure (for which God forgive me) but blessed be God there was none, nor anything that pleased me . . .

The reference to prostitutes was an indirect hint that he used their services far more frequently and spontaneously than he ever mentioned in the diary. Pepys was also disappointed by Mrs Palmer's singing and ventriloquist skills on this occasion.

The same day a letter arrived from Elizabeth with bad news. Pepys's wife was an increasing source of embarrassment, especially now that the Countess of Sandwich's attention had been brought to her conduct:

> This day I received a letter from my wife, which troubles me mightily, wherein she tells me how Ashwell did give her the lie to her teeth. And that thereupon my wife giving her a box on the eare, the other struck her again, and a deal of stir which troubles me. And that my Lady hath been told by my father or mother something of my wife's carriage, which altogether vexes me, and I fear I shall find a trouble of my wife when she comes home to get

down her head again, but if Ashwell goes I am resolved to have no more. But to live poorly and low again for a good while and save money and keep my wife within bounds. If I can, or else I shall bid Adieu to all content in the world. So to bed, my mind somewhat disturbed at this, but yet I shall take care by prudence to avoid the ill consequences which I fear, things not being gone too far yet, and this he<igh>th that my wife is come to being occasioned from my own folly in giving her too much head heretofore for the year past.

By 5 August Pepys was after Betty Lane again. This time he was successful but with an unexpected meeting that showed the dangers of being caught:

So to the Exchange, and thence home to dinner with my brother. And in the afternoon to Westminster hall and there found Mrs Lane, and by and by, by agreement we met at the Parliament stairs (in my <way> down to the boat who should meet us but my Lady Jemimah,* who saw me lead her but said nothing to me of her, though I stayed to speak to her† to see whether she would take notice of it or no) and off to Stangate and so to the Kingshead at Lambeth marsh, and had variety of meats and drinks, come to Xs,[17] but I did so towse her and handled her but could get nothing more from her though I was very near it. But as wanton and bucksome as she is she dares not adventure upon that business. In which I very much commend and like her.

Stayed pretty late and so over with her by water and being in a great sweat with my towsing of her I durst not go home by water but took coach.

---

* Lady Jemima Mountagu (later Carteret), daughter of the Earl and Countess of Sandwich.

† Lady Jemima.

Lady Jemima had ignored Betty Lane. She had already learned that women of status turned blind eyes to such matters. Her father, the Earl of Sandwich, had his own mistress, a woman called Elizabeth Becke in Chelsea 'that he spends his time and money upon' (as Pepys observed on 10 August 1663). Pepys managed to push Betty Lane almost to intercourse once again, but the fact that she still would not go that far made Pepys respect her more, or so he said. He was moderately grateful for being saved from himself and breaking his vows irretrievably.

On 7 August Pepys was at the Deptford dockyard on business, but the Bagwells materialized to importune him for a favour. Pepys revealed here his cynicism and scheming:

> ... young Bagwell and his wife waylayd me to desire my favour about getting him a better ship, which I shall pretend to be willing to do for them, but my mind is to know his wife a little better.

By the evening of 12 August, Elizabeth was home and the matter of getting rid of Mary Ashwell had arisen again. However, the next day (13 August) Mary made a complaint to Pepys about Elizabeth that made him reconsider where the fault really lay:

> And before going to bed, Ashwell begun to make her complaint, and by her I doth perceive that she hath received most base usage from my wife, which my wife sillily denyes, but it is impossible the wench could invent words and matter so perticularly, against which my wife hath nothing to say but flatly to deny, which I am sorry to see, and blows to have past, and high words even at Hinchingbrooke house* among my Lady's people, of which I am mightily shamed.
>
> I said nothing to either of them but let them talk. Till she was gone and left us abed, and then I told my wife my mind with great sobriety and grief. And so to sleep.

* The Sandwich family's country seat.

The following morning it was apparent that nothing was going to change Elizabeth's mind. Ashwell would have to go, Pepys conceded: 'we shall have no peace while she stays'. More tension followed on Sunday 16 August:

> Up and with my wife to church and finding her desirous to go to church, I did suspect her meeting of Pembleton, but he was not there, and so I thought my jealousy in vain, and writ the sermon with great quiet. And home to dinner very pleasant, only some angry words my wife could not forbear to give Ashwell. And after dinner to church again and there, looking up and down, I found Pembleton to stand in the Isle against us, he coming too late to get a pew. Which, Lord, into what a sweat did it put me. I do not think my wife did see him, which did a little satisfy me. But it makes me mad to see of what a jealous temper I am and cannot help it. Though let him do what he can, I do not see, as I am going to reduce my family, what hurt he can do me, there being no more occasion now for my wife to learn of him.

Mary Ashwell finally left on 25 August. By 27 August Pepys was told off by Elizabeth because he prevented her from enjoying herself:

> Up, after much pleasant talk with my wife and a little that vexes me, for I saw that she is confirmed in it that all that I do is by design, and that my very keeping of the house in dirt, and the doing of this and anything else in the house, is but to find her employment to keep her within and from minding of her pleasure. In which, though I am sorry to see she minds it, is true enough in a great degree.

On 30 August Pembleton came into church, to Pepys's horror:

> To church, I alone, in the afternoon and there see Pembleton come in and look up, which put me into a sweat and seeing not my wife

> there, went out again. But Lord. How I was afeared that he might, seeing me at church, go home to my wife, so much it is out of my power to preserve myself from jealousy. And so sot* impatient all the sermon. Home and find all well and no sign of anybody being there and so with great content playing and dallying with my wife and so to my office, doing a little business there among my papers, and home to my wife to talk. Supper and bed.

On 7 September Pepys claimed to be disgusted by the sight of prostitutes in Fleet Alley even though he had specifically gone to look at them:

> . . . and went all alone to the black spread Eagle in Bride lane and there had a chop of veale and some bread, cheese, and beer, cost me a shilling to my dinner, and so through fleete ally, God forgive me, out of an itch to look upon the sluts there, against which when I see them my stomach turned . . .

It seems only the wretchedness of the prostitutes' appearance made it impossible for Pepys to proceed which, perhaps, he might otherwise have done.

Just two days later (9 September) Pepys was outraged by Lord Sandwich's playing 'the beast and fool' with his mistress Elizabeth ('Betty') Becke in Chelsea:

> . . . I am ashamed to see my Lord so grossly play the beast and fool, to the flinging off of all Honour, friends, servants, and everything and person that is good, and only will have his private lust undisturbed with this common whore, his sitting up night after night alone, suffering nobody to come to them, and all the day too . . . and other poor courses to obtain privacy beneath his Honour. With his carrying her abroad and playing on his lute under her

* An archaic past tense form of 'sat'.

> window, and 40 other poor sordid things, which I am grieved to hear but believe it to no purpose for me to meddle with it, but let him go on till God Almighty and his own conscience and thoughts of his Lady and family do it.

Pepys of course did not 'keep' a mistress, in the sense of maintaining one. He was more inclined to secretive recreational encounters with a variety of women.

On 24 September Pepys was with Betty Lane again, torturing himself over the occasion and how he treated his wife. Nevertheless, he started by lying to her:

> In the afternoon telling my wife that I go to Deptford, I went by water to Westminster hall and there finding Mrs Lane, took her over to Lambeth, where we were lately, and there, did what I would with her but only the main thing, which she would not consent to, for which God be praised and yet I came so near that I was provoked to spend.* But, trust in the Lord, I shall never do so again while I live. After being tired with her company I landed her at White hall, and so home and at my office writing letters till 12 at night almost, and then home to supper and bed, and there found my poor wife hard at work, which grieved my heart to see that I should abuse so good a wretch, and that is just with God to make her bad to me for my wronging of her, but I do resolve never to do the like again. So to bed.

Once more Pepys had been thwarted from having intercourse with Betty, she fearing the consequences of pregnancy for an unmarried woman, though of course she had no idea that Pepys was probably sterile. The last line was an oath Pepys would never honour and it is interesting that he never apparently returned to the diary to amend comments like this. On 27 September he realized he had been punished:

---

* To ejaculate.

> So home to dinner, being a little troubled to see Pembleton look into the church as he used to do, and my wife not being there to go out again, but I do not discern in my wife the least memory of him.
>
> Dined, and so to my office a little, and then to church again, where a drowzy sermon, and so home to spend the evening with my poor wife. Consulting about her closet, clothes, and other things. At night to supper, though with little comfort, I finding myself both head and breast in great pain and which troubles me most my right eare is almost deaf. It is a cold which God Almighty in justice did give me while I sat lewdly sporting with Mrs Lane the other day with the broken window in my neck. I went to bed with a posset, being very melancholy in consideration of the loss of my hearing.

On 20 October Pepys used violence in a more justifiable context. Elizabeth needed defending from an assailant:

> . . . while I was in Kirtons shop,[18] a fellow came to offer kindness or force to my wife in the coach. But she refusing, he went away, after the coachman had struck him and he the coachman. So I being called went thither and the fellow coming out again of a shop, I did give him a good cuff or 2 on the chops, and seeing him not oppose me, I did give him another, at last found him drunk, of which I was glad, and so left him and home, and so to my office a while, and so home to supper and to bed.

The following day (21 October) Pepys decided to teach Elizabeth arithmetic, which he had been learning. He felt his role was to make her the accomplished wife he wanted:

> This evening after I came home, I begun[19] to enter my wife in Arithmetiq<ue> in order to her studying of the globes* and she

* Celestial and terrestrial globes.

> takes it very well. And I hope with great pleasure, I shall bring her to understand many fine things.

Elizabeth was soon bored and lonely again. Moreover, it appears that sexual intercourse resulted in pain (24 October):

> . . . so home to supper and to bed where to my trouble I find my wife begin to talk of her being alone all day, which is nothing but her lack of something to do, for while she was busy she never, or seldom, complained. She hath also a pain in the place which she used to have swellings in and that that troubles me is that we fear that it is my matter that I give her that causes it, it never coming but after my having been with her.

On 29 October Pepys visited the Guildhall in London where he met up with John Creed:

> After I had dined, I and Creed rose and went up and down the house and up to the ladies room, and there stayed gazing upon them. But though there were many and fine, both young and old, yet I could not discern one handsome face there which was very strange. Nor did I find the lady that young Dawes married so pretty as I took her for,[20] I having here an opportunity of looking much upon her very near . . . Being wearied with looking upon a company of ugly women, Creed and I went away, and took coach and through Cheapside . . .

The volatility of the Pepys marriage was exposed on 2 November by a trivial disagreement. Elizabeth believed she had caught their chambermaid Jane Gentleman[21] lying:

> . . . after supper there happening some discourse where my wife thought she had taken Jane in a lie, she told me of it mighty Tryumphantly, but I not seeing reason to conclude it a lie, was

> vexed and my wife and I to very high words, wherein I up to my chamber, and she by and by fallowed me up, and to very bad words from her to me, calling me perfidious and man of no conscience, whatever I pretend to, and I know not what. Which troubled me mightily, and though I would allow something to her passion, yet I saw again and again that she spoke but somewhat of what she had in her heart. But I tempered myself very well, so as that though we went to bed with discontent she yielded to me and began to be fond, so that being willing myself to peace, we did before we sleep become very good friends, it being past 12 a-clock, and so with good hearts and joy, to rest.

Elizabeth's temper was apparent on 3 November. After an argument with the maid Susan, Elizabeth had 'struck her'. Susan had run away before returning and pleading for a pardon.

Pepys was still in pursuit of Betty Howlett, but she was proving elusive. On 7 November 1663:

> . . . by coach abroad about several businesses to several places. Among others to Westminster hall where seeing Howlett's daughter going out of the other end of the hall, I fallowed her if I could to have offered talk to her and dallied with her a little. But I could not overtake her.

It is possible that Betty Howlett was trying to avoid Pepys. His interest in her never waned and later as Mrs Mitchell she served as one of his mistresses.

Elizabeth Pepys's gynaecological issues, which appear to have involved an abscess in her vulva, led to her being inspected by the surgeon Thomas Hollier (called by Pepys 'Hollyard') on 16 November. He had operated on Pepys in 1658:

> . . . in the evening Mr Hollyard came, and he and I about our great work to look upon my wife's malady in her secrets which he did,

> and it seems her great conflux of humours, heretofore that did use to swell there, did in breaking leave a hallow which hath since gone in further and further till now it is near 3 inches deep, but as God will have it, it doth not run into the bodyward but keeps to the outside of the skin and so he must be forced to cut it open all along, and which my heart I doubt will not serve for me to see done, and yet she will not have any body else to see it done, no, not her own maids, and therefore I must do it, poor wretch, for her. Tomorrow night he is to do it.

The following day, Hollier changed his mind. Pepys was characteristically concerned about his own sensibilities:

> So home, Mr Hollyard being come to my wife. And there she being in bed, he and I alone to look again upon her parts and there he doth find that, though it would not be much pain, yet she is so fearful, and the thing will be somewhat painful in the tending, which I shall not be able to look after, but must require a nurse and people about her so that upon second thoughts he believes that a fomentacion will do as well, and though it will be troublesome yet no pain, and what her maid will be able to do without knowing directly what it is for, but only that it may be for the piles. For though it be nothing but what is very honest, yet my wife is loath to give occasion of discourse concerning it.
>
> By this my mind and my wife's is much eased for I confess I should have been troubled to have had my wife cut before my face. I could not have borne to have seen it . . .

Pepys, with immaculate timing, then bent the surgeon's ear about his constipation.

Pepys's recorded infidelities had diminished since the summer after Elizabeth had returned home and during the time he was ill with constipation and other symptoms. On 22 December he was mischievous with a Mr Hawley, a former Axe Yard neighbour and who had also been a clerk to Sir George Downing (as Pepys had been from 1656 to 1660). Hawley was another fan of Betty Lane:

> I did go to Westminster hall, and there met Hawly, and walked a great while with him, among other discourse encouraging him to pursue his love to Mrs Lane, while God knows I had a roguish meaning in it.

Pepys wanted to encourage Betty to marry Hawley. Unaware of his probable infertility, avoiding intercourse was the only reliable means of preventing pregnancy. A married mistress was the perfect solution.

The year 1663 ended with Pepys reflecting on his marriage in a positive way, and comparing himself and Elizabeth to other couples (27 December):

> Up and to church alone and so home to dinner with my wife very pleasant and pleased with one another's company, and in our general enjoyment one of another, better we think then most other couples do.

Mr Hollier the surgeon was paid off for his work on 28 December though the future seemed uncertain:

> After dinner straight on foot to Mr Hollyard's and there paid him 3£ in full for his physic and work to my wife about her evill below, but whether it is cured forever or no I cannot tell, but he says it will never come to anything, though it may be it may ooze now and then a little. So home and find my wife gone out with Will (whom she sent for as she doth nowadays upon occasion) to have a tooth drawn, she having it seems been in great pain all day, and at night she came home with it drawn, and pretty well.

5

1664

I Did Arrive At What I Would, With Great Pleasure

During 1664 Pepys recorded his private life in ever greater detail, especially the pursuit of Mrs Bagwell. He started using polyglot when recording his liaisons, beginning with French. Pepys continued to be obsessed with economizing, occasioning more rows with his wife.

On 9 January, Pepys managed to combine giving his wife a lift with meeting Betty Lane again. Betty was menstruating and could not oblige him with more, but Pepys's wording once again indicates that much had gone on in the past without being recorded by him. Pepys also enquired after Betty Howlett, soon to be Mrs Mitchell:

> After dinner by coach I carried my wife and Jane to Westminster, leaving her at Mr Hunts, and I to Westminster hall, and there visited Mrs Lane and by appointment went out and met her at the Trumpet, Mrs Hare's, but the room being damp we went to the Bell tavern and there I had her company, but could not do as

> I used to do (yet nothing but what was honest) for that she told me she had those.* So I to talk about her having Hawly, she told me flatly no, she could not love him. I took occasion to enquire of Howletts daughter, with whom I have a mind to meet a little to see what mettle the young wench is made of, being very pretty, but she tells me she is already betrothed to Mrs Michell's son. And she in discourse tells me more, that Mrs Michell herself had a daughter before marriage, which is now near 30 year old. A thing I could not have believed.

On 11 January Elizabeth's domestic management skills came under question again, but she was quick to blame Will Hewer. Will had moved out into his own lodging but proved to be a distraction to the staff. Pepys recommended a beating for one of the maids but also discovered Will told a different tale:

> So home, where I found the house full of the washing and my wife mighty angry about Will's being here today talking with her maids, which she overheard, idling of their time, and he telling what a good maid my old Jane was, and that she would never have her like again. At which I was angry, and after directing her to beat at least the little girl. I went to the office and there reproved Will, who told me that he went thither by my wife's order, she having commanded him to come thither on Monday morning. Now God forgive me how apt I am to be jealous of her as to this fellow . . .

Pepys's uncle William Wight showed an unhealthy interest on 12 January in whether Elizabeth was pregnant. Pepys hoped this meant he planned something for them:

> . . . my wife did tell me how my Uncle did this day accost her alone, and spoke of his hopings she was with child, and kissing

* Meaning her period.

> her earnestly told her he should be very glad of it, and from all circumstances methinks he doth seem to have some intention of good to us, which I shall endeavour to continue more then ever I did yet.

A few days later (15 January) Pepys was more perplexed:

> So home and my wife tells me that my Uncle Wight hath been with her and played at cards with her, and is mighty inquisitive to know whether she is with child or no. Which makes me wonder what his meaning is, and after all my thoughts I cannot think, unless it be in order to the making his Will, that he might know how to do by me. And I would to God my wife had told him that she was.

Whatever was going on (which would not become clear until 11 May 1664), Pepys dealt with business first on 16 January before heading off to meet Betty Lane. This time he used the shorthand to record the more colourful details in French. As his sexual escapades intensified over the next few years, he developed this into a polyglot:

> I by water to Westminster hall and there did see Mrs Lane and *de là, elle* and I to the cabaret at the *Cloche* in the street *du roy* and there after some caresses, *je l'ay foutée*[1] *sous de la chaise deux* times and the last to my great pleasure *mais j'ai grand peur que je l'ay fait fere*[2] *aussi elle même. Mais* after I had done, *elle commençait parler* as before and I did perceive that *je n'avait fait rien de danger à elle. Et avec ça*, I came away and though I did make grand promises *à la contraire, nonobstant je ne le verrai pas* long time ['I by water to Westminster hall and there did see Mrs Lane and from there she and I to the cabaret at the Bell in King Street and there after some caresses, I fucked her under the chair 2 times, and the last to my great pleasure but I am very afraid that I made her do also herself. But after I had done, she began to speak as before and I did perceive that I had done nothing

> dangerous to her. And with that, I came away and though I did make grand great promises to the contrary, however I will not see her for a long time']. So by coach home and to my office . . .
>
> So home to supper and to bed. With my mind *un peu troublé pour ce que j'ai fait* today. But I hope it will be *la dernière de toute ma vie* ['So home to supper and to bed, with my mind a little troubled by what I did today. But I hope it will be the last of my whole life'].

Pepys apparently believed he might have hurt Betty. This was probably because she experienced an orgasm so intense that she momentarily lost the power of speech. Her speedy recovery reassured him all was well, but he feared, according to contemporary belief, that she now might fall pregnant (see next entry below).[3] Nonetheless, he clearly found vigorous and forceful sex exciting, and was sometimes unable to control himself (see, for example, 21 February 1665).

On 1 February Betty Lane told him she was not pregnant after all:

> Thence to Westminster hall and there met with diverse people, it being term time. Among others I spoke with Mrs Lane, of whom I doubted* to hear something of the effects of our last meeting about a fortnight or 3 weeks ago, but to my content did not.

Pepys's post as Clerk of the Acts meant that seeking his favour was in many people's interests. Sir William Warren was a timber merchant in Wapping and Rotherhithe. On 2 February he used the indirect form of a gift to Mrs Pepys:

> Then to the Change again, and thence off to the Sun taverne with Sir W. Warren, and with him discoursed long, and had good advice, and hints from him, and among things he did give me a pair of gloves for my wife wrapt up in paper which I would not open,

* Feared.

> feeling it hard, but did tell him my wife should thank him, and so went on in discourse. When I came home, Lord, in what pain I was to get my wife out of the room without bidding her go, that I might see what these gloves were, and, by and by, she being gone, it proves a pair of white gloves for her and 40 pieces in good gold which did so cheer my heart, that I could eat no victuals almost for dinner for joy to think how God doth bless us every day more and more. And more yet I hope he will upon the increase of my duty and endeavours. I was at great loss what to do, whether tell my wife of it or no which I could hardly forbear, but yet I did and will think of it first before I do, for fear of making her think me to be in a better condition, or in a better way of getting money, then yet I am.

On 3 February came one of the most remarkable passages in the diary concerning Pepys's sexual interests:

> This night late coming in my coach coming up Ludgate hill, I saw 2 gallants and their footmen taking a pretty wench, which I have much eyed lately set up shop upon the hill, a seller of ribband and gloves. They seem to drag her by some force, but the wench went, and I believe had her turn served, but God forgive me, what thoughts and wishes I had of being in their place.
>
> In Covent garden tonight, going to fetch home my wife, I stopped at the great Coffee house there, where I never was before . . .

Pepys had been titillated by the sight of a rape underway and wished he had been able to take part. Minutes later, he collected Elizabeth as if it was an entirely normal evening. The victim of course had little chance of help from any public official (but see below, 22 February).

News of another rape at Holborn emerged on 22 February, but this time Pepys only heard about it. On this occasion an attempt was made to cover it up because of the culprits being on the royal staff:

> The rape upon a woman at Turnstile the other day, her husband being bound in his shirt, they both being in bed together it being night, by 2 Frenchmen, who did not only lie with her but abused her with a Linke,* is hushed up for 300£. Being the Queen Mother's servants.

The hush money failed. Rape was recognized as a crime in the seventeenth century in England but proving it was extremely difficult. Successful prosecutions were extremely rare. In this instance, the assailants were found guilty and condemned in April.[4] That Pepys used the word 'rape' shows that he understood its meaning, but it is doubtful that he would have defined any of his own behaviour in the same context.

Pepys's uncle Wight's attention to Elizabeth was becoming a genuine concern by 26 February, but for the moment Pepys dismissed his worries:

> So rode home and there found my uncle Wight. 'Tis an odd thing as my wife tells me his caressing† her and coming on purpose to give her visitts, but I do not trouble myself for him at all but hope the best and very good effects of it.

The next day (27 February), Mrs Bagwell arrived to see Pepys at home, seeking preferment for her husband William. Pepys was uncertain how to proceed:

> Up, but weary, and to the office, where we sat all the morning. Before I went to the office there came Bagwell's wife to me to speak for her husband. I liked the woman very well and stroked her under the chin but could not find in my heart to offer anything uncivil to her, she being I believe a very modest woman.

---

* A torch, used to light the way.

† This does not mean physical caresses, but instead making a fuss of her.

Pepys continued to show restraint on 29 February, determining to have nothing more to do with Betty Lane (a vow he had not the slightest chance of keeping):

> . . . so to Westminster hall, and there talked with Mrs Lane and Howlett but the match with Hawley I perceive will not take. And so I am resolved wholly to avoid occasion of farther trouble with her.

Pepys's controlling nature occasioned another row with Elizabeth on 14 March:

> So to the Change and thence home where my wife and I fell out about my not being willing to have her have her gown laced, but would lay out the same money and more on a plain new one. At this she flounced away in a manner I never saw her nor which I could ever endure. So I away to the office, though she had dressed herself to go see my Lady Sandwich. She by and by in a rage fallows me, and coming to me tells me in spiteful manner like a vixen and with a look full of rancour that she would go buy a new one and lace it and make me pay for it, and then let me burn it if I would after she had done it, and so went away in a fury. This vexed me cruelly but being very busy I had not hand* to give myself up to consult what to do in it. But anon, I suppose after she saw that I did not fallow her, she came again to the office where I made her stay, being busy with another, ½ an hour, and her stomach† coming down we were presently friends. And so after my business being over at the office we out and by coach to my Lady Sandwich's with whom I left my wife, and I to White hall . . .

---

* The word 'hand' ('free hand') here was a colloquial equivalent of 'time on hand', i.e. P had no time available to deal with his wife at that moment.

† Her outraged pride.

On 26 March the gown was returned laced 'but will cost me a great deal of money, more then ever I intended, but it is but for once'. On 3 April Elizabeth wore it for him and he conceded it 'becomes her very nobly and is well made'.

On 15 March Pepys's younger brother Thomas died aged twenty-nine (he had been born on 18 June 1634). Two days earlier (13 March), Pepys reported that 'his disease is the pox' to his alarm. He changed his mind later. The funeral followed on 18 March, a necessity in a time when there was no means of preserving a body for any length of time. Pepys was fascinated by the experience of death and how the world moved on:

> . . . but Lord to see how the world makes nothing of the memory of a man, an hour after he is dead. And endeed, I must blame myself for though at the sight of him dead and dying, I had real grief for a while, while he was in my sight, yet presently after and ever since I have had very little grief endeed for him.

Thomas Pepys's affairs were soon to be the occasion of some disquiet, he emerging as a 'rogue in all respects'. It emerged that he had fathered a child by his maid and gone to elaborate lengths to try and have it taken by a beggar woman (6 April). The story must have hit home with Pepys who believed this was a risk that applied to him too, unaware he was probably sterile. He made no connection between his brother's behaviour and his own.

Pepys's jealousy, doubtless provoked unconsciously by his own adulterous activities, had not abated. On 4 April he went by water with an acquaintance to the Halfway House:

> And there found my wife who was gone with her maid Besse to have a walk. But Lord how my jealous mind did make me suspect that she might have some appointment to meet somebody. But I found the poor souls coming away thence so I took them back, and eat and drank, and then home, and after at the office a while, I home to supper and to bed.

The next day (5 April) Pepys was off to see Betty Lane again, still trying to encourage her to marry Mr Hawley. Betty was not available for sex, which suited Pepys's attempts to exercise self-control:

> I to Westminster hall and by and by, by agreement to Mrs Lanes lodging, whither I sent for a lobster, and with Mr Swayne[5] and his wife eat it, and argued before them mightily for Hawly. But all would not do, although I made her angry by calling her old, and making her know what herself is. Her body was out of temper for any dalliance, and so after staying there 3 or 4 hours but yet taking care to have my oath safe of not staying a ¼ of an hour together with her . . .

Back home, Pepys was not pleased by how Elizabeth addressed him, and assaulted her:

> . . . home myself, where I find my wife dressed as if she had been abroad, but I think she was not. But she answering me some way that I did not like I pulled her by the nose endeed to offend her, though afterwards to appease her I denied it, but only it was done in haste. The poor wretch took it mighty ill and I believe besides wringing her nose she did feel pain, and so cried a great while. But by and by I made her friends. And so after supper to my office a while, and then home to bed.

Using conciliatory language allowed Pepys to present himself as the rational party, he alone being able to calm things down, thus here 'I made her friends'. It is more likely Elizabeth gave in, fearing more physical punishment (see 18/19 December 1664 below).

On 18 April Pepys visited Hyde Park, trying to catch up with Elizabeth and his aunt Wight. He was horrified to realize he might have been seen in the shared hackney coach he had taken by some of the court elite. Having found them he:

> . . . did by coach, which I had agreed to wait for me, go with them all and Mr Hunt and a kinswoman of theirs, Mrs Steward, to Hide park, where I have not been since last year. Where I saw the King with his periwigg but not altered at all. And my Lady Castlemayne in a coach by herself in Yellow satin and a pinner* on. And many brave persons. And myself being in a hackney and full of people was ashamed to be seen by the world, many of them knowing me.

Pepys had an embarrassing moment on 21 April:

> . . . news comes my Lady Sandwich was come to see us so I went out, and running up (her friend however before me) I perceive by my dear Lady blushing that in my dining-room she was doing something upon the pott, which I also was ashamed of and so fell to some discourse, but without pleasure through very pity to my Lady.

Pepys's uncle Wight finally admitted his intentions towards Elizabeth on 11 May. He wanted her to bear a child for him who could be his heir (he and Elizabeth were not blood relations), another example of how a woman could be regarded at the time as a family commodity:

> My uncle Wight came to me to my office this afternoon . . . and from me went to my house to see my wife, and strange to think that my wife should by and by send for me after he was gone to tell me that he should begin discourse of her want of children and his also, and how he thought it would be best for him and her to have one between them, and he would give her 500£ either in money or jewels beforehand, and make the child his heyre. He commended her body and discoursed that for all he knew the thing was lawful. She says she did give him a very warm answer,

* A coif (close-fitting cap) with a pair of flaps.

> such as he did not excuse himself by saying that he said this in jest, but told her that since he saw what her mind was, he would say no more to her of it. And desired her to make no words of it. It seemed he did say all this in a kind of counterfeit laugh, but by all words that passed, which I cannot now so well set down, it is plain to me that he was in good earnest, and that I fear all his kindness is but only his lust to her. What to think of it of a sudden I know not, but I think not to take notice yet of it to him till I have thought better of it.

Encountering uncle Wight socially four days later (15 May) Pepys 'took no notice nor showed any different countenance'.

On 31 May, Pepys was at the office and took advantage of the absence of anyone else to spend time with Mrs Bagwell. She was still pursuing her husband's cause. It is unlikely to have been the first time since the last occasion when Pepys mentioned her (27 February 1664). Pepys remained unsure how to proceed:

> Dined at home, and so to the office where a great while alone in my office, nobody near, with Bagwell's wife of Deptford but the woman seems so modest that I durst not offer any courtship to her, though I had it in my mind when I brought her in to me. But I am resolved to do her husband a courtesy, for I think he is a man that deserves very well.

It would not be until 3 October 1664 that Pepys recorded making an advance to Mrs Bagwell.

Pepys was invited to be godfather to a child of 'Griffin' (Griffith), the Navy Office's doorkeeper. Pepys did not want Elizabeth to accompany him (12 June), and so began 'our great dispute':

> . . . the question was whether my wife should go and she having dressed herself on purpose, was very angry, and began to talk openly of my keeping her within doors before Creed, which vexed

> me to the guts, but I had the discretion to keep myself without passion and so resolved at last not to go, but to go down by water. Which we did by H. Russell* to the Halfway house and there eat and drank, and upon a very small occasion had a difference again broke out, where without any the least cause she had the cunning to cry a great while and talk and blubber which made me mighty angry in mind, but said nothing to provoke her because Creed was there. But walked home . . .

Once home, Elizabeth placated her husband:

> My wife made great means to be friends, coming to my bed's side and doing all things to please me and at last I could not hold out but seemed† pleased and so parted and I with much ado to sleep . . .

On 4 July an argument erupted which caused Pepys to be reminded of 'their differences', the time he and Elizabeth had temporarily separated around 1656:

> After dinner I walked homeward, still doing business by the way and at home find my wife this day of her own accord to have lain out 25s upon a pair of pendances for her eares which did vex me and brought both me and her to very high and very foul words from her to me, such as trouble me to think she should have in her mouth, and reflecting upon our old differences which I hate to have remembered. I vowed to break them or that she should go and get what she could for them again. I went with that resolution out of doors. The poor wretch afterwards in a little while did send out to change them for her money again. I fallowed Besse her messenger at the Change and there did consult and sent her back. I would not have them changed, being satisfied that she yielded.

---

* The Navy Office's waterman Henry Russell.

† 'pretended'.

Pepys had managed to assert the earrings (recorded as 'pendances' in longhand) as being in his gift. On 9 July he went:

> . . . home to my wife to supper and bed. Where we have not lain together because of the heat of the weather a good while, but now against her going into the country.

Despite the relief afforded by this occasion, Elizabeth's departure two days later for Brampton created an opportunity for Pepys in London. She was away until 6 August.

Pepys discovered on 20 July that Betty Lane was married (on 14 July). She was twenty-eight, unusually old for the time, as Pepys had pointed out on 5 April (above). Pepys was determined to meet up with her again, interested to see whether marriage had improved her abilities and emboldened now by the protection if she fell pregnant:

> But being at Westminster hall I met with great news that Mrs Lane is married to one Martin, one that serves Captain Marsh.[6] She is gone abroad with him today, very fine. I must have a bout with her very shortly to see how she finds marriage.

Betty's husband was Samuel Martin, whom Pepys despised.[7] Pepys fulfilled his plan the next day (21 July), and even smugly negotiated a further tryst with the obliging Betty, still calling her Lane. He flattered himself with what he could offer her, sneering at her cuckolded new husband and Betty's capabilities and loyalty as a wife. His description implied, very obliquely, that she had finally consented to intercourse with him.

> Thence to Westminster and to Mrs Lane's lodgings to give her joy. And there suffered me to deal with her as I hoped to do, and by and by her husband comes, a sorry, simple fellow, and his letter to her which she proudly showed me a simple, silly, nonsensical thing. A man of no discourse, and I fear married her to make a prize of,

> which he is mistaken in. And a sad wife I believe she will prove to him, for she urged me to appoint a time as soon as he is gone out of town to give her a meeting next week. And so by water with a couple of Cosens of Mrs Lane's and set them down at Queene hive and I through bridge home.*

He took up with Betty again just two days later (23 July), after toying with the idea of visiting a prostitute en route, continuing to use Betty's maiden name intermittently thereafter. He then returned to the prostitute:

> . . . walked toward Westminster and being in an idle and wanton humour walked through Fleet alley and there stood a most pretty wench at one of the doors. So I took a turn or 2, but what by sense of honour and conscience I would not go in. But much against my will took coach and away to Westminster hall, and there light of Mrs Lane, and plotted with her to go over the water. So met at Whitich stairs[8] in Chanel row, and over to the old house at Lambeth marsh and there eat and drank, and had my pleasure of her twice. She being the strangest woman in talk of love to her husband sometimes and sometimes again she doth not care for him. And yet willing enough to allow me a liberty of doing what I would with her.
>
> So spending 5s or 6s upon her I could do what I would, and after an hour's stay and more back again and set her ashore there again, and I forward to Fleetstreete, and called at Fleet alley, not knowing how to command myself, and went in and there see what formerly I have been acquainted with, the wickedness of these houses and the forcing a man to present expense. The woman endeed is a most lovely woman but I had no courage to meddle with her for fear of her not being wholesome, and so counterfeiting that I had

* P meant he walked from west to east over the north approach to London Bridge. Queene hive = Queenhithe, the small dock south of St Paul's.

> not money enough. It was pretty to see how cunning the Jade was, would not suffer me to have to do in any manner with her after she saw I had no money, but told me then I would not come again, but she now was sure I would come again. But I hope in God I shall not, for though she be one of the prettiest women I ever see, yet I fear her abusing me.
>
> So desiring God to forgive me for this vanity, I went home . . . weary of the pleasure I have had today and ashamed to think of it.

After Elizabeth arrived home on 6 August, she told him two days later that she had not been to the theatre while away. Pepys was delighted because that cancelled out the cost of his visits on 28 July and 4 August, 'it costing no more money then it would have done upon her, had she gone both her times that were due to her', and saved him breaking his vows.

On 15 August at the Trumpet tavern in King Street, Westminster, Pepys was annoyed to be confronted by Betty Lane/Martin now wanting help after her marriage. Pepys had just dropped his wife off:

> I and my wife to Mr Blagraves. They being none of them at home, I to the hall, leaving her there, and thence to the Trumpet whither came Mrs Lane and there begins a sad story how her husband, as I feared, proves not worth a farding* and that she is with child and undone, if I do not get him a place. I had my pleasure here of her, and she like an impudent jade depends upon my kindness to her husband, but I will have no more to do with her, let her brew as she hath baked. Seeing she would not take my counsel about Hawly. After drinking we parted . . .

Pepys treated Betty as solely responsible for her misfortune, and that she should have accepted his nominee for husband. Despite her

---

* = farthing, a quarter of a penny. An interesting example of contemporary pronunciation.

being both pregnant and distressed, he was prepared to have sex with her while dismissing her as promiscuous and worthless.

On 5 September, Pepys learned that Betty was still intending to come and speak to him:

> ... which I know is wholly to get me to do something for her to get her husband a place, which he is in no wise fit for.

The next day (6 September) he was anxiously hoping that Mrs Bagwell was going to arrive at the Navy Office:

> At noon home to dinner. Then to my office and there waited, thinking to have had Baggwell's wife come to me about business, that I might have talked with her but she came not.

The same day he expressed his admiration for Dorothy ('Doll') Stacey, a milliner at the New Exchange, when he collected some gloves for Elizabeth:

> So home, having called upon Doll, our pretty Change woman, for a pair of gloves trimmed with yellow ribbon (to <go with the> petticoat she[9] bought yesterday) which cost me 20s. But she is so pretty that God forgive me I could not think it too much which is a strange slavery that I stand in to beauty that I value nothing near it.

On 7 September Mrs Bagwell turned up at Pepys's office, after missing the scheduled meeting the previous day. Pepys was too busy to speak to her properly, but it was clear that he was now planning to seduce her:

> ... after dinner I out to my office taking in Bagwells wife, who I knew waited for me, but company came to me so soon that I could have no discourse with her as I intended of pleasure.

Pepys was also interested in Jane Welsh, the maid of his barber Richard Jervas. By 11 September, things were starting to look up:

> Thence going home went by Gervas's and there stood Jane at the door and so I took her in and drank with her, her maister and mistress being out of door. She told me how she could not come to me this afternoon but promised another time. So I walked home contented with my speaking with her . . .

The very next day (12 September):

> . . . walked to Jervas's where I took Jane in the shop alone, and there heard of her <that> her master and mistress were going out. So I went away and came again ½ an hour after. In the meantime went to the Abby and there went in to see the tombs with great pleasure. Back again to Jane, and there upstairs and drank with her, and stayed 2 hours with her kissing her. But nothing more. Anon took boat and by water to the neat-houses* over against Fox hall to have seen Greatorex dive,† which Gervas and his wife were gone to see, and there I found them (and did it the rather for a pretence for my having been so long at their house), but being disappointed of some necessaries to do it I stayed not but back to Jane but she could not go out with me . . .

By 19 September, when Pepys pursued Jane again, she had lost interest. He found her:

> . . . cold and not so desirous of a meeting as before, and it is no matter, I shall be the freer from the inconvenience that might fallow thereof. Besides offending God Almighty and neglecting my business.

---

* cattle houses/sheds.

† An experiment in diving bells in the Thames conducted by Ralph Greatorex (c. 1625–75), a mathematical instrument maker.

Further brief meetings followed in 1664 (7 and 28 November, only the latter proving possibly more fruitful, when he managed 'a little while' with Jane).

Elizabeth's hopes of having a child were dashed on 27 September:

> So home, where my wife having (after all her merry discourse of being with child) her months upon her, is gone to bed.

Another row followed on 29 September, this time about Elizabeth's method of balancing her accounts:

> Coming home tonight I did go to examine my wife's house accounts and finding things that seemed somewhat doubtful, I was angry though she did make it pretty plain, but confessed that when she doth misse a sum, she doth add something to other things to make it. And upon my being very angry, she doth protest she will here lay up something for herself to buy her a necklace with. Which madded me and doth still trouble me, for I fear she will forget by degrees the way of living cheap and under a sense of want.

On 1 October Betty Martin tried her luck again with Pepys:

> This morning Mrs Lane (now Martin) like a foolish woman, came to the Hors shoo* hard by and sent for me while I was at the office to come to speak with her by a note sealed up. I know to get me to do something for her husband, but I sent her an answer that I would see her at Westminster. And so I did not go, and she went away, poor soul.

Elizabeth being ill, Pepys spent Sunday 2 October visiting various churches, ending up at Clerkenwell church in a pew close to Frances Butler (whom he called 'Boteler' later in the same entry):

* The Horseshoe. A location near the Navy Office.

> … and there (as I wished) sat next pew to the fair Butler who endeed is a most perfect beauty still. And one I do very much admire myself for my choice of her for as a beauty. She having the best lower part of her face that ever I saw all days of my life.

After visiting the Countess of Sandwich, Pepys returned to the church at Clerkenwell, his hopes up. By the time he returned home, so were Elizabeth's suspicions. Complications followed when Betty Martin turned up:

> So away back to Clerkenwell church thinking to have got sight of *la belle* Boteler again, but failed, and so after church walked all over the fields home, and there my wife was angry with me for not coming home and for gadding abroad to look after beauties, she told me plainly, so I made all peace, and to supper. This evening comes Mrs Lane (now Martin) with her husband to desire my help about a place for him, it seems poor Mr Daniel is dead, of the Victualling Office. A place too good for this puppy to fallow him in. But I did give him the best words I could …

The next day (3 October) Pepys met Jane Welsh at his barber's 'and stroked her under the chin'. In the afternoon Mrs Bagwell arrived:

> But meeting Bagwell's wife at the office before I went home I took her into the office and there kissed her only. She rebuked me for doing it, saying that did I do so much to many bodies else it would be a stain to me. But I do not see but she takes it well enough, though in the main I believe she is very honest. So after some kind discourse we parted, and I home to dinner …

Elizabeth Bagwell's rejection was probably a careful tactic. She had also hinted that Pepys's reputation preceded him. His earlier comments suggest that both she and her husband were complicit in the campaign to improve his professional opportunities, and she was the bait. Timing was everything, but she may also have underestimated the threat Pepys posed.

There were, along the way, opportunities simply to stare at women who took his fancy. On 9 October:

> Thence, it being time enough, to our own church, and there stood wholly privately at the great doore to gaze upon a pretty lady, and from church dogged* her home whither she went to a house near Tower hill, and I think her to be one of the prettiest women I ever see.

By 20 October Mrs Bagwell hinted that she would be more accommodating, unless of course she had resigned herself to there being no alternative. The persistent Pepys groomed her:

> Then I to my office, where I took in with me Bagwells wife and there I caressed her and find her every day more and more coming with good words and promises of getting her husband a place, which I will do.

The Martins were less subtle. On 21 October Betty's husband Samuel came on his own:

> . . . to trouble me again to get him a Lieutenant's place for which he is as fit as a fool can be. But I put him off like an asse as he is, and so setting my papers and books in order I home to supper and to bed.

Pepys took Elizabeth Bagwell out by appointment on 3 November. He indulged in some of his characteristic self-delusion

---

* 'dogged' = 'with determination', i.e. 'with determination <followed> her home'. Several words in this passage are blotched and messy.

when she resisted his advances, and his hopes that he would back off from her:

> At noon to the Change and thence by appointment was met with Bagwells wife and she fallowed me into Moore fields and there into a drinking house. And all alone eat and drank together. I did there caress her, but though I did make some offer did not receive any compliance from her in what was bad, but very modestly she denied me, which I was glad to see and shall value her the better for it. And I hope never tempt her to any evil more.

Pepys was circumspect about what happened with Mrs Bagwell on 8 November, but it seems improbable the meeting was restricted to polite conversation. She cannot now have come unaware of what might follow on later occasions:

> I to my office where Bagwell's wife stayed for me and together with her a good while, to meet again shortly. So all the afternoon at my office. Till late and then to bed. Joyed in my love and ability[10] to fallow my business.

On previous occasions Pepys had been worried about his susceptibility to distractions. Now he seems to have been able to combine work with such diversions.

On 15 November another meeting with Mrs Bagwell followed, this time removed to the safety of a more remote location beyond Moorfields, just to the north of the City. His description of the encounter avoided specifics, Pepys having not yet eased himself into the habitual use of polyglot. He must have ejaculated, but he was not explicit about whether he had coerced her to have intercourse:

> . . . after office done (where much business, but little done), I to the Change, and thence Bagwell's wife with much ado fallowed me through Moor fields to a blind alehouse, and there I did caress

> her and eat and drink and many hard looks and sithes* the poor wretch did give me, and I think verily was troubled at what I did, but at last after many protestings by degrees I did arrive at what I would, with great pleasure. And then in the evening, it raining, walked into town to where she knew where she was and then I took coach and to White hall to a Committee of Tanger, where, and everywhere else, I thank God, I find myself growing in repute . . .

On 18 November Pepys expressed how ashamed he was to hear William Craven, 1st Earl of Craven, who oversaw distributing royal lottery concessions, use an inappropriate metaphor:

> But I had the advantage this day to hear Mr Williamson discourse, who come to be a contractor with others for the Lotterys, and endeed I find he is a very logical man and a good speaker.
>
> But it was so pleasant† to see my Lord Craven, the chaireman, before many persons of worth and grave, use this comparison in saying that certainly these that would contract for all the lotteries would not suffer us to set up the Virginia Lottery for plate before them. 'For,' says he, 'if I occupy a wench first, you may occupy her again your heart out, you can never have her maiden-head after I have once had it.' Which he did <say> more loosely, and yet as if he had fetched a most grave and worthy instance. They made mirth but I and others were ashamed of it.

Craven's observation reflects an elite male culture in which subjecting a young girl to sex, specifically a virgin, was taken for granted (Pepys expressly referred to this himself on 13 November 1668).

On 6 December, a pregnant Betty Martin pursued Pepys at Westminster Hall, desperate for him to help her husband (Pepys continuing to use her maiden name, either out of habit or because

---

* 'blind' = remote, off the beaten track; 'sithes' = sighs.

† In the obsolete sense of 'facetious', unless P omitted 'not' after 'was'.

it eased his conscience). Pregnancy was no obstacle and nor was the risk of sex with a woman in her own home:

> So by and by Mrs Lane comes and plucks me by the cloak to speak to me and I was fain* to go to her shop, and pretending to buy some bands made her go home, and I by and by fallowed her and there did what I would with her, and so after many discourses and her intreating me to do something for her husband which I promised to do, and buying a little band of her, which I intend to keep to.[11] I took leave there coming a couple of footboys to her with a coach to fetch her abroad I know not to whom. She is great with child and she says I must be godfather. But I do not entend it.[12]

Mrs Bagwell's arrival on 7 December momentarily pricked Pepys's flexible conscience:

> Lay long then up, and among others Bagwell's wife coming to speak with me put new thoughts of folly into me. Which I am troubled at.

On 15 December, Pepys was looking for another suitable place to meet Mrs Bagwell:

> . . . I abroad to the carriers to see some things sent away to my father against Christmas, and thence to Moore fields and there up and down to several houses to drink to look for a place *pour rencontrer la femme de je sais quoy* ['to meet the wife of I know who'] against next Monday, but could meet none . . .

The French words were written in shorthand but unlike the surrounding text the symbols are more spaced out and larger. Pepys had slowed down as he decided how to form the words.

---

* Obliged, but willingly.

The following day (16 December) Pepys tried to track '*la femme de* Bagwell' down at Deptford where she and her husband lived, 'but failed'.

On 18 December Pepys lost his temper again with Elizabeth but this time the row was much more serious and even dangerous. Typically for Pepys, he was far more concerned about what other people would think. The following day (19 December) he wrote down what had happened:

> Going to bed betimes last night we waked betimes. And from our people's being forced to take the key to go out to light a candle I was very angry and begun to find fault with my wife for not commanding her servants as she ought. Thereupon she giving me some cross answer I did strike her over her left eye such a blow as the poor wretch did cry out and was in great pain, but yet her spirit was such as to endeavour to bite and scratch me. But I cog<g>ing* with her made her leave crying, and sent for butter and parsley, and friends presently one with another and I up vexed at my heart to think what I had done, for she was forced to lay a poultice or something to her eye all day and is black. And the people of the house observed it.

Despite what he had done to Elizabeth, Pepys was still hopeful of meeting Mrs Bagwell that very day, but he did not find her waiting for him. He wrote 'Bagwell' in shorthand, as he gradually became more concerned about secrecy. Pepys then killed time but had to resort to subterfuge to placate Elizabeth:

> Thence home and not finding Bagwell's wife as I expected, I to the Change and there walked up and down and then home, and she being come I bid her go and stay at Mooregate for me, and after going up to my wife (whose eye is very bad, but she is in very good

* Caressing, wheedling.

> temper to me) and after dinner I to the place and walked round the fields again and again, but not finding her I to the Change, and there found her waiting for me and took her away, and to an alehouse and there I made much of her, and then away thence and to another and endeavoured to caress her, but *elle ne voulut*[13] *pas* ['she desired not'], which did vex me, but I think it was chiefly not having a good easy place to do it upon.

Next day (20 December) the frustrated Pepys, despite having an injured wife, was back in Deptford looking for Mrs Bagwell. He even walked there with William Bagwell, taking care to remain unnoticed. In this transcription, Pepys's phonetic French spellings are retained:

> Up and walked to Deptford where after doing something at the yard I walked, without being observed, with Bagwell home to his house and there was very kindly used, and the poor people did get a dinner for me in their fashion. Of which I also eat very well. After dinner I found occasion of sending him abroad, and then alone *avec elle je tentoy à ferer ce que je vodre et contre sa force je le fesoy, bien que pas à mon contentement* ['alone with her I tried to do what I would and against her resistance I did it, although not to my satisfaction']. By and by he coming back again I took leave and walked home.

The clear implication was that Pepys had raped Elizabeth Bagwell, and was disappointed by the experience. It was not the only time (see 20 February 1665 below).[14]

Here, still trying to find ways to write French in shorthand, Pepys came up with *tentoy* for *tentais*, *vodre* for *voudrais*, and *fesoy* for *faisais*. Latham and Matthews supplied *faire* but *ferer* is certain. The old French verb *ferir* ('to strike/injure') seems most unlikely on this occasion, so Pepys must have meant something like 'to do'. These illustrate how difficult French is to write in Shelton's shorthand, unlike Spanish which Pepys soon began to use more often instead.

Both William and Elizabeth Bagwell were operating together to draw Pepys in, but whether she had any choice in the matter is a moot point. That she was prepared to resist Pepys suggests she was unhappy. On 21 February 1665 he used so much force on her that he hurt himself (see next chapter). Later in 1665, on 12 and 22 August, it became apparent that William Bagwell's parents were also involved in facilitating her availability to Pepys.

A few days later, on New Year's Eve, Pepys set down his feelings about 1664 without a hint of irony, announcing that:

> My family is my wife, in good health, and happy with her. Her woman Mercer, a pretty, modest, quiet maid. Her chambermaid Besse. Her cook maid Jane. The little girl Susan, and my boy, which I have had about ½ a year, Tom Edwards, which I took from the King's Chapell. And a pretty and loving quiet family I have as any man in England.

More significantly, he also noted that over Christmas he had purged his papers:

> This Christmas I judged it fit to look over all my papers and books and to tear all that I found either boyish or not to be worth keeping or fit to be seen if it should please God to take me away suddenly.

The papers Pepys destroyed are unknown. The decision illustrated the importance he attached to curating his archives. This has always seemed strange, given that the six diary volumes were carefully preserved, despite their contents. The papers he disposed of may have included those relating to his temporary separation from Elizabeth in the late 1650s (see 13 August 1661).

6

1665

In The End I Had My Will Of Her

The decisive event of 1665 was the plague, which seems to have encouraged Pepys to become more reckless and coercive in his infidelities. He habitually now deployed his polyglot to record some of the detail.

During a 'hard frost', Pepys had a busy day on Monday 2 January 1665. The novelty of sex with Mrs Bagwell had temporarily abated. Having arranged to meet Jane Welsh the following Sunday (when he was unable to find her), he found time to visit the Swan in New Palace Yard:

> . . . and there did sport a good while with Herbert's young kinswoman without hurt, though they being abroad, the old people.

Herbert's young kinswoman was probably Sarah Udall, whom Pepys continued to pursue (see 20 January below, and 23 March 1665), and subsequently her sister Frances (with force). This distraction was the preamble to another liaison that followed immediately:

Then to the hall, and there agreed with Mrs Martin and to her lodgings which she hath now taken to lie in, in Bow streete. Pitiful poor things yet she thinks them pretty, and so they are for her condition I believe good enough. Here I did *ce que je voudrais avec* ['what I would with'] her most freely, and it having cost 2s in wine and cake upon her, I away sick of her impudence, and by coach to my Lord Brunker's by appointment in the piazza in Cov<ent> Guarding.

Pepys was back to the Swan and Sarah Udall on 20 January:

Thence to the Swan at noon and there sent for a bit of meat and dined and had my *baiser* of the *fille* of the house there. But nothing *plus* ['had my kiss of the girl of the house there. But nothing more'].

On 23 January Pepys decided to pursue Jane Welsh at his barber Jervas's again. She was not in but he soon found that Mrs Bagwell had arrived at his office:

Thence to Jervas's my mind, God forgive me, running too much after *sa fille* ['his girl'][1] but *elle* not being within I away by coach to the Change. And thence home to dinner and finding Mrs Bagwell waiting at the office after dinner, away *elle* and I to a cabaret where *elle* and I have *été* ['she and I have been'] before and there I had her company *tout l'après-dîne* and had *mon plein plaisir* of *elle* ['all after dinner and had my full pleasure of her'].* But strange to see how a woman, notwithstanding her greatest pretences of love *a son mari* ['for her husband'] and religion, may be *vaincue* ['overcome'].

... So to my office a little but being minded to make an end of my pleasure today that I might fallow my business I did take coach and to Jervas's again thinking *avoir rencontré* Jane, *mais elle*

---

* An early example of P's alliterative tendencies in the polyglot. Wheatley, despite including this passage from Bright's transcription (left out of Bright's own edition), omitted the *l'après-dîne* and *plein*.

n'était pas dedans ['to have met Jane but she was not within']. So I back again and to my office, where I did with great content *ferais* ['make'][2] a vow to mind my business, and *laisser aller les femmes* ['to let go women'] for a month, and am with all my heart glad to find myself able to come to so good a resolution, that thereby I may follow my business. Which and my honour thereby lies a bleeding. So home to supper and to bed.

On 27 January Jane Welsh arrived with news:

I made me ready and found Jane Welsh, Mr Jervas his maid, come to tell me that she was gone from her master and is resolved to stick to this sweetheart of hers, one Harbing (a very sorry little fellow, and poor) which I did in a word or 2 endeavour to dissuade her from. But being unwilling to keep her long at my house I sent her away and by and by followed her to the Exchange, and thence led her about down to the 3 Cranes, and there took boat for the Falcon, and at a house looking into the fields there took up and sat an hour or 2 talking and discoursing and *faisant ce que je voudrais quant à la toucher* but she would not *laisser me ferais l'autre* thing, though I did what I *pouvais* to have got her *à me le laisser.* But I did enough to *ferais grand plaisir à moy-même* ['discoursing and doing what I would as far as touching her but she would not leave me to do the other thing, though I did what I could to have got her to leave it to me. But I did enough to do great pleasure to myself'].

Thence having endeavoured to make her think of making herself happy by staying out her time with her master and other counsels, but she told me she could not do it, for it was her fortune to have this man, though she did believe it would be to her ruin. Which is a strange stupid thing to a fellow of no kind of worth in the world and a beggar to boot.

On 4 February Pepys made a scathing comment about Elizabeth after having a dispute about paying the cookmaid Jane who had only been with them since late June 1664:

> In the evening was sent to by Jane that I would give her her wages. So I sent for my wife to my office, and told her that rather then be talked on I would give her all her wages for this Quarter coming on, though 2 months is behind. Which vexed my wife, and we begun to be angry, but I took myself up and sent her away. But was cruelly vexed in my mind that all my trouble in this world almost should arise from my disorders in my family and the indiscretion of a wife that brings me nothing almost (besides a comely person) but only trouble and discontent.

On Valentine's Day 1665, Mrs Bagwell was back and offering her services. Pepys managed to exercise some self-control, mindful of his vow on 23 January to stay away from women for a month:

> I up about business and, opening the doore there was Bagwell's wife with whom I talked afterwards and she had the confidence to say she came with a hope to be time enough to be my Valentine, and so endeed she did. But my oath preserved me from losing any time with her.

On 19 February Pepys was outraged by a discovery and ordered his maid Susan to be beaten and confined to the cellar, making such a commotion that their neighbours could hear:

> ... hearing by accident of my mayds their letting in a rogueing Scotch woman that haunts the office to help them to wash and scour in our house and that very lately, I fell mightily out, and made my wife, to the disturbance of the house and neighbours, to beat our little girle, and then we shut her down into the siller* and there she lay all night.

---

* = 'cellar'.

Susan was probably already by this time routinely being subjected to Pepys's roaming hands (see 6 August, this year, below).

Six days after Valentine's Day (20 February), and exactly twenty-eight days after his oath, Pepys gave in to temptation with Mrs Bagwell whom only a few days before he had boasted about resisting. The entry also contains a reference to Elizabeth Pepys mocking her husband's interest in the maids:

> Thence to the office, and there found Bagwells wife whom I directed to go home and I would do her business, which was to write a letter to my Lord Sandwich for her husband's advance into a better ship as there should be occasion. Which I did, and by and by did go down by water to Deptford yard, and then down further, and so landed at the lower end of the town, and it being dark did privately *entrer en la maison de la femme de* Bagwell ['privately enter the house of Bagwell's wife'], and there had *sa* company,[3] though with a great deal of difficulty, *néanmoins enfin j'avais ma volonté d'elle* ['nevertheless, in the end I had my will of her']. And being sated therewith I walked home to Redriffe, it being now near 9 a-clock, and there I did drink some strong waters and eat some bread and cheese and so home. Where at my office my wife comes and tells me that she hath hired a chamber maid, one of the prettiest maids that ever she see in her life, and that she is really jealous of me for her. But hath ventured to hire her from month to month. But I think she means merrily.

Pepys prioritized having 'his will' in various contexts, helping provoke his coercive attitude to sex. It is clear from the 'difficulty' involved that he had had to apply considerable force to achieve his goal. He had injured himself in the struggle. The next morning (21 February):

> Up, and to the office (having a mighty pain in my forefinger of my left hand from a strain that it received last night in struggling *avec la femme que je* ['with the woman that I'] mentioned yesterday) . . .

That his left forefinger was affected suggests Pepys was using his left hand in a grip to hold Mrs Bagwell down, his right hand required for other purposes. She must have struggled to fight back, probably being left worse off than he was.

It is obvious what had happened. Pepys, however, was unconcerned about Elizabeth Bagwell's welfare. Many of those who wrote about Pepys in the past were reluctant to label him a rapist. John Wilson seemed only concerned that Pepys had hurt his finger and elsewhere referred to Mrs Bagwell's 'harlotry'. In his biography of Pepys, Richard Ollard ignored this occasion in his discussion of the Bagwell story, but at least regarded the circumstances surrounding Pepys's supervision of William Bagwell's career as 'more than usually revolting'.[4] Yet, there can be no doubt that Mrs Bagwell had been raped once again (see 20 December 1664 above).

Elizabeth Bagwell had no serious prospect of taking legal action against Pepys. In any case, it would have ended any chance of Pepys helping her husband. There was an engrained suspicion at the time that a woman's allegations were unreliable. She would have been more likely to risk her own reputation at a time when female chastity was so valued. 'As an act of social and sexual destruction, rape worked both <as> a literal and figurative silencing of women.'[5] Pepys knew that he could act with relative impunity. Moreover, William Bagwell's ship, the *Providence* (see 23 December 1665), was at sea in the war and his wife would have followed as best she could by staying in port towns. The ship was back in Deptford in July and her relations with Pepys resumed (see below).

Elizabeth Pepys's concerns about the new maid make it probable that she knew he casually touched their maids' breasts and sought kisses from them. She is less likely to have known about the extent of his philandering further afield. However, the maid arrived on 6 March (see below), and Pepys's hopes were dashed.

The tension mounted, even while in the background the threat of war with the Dutch was becoming a major preoccupation for Pepys. On the last day of the month (28 February), Pepys and Elizabeth had a furious row:

> Come home, I to the taking my wife's kitchen accounts at the latter end of the month, and there find 7s wanting. Which did occasion a very high falling out between us, I endeed too angrily insisting upon so poor a thing and did give her very provoking words calling her beggar, and reproaching her friends, which she took very stomachfully* and reproached me justly with mine and I confess being myself I cannot see what she could have done less. I find she is very cunning and when she least shows it hath her wit at work but it is an ill one, though I think not so bad but with good usage I might well bear with it, and the truth is I do find that my being over-solicitous and jealous and froward and ready to reproach her doth make her worse. However, I find that now and then a little difference doth do no hurt. But too much of it will make her know her force too much. We parted after many high words very angry, and I to my office to my month's accounts, and find myself worth 1270£. For which the Lord God be praised.

The following morning (1 March) they made up, but Pepys resented handing over money promised to Elizabeth to buy clothes:

> Up. And this day being the day that by a promise a great while ago made to my wife I was to give her 20£ to lay out in clothes against Easter, she did, notwithstanding last night's falling out, come to peace with me and I with her, but did boggle mightily at the parting with my money but at last did give it her and then she abroad to buy her things and I to my office where busy all the morning.

The new maid called Mary arrived on 6 March. Pepys was very unimpressed, and did not consider whether Elizabeth had made a joke at his expense. This inclination to take things literally was typical of his personality:

---

* Proudly, haughtily.

> ... instead of handsome, as my wife spoke and still seems to reckon, is a very ordinary wench, I think. And therein was mightily disappointed.

Although Pepys had already broken his oath of 23 January 1665, he was relieved to find on 9 March that circumstances were to prevent him breaking it again (he had perhaps renewed it) just as he was leading himself into temptation, once more with Betty Martin:

> ... I to Westminster where I hear Mrs Martin is brought to bed of a boy and christened Charles.* Which I am very glad of, for I was fearful of being called to be a godfather to it. But it seems it was to be done suddenly and so I escaped. It is strange to see how a liberty and going abroad without purpose of doing anything doth lead a man to what is bad, for I was just upon going to her, where I must of necessity[6] have broken my oath or made a forfeit. But I did not, company being (I heard by my porter) with her and so I home again.

Four days later (13 March) Betty Martin was still anxiously pursuing her husband's interests:

> ... so I home and there meeting a letter from Mrs Martin desiring to speak with me, I (though against my promise of visiting her) did go, and there found her in her child-bed dress desiring my favour to get her husband a place. I stayed not long.

The same day, Pepys discovered that he both liked and loathed his wife's new blonde hair extensions:

> This day my wife begun to wear light coloured locks, quite white almost, which, though it makes her look very pretty, yet not being natural vexes me, that I will not have her wear them.

---

* No record of this christening could be traced.

Pepys was distracted by the prostitutes in Drury Lane on 21 March but veered away perhaps out of fear of venereal disease. He arrived home to find a gratuity from the Navy's contractor John Burrows, who supplied certain articles of clothing and other goods:

> In our way the coach drove through a lane by Drury lane where abundance of loose women stood at the doors which, God forgive me, did put evil thoughts in me but proceeded no further, blessed be God. So home, and late at my office, then home and there found a couple of state cups, very large, coming, I suppose, each to about 6£ a piece, from Burrows the Slopseller.

On 23 March Pepys managed to enjoy the company of both Sarah Udall at the Swan and Betty Martin, finding time to drop his wife off en route and considerately picking her up later:

> . . . thence abroad, carried my wife to Westminster by coach. I to the Swan, Herbert's, and there had much of the good company of Sarah and to my wish, and then to see Mrs Martin, who was very kind. 3 weeks of her month of lying in is over. So took up my wife and home . . .

Pepys had had his 'wish' of Sarah Udall, passing over how far the encounter went. Sarah was married in November 1666. Such records as exist suggest she was about the same age as Betty Martin (see Glossary of People and Places). Betty Martin was 'very kind' which implied she had consented to or actively sought sexual activity. She certainly did so on 27 March, despite having just borne her husband a child:

> Thence to Mrs Martin, who, though her husband is gone away, as he writes, like a fool into France, yet is as simple and wanton as ever she was. With much[7] I made myself merry and away.

Betty Martin soon discovered her husband kept a mistress too but decided that while he was away, she would keep herself for him. On 30 March Pepys was impressed by her restraint:

> Thence to see Mrs Martin, whose husband being it seems gone away and as she is informed he hath another woman whom he uses and hath long done as a wife, she is mighty reserved and resolved to keep herself so till the return of her husband. Which is a pleasant thing to think of her.

Betty Martin's principles probably had more to do with her fear of explaining a pregnancy while her husband was away.

On 3 April Pepys made one of his regular visits to the theatre, on this occasion the Duke's House theatre in Lincoln's Inn Fields. The party included his wife and her companion Mary Mercer. They watched a show called *Mustapha* which Pepys thought so poor 'that we were not contented with it at all'. There were, however, compensations, including the royal mistress and two actresses:

> All the pleasure of the play was the King, and my Lady Castlemaine was there. And pretty witty Nell at the King's house, and the younger Marshall sat next us, which pleased me mightily.

Nell Gwyn was to become another of Charles II's mistresses, but not until 1668. In April 1665 she was still only fifteen. The 'younger Marshall' was Rebecca, an actress like her elder sister Anne.

On 12 April Pepys visited Elizabeth, Lady Batten, second wife of the Surveyor of the Navy, Sir William Batten, and there saw Margaret, Lady Penn, wife of the Navy Commissioner and Pepys's neighbour, Sir William Penn. Evidently, certain women, at least those with no reason to suspect him, found something appealing about Pepys:

> ... there found a great many women with her in her chamber merry. My Lady Penn and her daughter, among others, where my Lady Pen flung me down upon the bed, and herself and others, one after another upon me, and very merry we were, and thence I home and called my wife with my Lady Pen to supper, and very merry as I could be ...

In late April the war against the Dutch was underway and the fleet had sailed. Navy business became more urgent for Pepys. By 30 April it had become apparent that the plague had arrived in London. 'God preserve us all', Pepys wrote, who, at least temporarily, seems to have been diverted from women, partly because of his oath. On 15 May the oath expired:

> ... to the Swan at Herbert's, and there the company of Sarah a little while, and so away and called at the Harp and Ball, where the maid, Mary, is very *formosa* ['beautifully formed'] but, Lord, to see in what readiness I am upon the expiring of my vowes this day to begin to run into all my pleasures and neglect of business.

On 18 May Pepys mused on his shortcomings:

> But Lord, to see how frail a man I am, subject to my vanities then can hardly forbear, though pressed with never so much business, my pursuing of pleasure ...

By 19 June Elizabeth Pepys had gone to visit her mother. The following day (20 June) was thanksgiving for the victory at sea off Lowestoft. Pepys celebrated in style with Sarah Udall:

> ... after dinner, to White hall with Sir W. Berkely in his coach. And so walked to Herbert's* and there spent a little time *avec la moça,*[8] *sin*

* The Swan.

> *hazer algo con ella que* kiss and *tocar ses mamelles, que me haza hazer la cosa a mi mismo con gran plaisir* ['with the wench without doing something with her other then kissing and touching her breasts, which makes me do the thing to myself with great pleasure']. Thence by water to Fox hall, and there walked an hour alone, observing the several humours of the citizens that were there this holyday, pulling of cherries[9] and God knows what. And so home to my office, where late . . . my wife came home when I came from the office.

Pepys became worried about the plague and visiting taverns though he did go to the Swan on 28 June, having discovered that Betty Martin had left London. Many others were now also preparing to escape the contagion and were packing up to go.

Pepys was back at the Swan on 3 July before moving on to another hostelry for more company with Sarah Udall:

> . . . so to the Swan, and there *demeurais un peu de temps con la fille* ['dallied a little while with the girl']. And so to the Harp and Ball and alone *demeurais un peu de temps besando la* ['dallied a short time kissing her'] and so away home and late at the office about letters, and so home.[10]

By 5 July Pepys was arranging to pack Elizabeth off to Woolwich for safety from the plague. Six days later (11 July) he was back at the Harp and Ball, meeting there a maid of his called Mary (she was sacked by Elizabeth by 9 November). Pepys had already met Mary there on several occasions:

> At 6 a-clock up and to Westminster (where and all the town besides, I hear, the plague encreases) and it being too soon to go to the Duke of Albemarle I to the Harp and Ball, and there made a bargain with Mary to go forth with me in the afternoon, which she with much ado consented to.

Pepys went on to the Duke of Albemarle's and then Trinity House:

> . . . and thence had Mary meet me at the New Exchange and there took coach and I with great pleasure took the ayre to Highgate, and thence to Hampstead. Much pleased with her company, pretty and innocent, and had what pleasure almost I would with her and so at night, weary and sweaty, it being very hot beyond bearing, we back again, and I set her down in St Martin's Lane.

Mrs Bagwell was back to see Pepys on 15 July but had competition:

> Up, and after all business done though late, I to Deptford. But before I went out of the office saw there young Bagwells wife returned, but could not stay to speak to her, though I had a great mind to it. And also another great lady, as to fine clothes, did attend there to have a ticket signed which I did do, taking her through the garden to my office, where I signed it and had a salute* of her, and so I away by boat to Redriffe . . .

Pepys visited Deptford again on 18 July, but he only reported that he had 'stayed a little while' before heading by water to visit Elizabeth in Woolwich, whom he had not seen for almost a week. This may be an example of an occasion when he had intended to see Mrs Bagwell but did not bother to record it, perhaps having been thwarted. On 19 July, Pepys went out late with a plan. Business could be conducted at almost any time of day or evening and likewise, domestic or social activities:

> Very late, I went away, it raining, but I had *un design pour aller à la femme de* Bagwell and did so, *mais ne savais obtener algun cosa de ella como yo quisiere sino tocar la* ['a design to go to Bagwell's wife and did so,

* A kiss.

> but knew not how to get something from her that I wanted but to touch her']. So away about 12 . . .

Pepys already knew of Mrs Elizabeth Burrows, daughter of a Mrs Crofts who worked at Westminster Hall, before 2 June 1665 when he first mentioned her. On that occasion Mrs Burrows, the wife of Anthony Burrows, a naval officer killed in action during 1665, was out. On 20 July Pepys was pleased to discover she was in:

> . . . and so to Mrs Crofts where I found and saluted Mrs Burrows who is a very pretty woman for a mother of so many children.

As a Navy widow, Elizabeth Burrows was soon compromised because all she had was the Navy ticket promissory note for her husband's wages. Later in 1665 she sought Pepys's attention and interest in her plight (see 21 December 1665 below). Her needs and looks provided him with an opportunity. During the research for this book, her marriage was identified as that between an Elizabeth Crofts and Anthony 'Barwis' on 28 April 1653 at St Mary Somerset in London. She was probably the woman of this name born in Westminster in 1637 (see Glossary of People and Places). She was thus at least about twenty-eight and could easily have had six or more pregnancies by the time she came into Pepys's orbit in 1665.

On 6 August, Pepys asked his servant Susan to deal with his hair. She had been first mentioned as a 'little girl' on 31 December 1663 along with a cookmaid. Now in 1665, his hands soon wandered:

> And dressed and had my head combed by my little girle, to whom I confess *que je sum demasiado* kind, *nuper ponendo saepe mes manos*[11] *in su dos choses de son* breast. *Mais il faut que je* ['that I am far too kind, lately often putting my hands on her 2 things of her breast. But it is necessary that I'] leave it lest it bring me to *alguno* ['some'] major inconvenience. So to my business in my chamber.

In this instance Pepys wrote out several of the French and Latin words in longhand (*sum*, *demasiado*, and *nuper*). 'Little girl' is a reference to Susan's physical size and junior status. 'Kind' meant lustfully disposed towards. Susan is likely to have been no older than her mid-teens.[12] She was in no position to resist her employer's attention, the only inhibiting factor here being his concern about consequences. Although this is the first time Pepys recorded touching Susan in a sexual way, he also made it clear that he was already habitually doing so. She fell ill in 1666 and seems to have recovered but suffered fits (diary, 1 and 12 May 1666).

On 11 August, the waterman Delkes arrived with his daughter Mrs Robins, seeking exemption for his son-in-law from being pressed into naval service. Pepys boasted that he resisted at least most of what was on offer, but had had ill-timed second thoughts:

> . . . in the morning a pleasant *rencontre* ['meeting'] happened in having a young married woman brought me by her father, old Delkes that carries pins always in his mouth, to get her husband off that he should not go to sea. *Uno ombre pouvait avoir* done any *cosa cum ella* ['A man could have done anything with her'], but I did *natha*[13] *sino besar* ['nothing but kiss'] her. After they were gone my mind run upon having them called back again, and I sent a messenger to Blackwall, but he failed so I lost my expectation.

The next day (12 August), Pepys was at Greenwich, with half a mind to meet up with his wife. Instead, he headed back to Deptford in the company of Mrs Bagwell's father-in-law (Owen Bagwell, the dockyard foreman).[14] As was usual at the time, the term '-in-law' was omitted:

> Coming back to Deptford, old Bagwell walked a little way with me, and would have me in to his daughter's, and there he being gone *dehors, ego* had my *volunté de su hija* ['he being gone outside, I had my will of his daughter'].

A few days later, on 15 August, Pepys recalled from the night before his dream involving the unobtainable Lady Castlemaine.

> Up by 4 a-clock and walked to Greenwich where called at Captain Cockes and to his chamber he being in bed. Where something put my last night's dream into my head, which I think is the best that ever was dreamed, which was that I had my Lady Castlemayne in my arms and was admitted to use all the dalliance I desired with her and then dreamt that this could not be awake, but that it was only a dream. But that since it was a dream, and that I took so much real pleasure in it, what a happy thing it would be if when we are in our graves (as Shakespeere resembles it) we could dream, and dream but such dreams as this, that then we should not need to be so fearful of death, as we are this plague time.

Pepys returned to the dockyard in Deptford on 22 August:

> . . . and by and by out at the back gate, and there saw the Bagwells wifes, mother and daughter, and went to them and went into the daughter's house with<out> the mother and *faciebam*[15] *la cosa que ego tenebam* a mind to *con ella* ['did the thing that I had a mind to with her']. And drinking and talking, by and by away, and so walked to Redriffe . . .

Pepys appears to have meant he had seen the two Bagwell wives, Alice Bagwell and her daughter-in-law Elizabeth Bagwell. The lack of punctuation and confused referencing is typical of Pepys who indicated here that Alice Bagwell was complicit in her daughter-in-law's sexual services in return for her son's advancement (see her husband Owen's actions on 12 August above).*

---

* On 30 November 1665, P committed a sexual act with the naval widow Elizabeth Burrows at the door of her mother's house.

On 23 August, Delkes the waterman was back with his daughter Mrs Robins, enticed there by Pepys. Pepys did not get what he wanted, but was optimistic:

> . . . comes by a practice of mine yesterday old Delks the waterman with his daughter Robins and several times to and again, he leaving her with me. About the getting of his son Robins off, who was pressed yesterday again. And *yo haze ella mettre su mano* upon *hemera pragma*[16] *hasta hazer me hazer la cosa in su mano. Pero ella no voulut permettre que je ponebam meam manum a ella* ['I made her put her hand upon my thing until making myself do the thing in her hand. But she would not let me put my hand on her'] but I do not doubt but ἀλλῳ χείρῳ[17] *de obtenir le* ['but <with> another laying on of hands to get it']. All the afternoon at my office mighty busy writing letters . . .

This entry has some of the most difficult polyglot in the diary. Some words are written in shorthand with incorrectly positioned consonants, thereby altering the medial vowels, possibly intentionally. The alliterative use of *hasta* with *hazer me hazer* ('until making myself do') is paralleled only once, on 18 February 1667. Greek words, the first pair in shorthand and the second in longhand, were very unusual for Pepys. They were blundered and are challenging to make sense of.

The entry appears to be an elaborate play on the word 'hand', as well as involving alliteration based on 'h' and 'm' and the rhyming suffixes of the inflected Greek words. The Greek supplied Pepys with a pun on what he had written in Spanish. He was apparently referring to the prospect of more successfully forcing Mrs Robins to provide manual stimulation on another occasion. Pepys avoided writing such complicated polyglot thereafter; although he knew Greek, he rarely used it, and his competence seems to have been limited.[18]

Elizabeth Pepys fell out with her companion Mercer a few days later, informing her husband on 29 August. Pepys had to restrain himself:

In the morning waking, among other discourse my wife begun to tell me the difference between her and Mercer, and that it was only from restraining her to gad abroad to some Frenchmen that were in the town which I do not wholly, yet in part believe, and for my quiet would not enquire into it.

By 2 September Pepys was back with Mrs Bagwell:

After dinner I to Deptford and there took occasion to *andar a la casa de la gunaica de mi Minusier* and did what I had a mind *a hazer con la* and *volvio* ['to go to the house of the wife of my Carpenter and did what I had a mind to do with her and went back'].[19]

It is not difficult to understand one of the reasons for Pepys's recklessness. He lived at a time when death was everywhere, and in 1665 that had never been clearer. On 4 September:

But it troubled me to pass by Come Farme* where about 21 people have died of the plague. And 3 or 4 days since I saw a dead corpse in a Coffin lie in the Close unburyed. And a watch is constantly kept there night and day to keep the people in. The plague making us cruel as dogs one to another.

On 5 October Pepys allowed himself a distraction or two while en route to see John Evelyn at his home, Sayes Court in Deptford. Evelyn would have been appalled, had he known:

I walked through Westminster to my old house, the Swan, and there did pass some time with Sarah, and so down by water to Deptford and there to my Valentine [Mrs Bagwell]. Round about and next door on every side is the plague, but I did not value it, but there did what I would *con ella* ['with her'] and so away to Mr

* In Blackheath, a short distance from Deptford and Greenwich.

> Evelings to discourse of our confounded business of prisoners, and sick and wounded seamen wherein he and we are so much put out of order. And here he showed me his gardens, which are for variety of Ever-greens, and hedges of Holly, the finest things I ever see in my life.

On 16 October Thomas Povey bemoaned the state of the Restoration court and its decadence while he and Pepys walked to Syon House:

> . . . in our way he discoursing of the wantonness of the Court and how it minds nothing else. And I saying that that would leave the King shortly if he did not leave it, he told me 'No', for the King doth spend most of his time in feeling and kissing them naked all over their bodies in bed. And contents himself without doing the other thing but as he finds himself included, but this lechery will never leave him.

One wonders what Povey would have made of some of Pepys's other social activities. On 23 October Pepys came home to Greenwich (where he lived during the plague) to find Sir Thomas, 2nd Baron Rutherford, waiting for him. Rutherford seems to have been as free with his hands, or at least wanted to be, as Pepys was. The meeting is useful evidence that Pepys was not alone in his tendencies:

> We supped together and sat up late, he being a mighty wanton man with a daughter-in-law* of my landlady's, a pretty conceited woman big with child and he would be handling her breasts which she coyly refused.

---

* Mrs Rebecca Daniels. See 21 December 1665.

Meanwhile, Pepys was increasingly exercised by the prize goods scandal. This erupted in late 1665 after Sandwich prematurely allowed the distribution of captured Dutch cargoes before the Admiralty had declared them. The result was that the King issued instructions 'to examine most severely all that had been done in the taking out any with or without order, without respect to my Lord Sandwich at all' (12 October). Sandwich was temporarily relieved of his post and the ructions rumbled on for several years. Pepys, for his part, swiftly disposed of the spices he had purchased from one of the Dutch vessels.[20]

On 5 November, Pepys visited Evelyn once again. Evelyn showed Pepys his draft text of a major work about gardening (*Elysium Britannicum*) but this was not published until modern times. Then Captain Cocke arrived:

> Here comes in, in the middle of our discourse, Captain Cocke as drunk as a dog but could stand and talk and laugh. He did so joy himself in a brave woman that he had been with all the afternoon, and who should it be but my Lady Robinson. But very troublesome he is with his noise and talk, and laughing, though very pleasant.
>
> With him in his coach to Mr Glanvills, where he sat with Mrs Penington and myself a good while talking of this fine woman again and then went away. Then the lady and I to very serious discourse ... After an hour's talk we to bed, the lady mightily troubled about a pretty little bitch she hath, which is very sick, and will eat nothing, and the worst was, I could hear her in her chamber bemoaning the bitch, and by and by taking her into bed with her. The bitch pissed and shit a bed, and she was fain to rise and had coals out of my chamber to dry the bed again.

Judith Penington soon became of more interest, even though she was almost forty years old, but apparently unmarried. Her brother Isaac, the Quaker leader, appears to have thought her wanton (see

Glossary of People and Places). On 8 November Pepys was after Mrs Bagwell, but determined not to be spotted:

> . . . by water to Deptford and there did order my matters so, walking up and down the fields till it was dark night, that *je alloy à la maison* ['I went to the house'] of my valentine, and there *je faisais* whatever *je voudrais avec* her ['I did whatever I would with her'], and about 8 at night did take water, being glad I was out of the town, for the plague it seems rages there more then ever. And so to my lodgings . . .

On 9 November, Pepys learned that Elizabeth had sacked her maid Mary, whom he had been meeting at the Harp and Ball. He was worried whether he was the reason:

> W. Hewer did tell me my wife will be here tomorrow and hath put away Mary, which vexes me to the heart, I cannot helpe it though it may be a folly in me, and when I think seriously on it, I think my wife means no ill design in it, or, if she do, I am a fool to be troubled at it, since I cannot help it.

Pepys thought Judith Penington to be a modest and refined woman, but discovered she was unusually forward when on 13 November he and Captain Cocke headed:

> . . . to Glanvills, and there he and I sat talking and playing with Mrs Penington whom we found undressed in her smock and petticoats by the fireside, and there we drank and laughed, and she willingly suffered me to put my hand in her bosom very wantonly and keep it there long. Which methought was very strange, and I looked upon myself as a man mightily deceived in a lady, for I could not have thought she could have suffered it by her former discourse with me. So modest she seemed, and I know not what.

Pepys met Judith again in the company of George Cocke on 26 November:

I walked with a lanthorn, weary as I was, to Greenwich but it was a fine walk, it being a hard frost. And so to Captain Cocke's, but he I found had sent for me to come to him to Mrs Penington's, and there I went, and we were very merry, and supped. And Cock being sleepy he went away betimes. I stayed alone talking and playing with her till past midnight. She suffering me *a hazer* whatever *ego voulu*[21] *avec ses mamelles* ['to do whatever I wanted with her breasts']. And I almost led her to discourse to make her *tocar mi cosa* naked which *ella* did *presque* ['touch my naked thing which she almost did'] and did not refuse. Much pleased with her company we parted and I home to bed at past one, all people being in bed thinking I would have stayed out of town all night.

The next day (27 November) Pepys visited Sarah Udall at the Swan, and went further than she was willing to go:

I to the Swan, and there found Sarah all alone in the house and I had the opportunity *a hazer* what I *tenia*[22] a mind *á hazer con ella* only *con* my hands ['to do what I had a mind to do with her only with my hands']. But she was vexed at my offer *a tocar la* under *sus jupes* ['to touch her under her skirts'] but I did once, *non obstant* ['notwithstanding'] all that.

On 4 December he was back with Judith Penington, his wife having returned to London:

So late by water home, taking a barrel of oysters with me and at Greenwich went and sat with Madam Penington *con la quelle je faisais* almost whatever *je voudrais. Con mi mano, sino tocar la chose même* ['with whom I did almost whatever I would. With my hand, if

> not to touch the very thing'] and I was very near it and made her undresse her head and sit dishevelled all night sporting till 2 in the morning and so away to my lodging almost cloyed* with this dalliance and so bed.

On 6 December Pepys was catapulted almost into ecstasy by music, illustrating the intensity of his physical senses:

> ... so with my wife walked and Mercer to Mrs Pierces where Captain Rolt and Mrs Knipp, Mr Coleman and his wife, and Laneare, Mrs Worship and her singing daughter, met, and by and by unexpectedly comes Mr Pierce from Oxford. Here the best company for Musique I ever was in, in my life, and wish I could live and die in it, both for musique[23] and the face of Mrs Pierce, and my wife and Knipp who is pretty enough but the most excellent, mad-humourd thing, and sings the noblest that ever I heard in my life, and Rolt with her, some things together most excellently. I spent the night in ecstasy almost ...

On 16 December Pepys managed the feat of hands-free masturbation, apparently based on fantasizing about Betty Howlett (his description is ambiguous):

> ... I did see Betty Howlet come after the sickness to the hall. Had not opportunity to salute her as I desired but was glad to see her and a very pretty wench she is. Thence back landing at the Old Swan and taking boat again at Billingsgate, and setting ashore we home and I to the office lying down close in my boat and there, without use of my hand, had great pleasure, and the first time I did make trial of my strength of fancy of that kind without my hand, and had it complete *avec la fille que* I did see *au jour dhuy* ['with the girl that I did see today'] in Westminster hall.

---

* worn out, glutted.

20 December proved to be a busy day:

> So home to Greenwich, and thence I to Mrs Penington and had a supper from the King's head for her and there mighty merry and free as I used to be with her. And at last, late I did pray her to undress herself into her nightgown that I might see how to have her picture drawn carelessly (for she is mighty proud of that conceit) and I would walk without in the street till she had done. So I did walk forth and whether I made too many turns or no in the dark cold frosty night between the 2 walls up to the park gate I know not, but she was gone to bed when I come again to the house, upon pretence of leaving some papers there, which I did on purpose by her consent. So I away home, and was there sat up for to be spoken with my young Mrs Daniel to pray me to speak for her husband to be a Lieutenant. I had the opportunity here of kissing her again and again, and did answer that I would be very willing to do him any kindness and so parted and I to bed . . .

The following day (21 December) Mrs Daniels, who was pregnant, obliged Pepys with a meal and more attention. He was pleased to see Elizabeth Burrows again:

> Coming home and going to bed the boy tells me his sister Daniel hath provided me a supper of little birds killed by her husband, and I made her sup with me, and after supper were alone a great while, and I had the pleasure of her lips. She being a pretty woman, and one whom a great belly becomes as well as ever I saw any. She gone, I to bed. This day I was come to by Mrs Burrows of Westminster, Lieutenant Burrows (lately dead) his wife, a most pretty woman and my old acquaintance. I had a kiss or 2 of her, and a most modest woman she is.

By 15 June 1666 (see next chapter) she was actively seeking Pepys's financial assistance.

On 23 December Pepys wrote to Sir William Coventry seeking a position as ship's carpenter for William Bagwell. It was not the first time (see above 9 July 1663). This extract is from Pepys's letter, not the diary:

> I must become a suitor to you for one to whom you have already been kind for my sake, and am from the good character I have of his care and diligence led again to move you on his behalf. It is for one Bagwell, carpenter formerly of the *Dolphin*, now of the *Providence*, who tells me he hears Clements, carpenter of the *Swiftsure*, is promised the new *London* in consideration of his loss in the old one. If so, and that the *Swiftsure* be not engaged, indeed I think your favour to this man be well placed . . . [24]

Coventry of course was unlikely to be aware of the advance compensation for Pepys's trouble in the matter made on her husband's behalf by Mrs Bagwell.

Although the plague continued, the year ended with Pepys feeling chastened but optimistic:

> I have raised my estate from 1300£ in this year to 4400£. I have got myself greater interest, I think, by my diligence and my employments increased by that of Treasurer for Tanger, and Surveyor of the Victuals.
>
> It is true we have gone through great melancholy because of the great plague, and I put to great charges by it, by keeping my family long at Woolwich, and myself and another part of my family, my clerks, at my charge at Greenwich, and a maid at London. But I hope the King will give us some satisfaction for that. But now the plague is abated almost to nothing, and I intending to get to London as fast as I can my family, that is my wife and maids, having been <there> these 2 or 3 weeks . . .*

* P means he had been back in London for two to three weeks but omitted 'there' or an equivalent.

My whole family hath been well all this while, and all my friends I know of, saving my aunt Bell, who is dead, and some children of my Cos<en> Sarah's, of the plague. But many of such as I know very well, dead. Yet to our great joy the town fills apace and shops begin to be open again. Pray God continue the plague's decrease. For that keeps the Court away from the place of business, and so all goes to rack as to public matters, they at this distance not thinking of it.

7

1666

She Would Now Have Done Anything

During 1666 Pepys became more frustrated by what he perceived as Elizabeth's shortcomings. Pepys was preoccupied with his busy public life and his accelerating interest in a wider variety of women.

Visiting Lord Brouncker's residence in Covent Garden on 2 January Pepys was delighted to encounter the actress and singer Elizabeth Knepp (or Knipp). He was mesmerized by her. His conduct at their first meeting appears startling now:

> . . . above all my dear Mrs Knipp, with whom I sang, and in perfect pleasure I was to hear her sing, and especially her little Scotch song of *Barbary Allen*. And to make our mirth the completer, Sir Jo. Minnes was in the highest pitch of mirth and his Mimicall tricks, that ever I saw, and most excellent pleasant company he is and the best Mimique that ever I saw, and certainly would have made an excellent Actor and now would be an excellent teacher of Actors. Thence, it being post night,

> against my will took leave but before I come to my office, longing for more of her company, returned and met them coming home in coaches, so I got into the coach where Mrs Knipp was and got her upon my knee (the coach being full) and played with her breasts and sung, and at last set her at her house and so good night.

Pepys's attentions wandered elsewhere as freely as his hands, Elizabeth being still in Woolwich. Pepys had already commented on his Greenwich landlady's daughter Frances Tooker, apparently only in her mid-teens at most. On 11 October 1665 Pepys had referred to her as 'a very pretty child', supplying her first name ('Fr:') on 26 October. On 5 January he met up with 'Mrs Tooker' and made his first move:

> So home and to my papers for lack of company but by and by comes little Mrs Tooker and sat and supped with me and I kept her very late talking and making her comb my head, and did what I will with *elle et tenia*[1] *grande plaisir con ella, tocanda sa cosa con mi cosa* and *hazendo la cosa par cette moyen* ['what I will with her and had great pleasure with her, touching her thing with my thing and doing the thing by this means']. So late to bed.

On 29 January Pepys and John Evelyn discussed the decadence of the court. Pepys was most impressed with Evelyn's views, despite his own lifestyle:

> I was called away before dinner ended to go to my company who dined at our lodgings. Thither I went with Mr Eveling (whom I met) in his coach going that way. But finding my company gone but my Lord Brouncker left his coach for me, so Mr Eveling and I into my Lord's coach, and rode together with excellent discourse till we come to Clapham. Talking of the vanity and vices of the Court, which makes it a most

> contemptible thing. And endeed in all his discourse I find him a most worthy person.

On 20 February Pepys heard news of Betty Martin and reverted again to her maiden name (Lane). It is likely that someone who knew he would be interested passed on the information. Moreover, Frances Tooker came to stay but there is no mention of her being approached by Pepys:

> I away to Westminster hall and there hear that Mrs Lane is come to town. So I stayed loitering up and down till anon she comes and agreed to meet at Swayn's and there I went anon and she come, but stayed but little, the place not being private. I have not seen her since before the plague. So thence parted and *rencontrais à* her last *logis*, and in the place did *hazer* what I *tenia* a mind *para fere*[2] *con* her ['and met at her last lodgings, and in the place did do what I had a mind to do with her']. At last she desired to borrow money of me, 5£, and would pawn gold with me for it, which I accepted and promised in a day or 2 to supply her. So away home to the office, and thence home, where little Mrs Tooker stayed all night with us, and a pretty child she is and happens to be niece to my beauty that is dead, that lived at the Jackeanapes, in Cheapside. So to bed, a little troubled that I have been at 2 houses this afternoon with Mrs Lane that were formerly shut up of the plague.

Pepys provided the money on 28 February (below). On the 23rd Knepp paid a visit, to Pepys's delight. She had come to visit Elizabeth, who was out:

> . . . so I fain to entertain her, and took her out by coach to look my wife at Mrs Pierces and Unthankes but find her not, so back again, and then my wife comes home, having been buying of things. And at home I spent all the night talking with this baggage, and teaching her my song of *Beauty retire* which she sings and makes go

> most rarely, and a very fine song it seems to be.* She also entertained me with repeating many of her own and others' parts of the playhouse, which she do most excellently and tells me the whole practices of the playhouse and players, and is in every respect most excellent company. So I supped, and was merry at home all the evening, and the rather it being my Birthday, 33 years. For which God be praised that I am in so good a condition of health and estate, and everything else as I am, beyond expectation, in all. So she to Mrs Turner's to lie, and we to bed. Mightily pleased to find myself in condition to have these people come about me and to be able to entertain them and have the pleasure of their qualities, then which no man can have more in this world.

On 26 February Pepys explained how he was giving in to Elizabeth for an easier life:

> And an hour after was waked with my wife's quarrelling with Mercer, at which I was angry, and my wife and I fell out. But with much ado to sleep again, I beginning to practise more temper, and to give her her way.

By 28 February he was with Betty Martin again on what proved to be a rather complicated day (confusingly calling her by both Martin and her maiden name Lane):

> ... going out of the hall was called to by Mrs Martin. So I went to her and bought 2 bands† and so parted and by and by met at her chamber and there did what I would, and so away home and there find Mrs

---

* 'Baggage' means Elizabeth Knepp, here being used to suggest she was affably saucy. *Beauty Retire* was P's setting of some of the text of Sir William Davenant's *The Siege of Rhodes*. Recordings of the song, the sheet music for which has survived and is held by P in the Hayls painting, can be found online today.

† Small panels of linen worn at the throat secured with a tie.

Knipp, and we dined together, she the pleasantest company in the world. After dinner I did give my wife money to lay out on Knipp, 20s, and I abroad to White hall to visit Colonel Norwood, and then Sir G. Carteret . . . Thence to the Palace yard to the Swan and there stayed till it was dark, and then to Mrs Lanes, and there lent her 5£ upon 4£ 01s in gold. And then did what I would with her, and I perceive she is come to be very bad and offers anything, that it is dangerous to have to do with her, nor will I see <her> any more a good while.

Typically for Pepys, he finished February 1666 determined to mend his ways:

And thus ends this month with my mind full of resolution to apply myself better from this time forward to my business then I have done these 6 or 8 days. Visibly to my prejudice both in quiet of mind and setting backward of my business, that I cannot give a good account of it as I ought to do.

Pepys was becoming reconciled to his nature. On 9 March:

. . . to Sir W. Batten's and there Mrs Knipp coming we did spend the even<ing> together very merry, she and I singing and, God forgive me, I do still see that my nature is not to be quite conquered, but will esteem pleasure above all things, though yet in the middle of it, it hath reluctancy after my business, which is neglected by my fallowing my pleasure. However, music and women I cannot but give way to, whatever my business is.

Pepys decided on 10 March that he was better off making the most of life:

The truth is I do indulge myself a little the more pleasure, knowing that this is the proper age of my life to do it, and out of my observation that most men that do thrive in the world do forget

> to take pleasure during the time that they are getting their estate, but reserve that till they have got one and then it is too late for them to enjoy it with any pleasure.

On 14 March Pepys decided to seek out prostitutes in some of their well-known haunts off Drury Lane:

> Thence to walk all alone in the fields behind Grays Inne, making an end of reading over my dear *Faber Fortunae* of my Lord Bacon's, and thence, it growing dark, took 2 or 3 wanton turns about the idle places and lanes about Drury lane, but to no satisfaction, but a great fear of the plague <among>[3] them, and so anon I walked by invitation to Mrs Pierce's, where I find much good company, that is to say, Mrs Pierce, my wife, Mrs Worship and her daughter, and Harris the player, and Knipp, and Mercer, and Mrs Barbary Sheldon, who is come this day to spend a week with my wife. And here with music we danced, and sung and supped, and then to sing and dance till past one in the morning . . .

The casual mention of 'wanton turns about' the back streets around Drury Lane 'to no satisfaction' implies that Pepys went there more often, probably with greater success. If so, these visits normally went unrecorded.

On 18 March Pepys sent Betty Martin's husband Samuel out shopping:

> To Herbert's and drank and thence to Mrs Martin's and did what I would with her, her husband going for some wine for us. The poor man I do think would take pains if I can get him a purser's place, which I will endeavour.

By May 1666 Pepys had obtained a Navy purser post for Samuel Martin, the first of several.[4] Pursers were able to profit from selling food and clothes privately to sailors. Pepys was in two minds about providing him with jobs. Martin's absence at sea made sexual relations with Betty potentially riskier, but he also supplied Pepys with information about how to make money and Pepys of course felt obliged to offer a quid pro quo for Betty's amenability.

On 23 March Pepys discovered that Frances Tooker had come to stay again:

> Up and going out of my dressing room, when ready to go downstairs, I spied little Mrs Tooker, my pretty little girl, which it seems did come yesterday to our house to stay a little while with us, but I did not know of it till now. I was glad of her coming, she being a very pretty child, and now grown almost a woman.

On this occasion he makes no mention of assaulting Frances again, presumably because in his own house that would have been too dangerous.

The same day, Pepys was pleased to hear that Betty Howlett was married to Michael Mitchell, his elder brother (who had been betrothed to Betty) having died in the plague. The wedding occurred on 27 February 1666 in Canterbury, Betty being about twenty years old:

> I am mighty glad of this match, and more that they are likely to live near me in Thames street. Where I may see Betty now and then, whom I from a girl did use to call my second wife, and mighty pretty she is.

On 6 April Elizabeth set out for Brampton once again. Five days later (11 April) Mrs Bagwell arrived to see Pepys, but he did not enlarge on what happened. She had, like many navy wives, stayed in lodgings in or near Portsmouth while her husband was working in the dockyard there:

> This noon Bagwell's wife came to me to the office after her being long at Portsmouth.

Pepys was subjected on 17 April to 'my heart tempting me 1000 times to go abroad about some pleasure or other' but managed to restrain himself. However, Pepys bumped into his barber's servant Jane Welsh on 18 April to discover her marriage plans were in ruins:

> . . . spying out of my coach Jane that lived heretofore at Jervas my barber's I went a little further and stopped and went on foot back and overtook her, taking water at Westminster bridge* and spoke to her, and she telling me whither she was going, I over the water and met her at Lambeth and there drank with her, she telling me how he that was so long her servant did prove to be a married man, though her maister told me (which she denies) that he had lain with her several times in his house.
>
> There left her *sin hazer alguna cosa con ella* ['without doing something with her'], and so away by boat to the Change . . .

Pepys never mentioned her again. He had presumably hoped that if she had married, he would have been able to proceed further in his relations with her. Pepys eventually returned home where he found Elizabeth's companion Mary Mercer:

> . . . home and to bed. *Apres ayant tocado les mamelles de* Mercer *que eran ouverts, con grand plaisir* ['After having touched Mercer's breasts that were uncovered, with great pleasure'].

Here was Pepys freely handling his wife's companion's breasts as he walked through the door. He probably meant that she was wearing

* The first true Westminster Bridge was built 1739–50; P meant the facility consisting of a quay and ferry for crossing to Lambeth.

a décolletage dress exposing her cleavage in contemporary style. Elizabeth was away but she returned the next day (Thursday 19 April) unexpectedly early to Pepys's disquiet:

> Anon comes home my wife from Brampton. Not looked for till Saturday, which will hinder me of a little pleasure but I am glad of her coming.

By 19 June 1666 (see below) it was clear Pepys was accustomed to handling Mercer's breasts routinely. Elizabeth must have been aware of, and overlooked, a certain amount of her husband's casual man-handling of her female companions and servants, who experienced it as an occupational hazard.

Despite his concerns that Elizabeth's homecoming might stop his antics, Pepys was able to start the day enjoying his wife's company before moving on to a mistress. On 20 April:

> Up and after an hour or 2's talk with my poor wife, who gives me more and more content every day then other, I abroad by coach to Westminster and there met with Mrs Martin, and she and I over the water to Stangate[5] and after a walk in the fields to the King's head, and there spent an hour or 2 with pleasure with her, and eat a tansy* and so parted. And I to the New Exchange . . .

Part of Pepys's grooming technique was to inveigle himself into casual social contact with the families of women he had targeted. On Sunday 13 May he went to St Margaret's, Westminster (where, indeed, he had married Elizabeth over a decade before). Here he privately admitted his cynical intentions:

> At this church I spied Betty Howlett who endeed is mighty pretty and struck me mightily. After church time, standing in the

* A pudding.

> church yard, she spied me so I went to her, her fathers and mothers and husband being with her. They desired and I agreed to go home with Mr Michell and there had the opportunity to have salute<d> 2 or 3 times Betty and make an acquaintance which they are pleased with, though not so much as I am or they think I am. I stayed here an hour or more chatting with them in a little sorry garden of theirs by the Bowling Alley . . .

At the end of the day, he spent 'an hour with my wife pleasantly in her closet' before going to bed. On 16 May Pepys was tormented by his temptations:

> . . . I going down to Deptford and Lord to see with what itching desire I did endeavour to see Bagwell's wife but failed, for which I am glad, only I observe the folly of my mind that cannot refrain from pleasure at a season above all others in my life requisite for me to show my utmost care in.[6]
>
> I walked both going and coming, spending my time reading of my Civill and Ecclesiastical law-book.

The book was Thomas Ridley's 1607 survey, Pepys owning a 1662 edition. It contains several references to the evils and consequences of adultery (see Introduction).[7]

Pepys would have to wait until 13 June to see Mrs Bagwell. But four days later (20 May):

> I out to Westminster and straight to Mrs Martin's and there did what I would with her, she staying at home all the day for me. And not being well pleased with her over-free and loose company I away to Westminster Abbey . . .

A week later (27th), Pepys tried again but found Betty was with her husband and Mrs Burrows, 'the pretty', and had to content himself with 'an hour or 2' of their company.

On the anniversary of the Restoration (29 May), Elizabeth decided to entice her husband:

> . . . I with a merry heart home to my office, and thither my wife comes to me, to tell me, that if I would see the handsomest woman in England, I shall come home presently; and who should it be but the pretty lady of our parish, that did heretofore sit on the other side of our church, over against our gallery, that is since married; she with Mrs Anne Jones, one of this parish, that dances finely, and Mrs <no name supplied> sister did come to see her this afternoon, and so I home and there find Creed also come to me. So there I spent most of the afternoon with them, and endeed she is a pretty black woman,* her name Mrs Horesely. But Lord to see how my nature could not refrain from the temptation but I must invite them to go to Fox hall to Spring Garden though I had freshly received minutes of a great deal of extraordinary business. However, I could not help it but sent them before with Creed, and I did some of my business and so after them, and find them there in an Arbour and had met with Mrs Pierce and some company with her. So here I spent 20s upon them and were pretty merry. Among other things, had a fellow that imitated all manner of birds and dogs and hogs with his voice, which was mighty pleasant. Stayed here till night then set Mrs Pierce in at the New Exchange and ourselfs took coach, and so set Mrs Horsly home, and then home ourselfs . . .

Pepys enjoyed himself in the way he preferred on Sunday 3 June. Betty Martin was now around several months into her pregnancy (see 25 July below):

> I to St. Margaret's Westminster and there saw at church my pretty Betty Michell. And thence to the Abbey and so to Mrs Martin and

* Dark-haired, dark-complexioned.

> there did what *je voudrais avec* her both *delante*[8] and backward which is also *muy bon plazer* ['did what I would with her both forward and backward, which is also very good pleasure'].

Pepys was unsettled by an unusual sight at Whitehall on 12 June:

> Walking here in the galleries I find the Ladies of Honour dressed in their riding garbs with coats and doublets with deep skirts just for all the world like mine, and buttoned their doublets up the breast, with perriwigs and with hats so that, only for a long petticoat dragging under their men's coats, nobody could take them for women in any point whatever. Which was an odde sight and a sight did not please me . . .
>
> Thence down by water to Deptford and there late, seeing some things dispatched to the fleet and so home (thinking endeed to have met with <Mrs> Bagwell[9] but I did not) . . .

Given his comment the next day, this failed assignation probably followed Mrs Bagwell coming to him at the office to arrange a meeting, but which Pepys did not record. After a long day on 13 June when he lost some lobsters he had bought, and witnessed the moving sight of a dozen loyal seamen attending the funeral of the naval officer Sir Christopher Myngs who had been killed during the Four Days Battle (see 23 June below), Pepys set out for the evening:

> . . . went down by water to Deptford, it being very late. And there I stayed out as much time as I could and then took boat again homeward. But the officers being gone in, returned and walked to Mrs Bagwell's house and there (it being by this time pretty dark and past 10 a-clock) went into her house and did what I would. But I was not a little fearful of what she told me but now, which is that her servant was dead of the plague. That her coming to me yesterday was the first day of her coming forth, and that she had new whitened the house all below stairs, but

that above stairs they are not so fit for me to go up to, they being not so.

On 15 June was visited again by the naval widow Mrs Burrows (see 21 December 1665 above). She was now desperate for money. The visit left him hopeful that she would be more obliging in future:

> So to the office and thither came my pretty widow Mrs Burrows, poor woman, to get her ticket paid for her husband's service. Which I did pay her myself and did *bezar* her *muchas vezes* ['kiss her many times'] and I do hope may thereafter have some day *mas de su* ['more of her'] company.

On 19 June Pepys confided in himself about how enticing he found Mary Mercer:

> . . . at my business till late at night, then with my wife into the garden and there sang with Mercer. Whom I feel myself begin to love too much by handling of her breasts in a morning when she dresses me, they being the finest that ever I saw in my life, that is the truth of it.

It is probable Elizabeth knew how Pepys treated Mercer. Moreover, there was tension between the two women, it being equally likely that Elizabeth was agitated by the attention Pepys was paying her companion. On 23 June:

> . . . I to my papers but vexed at what I heard but a little of this morning before my wife went out, that Mercer and she fell out last night, and that the girl is gone home to her mother's for all together.* This troubles me, though perhaps it may be an ease to me of so much charge. But I love the girle, and another we must be forced to keep I do foresee and then shall be sorry to part with her.

* Permanently, for the foreseeable future.

After negotiations, however, Mercer returned the same day, setting Pepys's mind at rest. In the evening William Bagwell caught up with Pepys, keen to bring news to his patron. He had been at the Four Days Battle (1–4 June 1666), a major engagement in the Anglo-Dutch War:

> From Deptford I walked to Redriffe and in my way was overtaken by Bagwell, lately come from sea in the *Providence*, who did give me an account of several particulars in the late fight and how his ship was deserted basely by the *York*, Captain Swanly, commander.

On 1 July Pepys went down to Deptford in search of Mrs Bagwell, her husband being returned to the fleet:

> . . . thinking to have seen Bagwell's wife, whose husband is gone yesterday back to the fleet, but I did not see her, so missed what I went for . . .

In an interesting digression about the visit to Deptford that reveals his capacity for compassion, Pepys considered the tragic consequences of a Navy so short of money that it was unavoidably dependent on the enforced recruitment of 'pressed men' into service:

> . . . so back to the Tower several times about the business of the pressed men, and late at it till 12 at night, shipping of them. But Lord, how some poor women did cry, and in my life I never did see such natural expression of passion as I did here. In some women's bewailing themselfs and running to every parcel of men that were brought, one after another, to look for their husbands, and wept over every vessel that went off, thinking they might be there, and looking after the ship as far as ever they could by moone light, that it grieved me to the heart to hear them. Besides, to see poor patient labouring men and housekeepers, leaving poor wifes and

families, taking up on a sudden by strangers, was very hard, and that without press-money, but forced against all law to be gone. It is a great tyranny.

The next day (2 July) at Deptford:

Here I meant to have spoke with Bagwell's *moher* ['wife'][10] but her face was sore, and so I did not, and returned . . .

Pepys did not explain why Mrs Bagwell had a sore face, but being struck by her husband before he went to sea is likely. Given how on his behalf William Bagwell and his parents had coerced her into compromising herself permanently with Pepys (who also struck his own wife), physical force and punishment would scarcely be surprising.

On 10 July Pepys was confronted at the Navy Office by a crowd of around 300 women demanding money for their husbands and others who were now Dutch prisoners. 'I do most heartily pity them and was ready to cry to hear them. But cannot help them', though he did slip some money to one. However, as he well knew, this was also a route that could be used for securing sexual favours, as with Mrs Burrows.

The next day (11 July), Pepys went to Westminster in search of Betty Martin and later in the day headed to his lodging in Greenwich:

. . . doing several things by the way and there failed of meeting Mrs Lane . . . to Mrs Clerkes and there I had a good bed, and well received, the whole people rising to see me, and among the rest young Mrs Daniel, whom I kissed again and again alone, and so by and by to bed and slept pretty well . . .

On 12 July Pepys managed to spend time with Mrs Burrows, who was still seeking her dead husband's pay, but this required complicated arrangements:

> At the office all the morning. At noon home and thought to have slept, my head all day being full of business and yet sleepy and out of order and so I lay down on my bed in my gowne to sleep, but I could not. Therefore about 3 a-clock up and to dinner and thence to the office, where Mrs Burroughs my pretty widow was and so I did her business and sent her away by agreement, and presently I by coach after and took her up in Fanchurch street. And away through the City, hiding my face as much as I could. But she being mighty pretty and well enough clad, I was not afeared but only lest somebody should see me and think me idle. I sit though[11] with her and so into the fields Uxbridge way, a mile or 2 beyond Tyburn, and then back and then to Paddington and then back to Lyssen green,* a place the coachman led me to (I never knew in my life) and there we eat and drank and so back to Char<ing> Cross and there I set her down. All the way most excellent pretty company. I had her lips as much as I would, and a mighty pretty woman she is and very modest and yet kind in all fair ways.
>
> All this time I passed with mighty pleasure, it being what I have for a long time wished for, and did pay this day 5s forfeit for her company.

Pepys managed a visit to Mrs Bagwell in Deptford on 18 July 'having stayed there a while, away home'. He, presumably, did not need any longer to specify to himself what had taken place.

Pepys was back to the pregnant Betty Martin on 25 July, apparently taking some malicious pleasure in deceiving Betty about her husband's whereabouts, and encouraging her belief that her husband was at sea:

> I away to Mrs Martin's new lodgings where I find her, and was with her alone but Lord how big she is already. She is, at least seems, in

* Now Lisson Grove, a short distance north-east of Paddington, and then still rural.

> mighty trouble for her husband at sea, when I am sure she cares not for him, and I would not undeceive her though I know his ship is one of those that is not gone but left behind without men.

Meeting Mrs Burrows again on 25 July in Westminster, Pepys was less impressed by her who 'being undressed did appear a mighty ordinary woman'. By 'undressed' Pepys meant she was not dressed up in her best to be seen socially.

On 1 August Pepys enjoyed an evening with his female acquaintances which he called 'innocent pleasure' but was anxious not to be spotted. This was the first time Betty Martin's younger sister Doll Lane (b. 1646), aged almost twenty, was mentioned. Evidently, her established elder sister, who was now thirty, had drawn Doll into her social circle. Doll had perhaps moved down from their home in East Retford to join Betty after their mother Anne was buried there on 30 October 1662:

> . . . after dinner to Mrs Martin's and there find Mrs Burroughs and by and by comes a pretty widow, one Mrs Eastwood, and one Mrs Fenton a maid. And here merry kissing and looking on their breasts, and all the innocent pleasure in the world. But Lord to see the dissembling of this widow how upon the singing of a certain Jigg by Doll, Mrs Martin's sister, she seemed* to be sick and fainted and God knows what because the Jigg which her husband (who died this last sickness) loved.[12] But by and by I made her as merry as is possible, and towsed and tumbled her as I pleased, and then carried her and her sober pretty kinswoman Mrs Fenton home to their lodgings in the new market† of my Lord Treasurers, and there left them. Mightily pleased with this afternoon's mirth. But in great pain to ride in a coach with them, for fear of being seen.

---

* Feigned, pretended.

† Southampton Market, near Holborn, built by Thomas Wriothesley, 4th Duke of Southampton and Lord Treasurer 1660–67.

It was just as well Pepys had been alone with them. Elizabeth did not take kindly to his visitors on 6 August. Pepys was crucified with embarrassment, and found himself apologizing instead for his wife's conduct:

> ... after dinner in comes Mrs Knepp, and I being at the office went home to her, and there I sat and talked with her, it being the first time of her being here since her being brought to bed. I very pleasant with her; but perceive my wife hath no great pleasure in her being here, she not being pleased with my kindness to her. However, we talked and sang and were very pleasant. By and by comes Mr Pierce and his wife (the first time she also hath been here since her lying-in, both having been brought to bed of boys, and both of them dead). And here we talked and were pleasant only my wife in a chagrin humour, she not being pleased with my kindness to either of them. And by and by she fell into some silly discourse wherein I checked her which made her mighty pettish, and discoursed very offensively to Mrs Pierce which did displease me, but I would make no words but put the discourse by as much as I could (it being about a report that my wife said was made of herself and meant by Mrs Pierce that she was grown a gallant, when she had but so few suits of clothes these 2 or 3 years, and a great deal of that silly discourse) and by and by Mrs Pierce did tell her that such discourses should not trouble her for there went as bad on other people, and perticularly of herself at this end of the town (meaning my wife) that she was crooked, which was quite false, which my wife had the wit not to acknowledge herself to be the speaker of, though she hath said it 20 times.
>
> But by this means we had little pleasure in their visit, however, Knipp and I sang, and then I offered them to carry them home, and to take my wife with me, but she would not go. So I with them, leaving my wife in a very ill humour and very slighting to them, which vexed me. However, I would not be removed from my civility to them but sent for a coach, and went with them

> and, in our way, Knipp saying that she come out of doors without a dinner to us, I took them to old Fishstreete ... And here we talked of the ill humour of my wife, which I did excuse as much as I could, and they seemed to admit of it, but did both confess they wondered at it ...
>
> So I home ... and there find my wife mightily out of order, and reproaching of Mrs Pierce and Knipp as wenches, and I know not what. But I did give her no words to offend her and quietly let all pass, and so to bed without any good looke or words to or from my wife.

Elizabeth regarded these women as threats for obvious reasons. A woman like Mrs Knepp could promote her husband's interests, which Elizabeth could not. Pepys was visibly embarrassed in public by his wife's failure to live up to his expectations.

Pepys had another excursion with Mrs Burrows on 8 August after dealing with her business. The day began at St James's Park, organized by Pepys to try and charm her into acquiescing and calling it his 'sport':

> ... I into the Park and there I met with Mrs Burroughs by appointment and did agree (after discoursing upon some business of hers) for her to meet me at New Exchange, while I by coach to my Lord Treasurer's and then called at the New Exchange, and thence carried her by water to parliament stayres, and I to the Exchequer about my Tanger Quarters tallies, and that done I took coach and to the west door of the abby where she came to me, and I with her by coach to Lissen greene where we were last, and stayed an hour or 2 before dinner could be got for us, I in the meantime having much pleasure with her, but all honest. And by and by dinner came up, and then to my sport again but still honest, and then took coach and up and down in the country toward Acton, and then toward Chelsy, and so to Westminster, and there set her down where I took her up, with mighty pleasure in her company, and so I by coach home ...

The principal event of the whole diary was the Great Fire of London in September 1666. Pepys's unmatched account of the disaster has overshadowed most of the rest of the diary. In the aftermath of the Fire Pepys arranged to see Mrs Bagwell on Monday 10 September:

> ... calling at Deptford intending to Bagwell but <she> did not *ouvrir la porta como yo* ['open the door as I'] did expect. So down late to Woolwich and there find my wife out of humour and indifferent as she uses upon her having such liberty abroad.

The next day (11th) Pepys made good his disappointment by heading to Deptford and 'there spoke with <Mrs> Bagwell and agreed upon tomorrow'. Pepys tried Mrs Bagwell again on 12 September, but only after seeing the pregnant Betty Martin first, managing an appointment with Elizabeth's brother Balty in between:

> Thence to Martin and there did *tout ce que je voudrais avec* ['all that I would with'] her and drank and away by water home and to dinner, Balty and his wife there. After dinner I took him down with me to Deptford and there by the *Bezan* loaded above ½ my goods* and sent them away. So we back home, and then I found occasion to return in the dark and to <Mrs> Bagwell and there *nudo in lecto con ella* did do all that I desired but though I did intend *para aver demorado con ella toda la* night, yet when I had done *ce que je voudrais* I did hate both *ella* and *la cosa* and taking occasion from the uncertainty of *su marido*'s return *esta noch*e did me *lever* ['and there naked in bed with her did do all that I desired but though I did intend to have stayed with her all the night, yet when I had done what I would I did hate both her and the thing and taking occasion from the uncertainty of her husband's return tonight did rouse myself'] and so away home late ...

* P's share of prize goods. The *Bezan* was a Dutch yacht given to Charles II by the Dutch East India Company.

Pepys's self-loathing was turned into hatred both for Mrs Bagwell and the sex. On 1 October he headed to Whitehall and publicly embarrassed himself, which showed how reckless he could be:

> . . . and there did hear Betty Michell* was at this end of the town and so without breach of vow did stay to endeavour to meet with her and carry her home but she did not come so I lost my whole afternoon. But pretty how I took another pretty woman for her, taking her a clap on the breech thinking verily it had been her.[13]

Pepys returned to Betty Martin in Westminster on 12 October:

> . . . to the Swan and there sent for a piece of meat and dined alone and played with Sarah, and so to the hall a while and thence to Mrs Martin's lodging and did what I would with her. She is very big and resolves I must be godfather.

Betty was now more than seven months pregnant. He was back with her on 14 October in search of Mrs Burrows who was not there. He did not elaborate further. The following week he met up with Betty again on 21 October, but this time met her sister Doll as well:

> This afternoon I went to see and sat a good while with Mrs Martin and there was her sister Doll with whom, contrary to all expectation, I did what I would and might have done anything else.

Despite it being Elizabeth's twenty-sixth birthday, Pepys headed out to see Betty Mitchell on 23 October before going on to Deptford, claiming to have done her and her husband a great kindness. Here he used the term 'poor wretch', which he usually applied to his wife though he regarded Betty Mitchell as his 'second wife':

---

* Written 'B.M.'

> . . . I down by water to Shadwell to see Betty Michell, the first time I was ever at their new dwelling since the fire. And there find her in the house all alone. I find her mighty modest. But had her lips as much as I would. And endeed she is mighty pretty, that I love her exceedingly. I paid her 10£ 1s that I received upon a ticket for her husband which is a great kindness I have done them. And having kissed her as much as I would, I away, poor wretch, and down to Deptford . . . Bagwell's wife, seeing me come the fields way, did get over her pales* to come after and talk with me. Which she did for a good way and so parted and I home and to the office and very busy.

The money probably came from his own funds, effectively paid to Betty Mitchell in return for services rendered. His wife was unmentioned in the entry for the day.

Pepys drank with Doll Lane ('A bad face, but good-bodied girl') again at the Dog tavern in Westminster on 26 October but 'did nothing but salute and play with her and talk'. There was more fun on Sunday 28 October. Pepys used his playful language, designed to make the occasion seem harmless. It is not clear whether his brother John was with him while he was with the women, but it is likely John knew what was going on:

> I with my brother to White hall and he to Westminster Abby. I presently to Mrs Martin's and there met widow Burroughs and Doll and did tumble them all the afternoon as I pleased, and having given them a bottle of wine I parted and home by boat (my brother going by land) . . .

On 1 November Pepys managed to have a tryst with Mrs Bagwell in his office, Elizabeth, who had increasingly become an incidental character in Pepys's days, conveniently having gone to Shadwell:

---

* Fence posts.

> I to my office where I took in Mrs Bagwell and did what I would with her and so she went away, and I all the afternoon till almost night there and then, my wife being come back, I took her and set her at her brother's, who is very sick, and I to White hall . . .

Pepys was a little concerned on 7 November (on which the plague was commemorated) that he had been seen meeting Doll Lane. Pepys was trying to be vigilant, but had surely been spotted on other occasions and had not realized:

> Thence to Westminster hall and, it being fast day, there was no shops open, but meeting with Doll Lane did go with her to the Rose tavern, and there drank and played with her a good while. She went away, and I stayed a good while after, and was seen going out by one of our neighbours near the office and 2 of the hall people that I had no mind to have been seen by, but there was no hurt in it nor can be alleged from it. Therefore I am not solicitous in it . . .

Given that Pepys was so worried about being spotted, he must have been in a private room with Doll. The word 'played' was a euphemism for significant sexual activity, which a private room would have facilitated.

Although Mary Mercer had been sacked on 3 September, she did come to see Elizabeth on 8 November. The following day (9 November), which had been very dramatic because of a fire at Whitehall, she travelled with Pepys back home. Elizabeth must have been in the coach too (the chaos caused by the fire had led to a shortage of coaches):

> We got well home and in the way I did *con mi mano tocar la jambe de* Mercer *sa chair.*[14] *Elle retirait sa jambe modestement* but I did *tocar sa peau* with my naked hand. And the truth is, *la fille* hath something that is *assez jolie* ['and in the way I did with my hand touch Mercer's leg

> <on> her flesh. She pulled her leg back modestly, but I did touch her skin with my naked hand. And the truth is, the girl hath something that is pretty enough']. Being come home, we to cards, till 2 in the morning, and drinking lamb's-wool.*

On Sunday 11 November Pepys went to St Olave's, across the road from the Navy Office, with Betty Mitchell. Betty Mitchell had been mentioned on numerous occasions and was a favourite of Pepys, but the relationship had so far been limited to fooling about and kissing. On this occasion Pepys masturbated at the thought of her during the service, both she and his wife present:

> Anon to church, my wife and I and Betty Michell, her husband being gone to Westminster. Here at church (God forgive me) my mind did *courir* ['run'] upon Betty Michell so that I doth *hazer con mi cosa in la eglisa même* ['I doth do <it> with my thing even in the church'].[15]

On 22 November, Pepys was outraged by Elizabeth's decision to expose her cleavage:

> At noon home to dinner where my wife and I fell out, I being displeased with her cutting away a lace hankercher sewed about the neck down to her breasts almost out of a belief, but without reason, that it is the fashion. Here we did give one another the lie too much, but were presently friends . . .

The same day Mrs Bagwell came to see Pepys, but it is not clear whether that was just before the argument with Elizabeth or afterwards. Pepys appears to have forgotten about the meeting, only adding it to the end of the day's entry when writing up Mrs Burrows's visit:

---

* Lamb's-wool was a beverage of ale, apples, sugar, and nutmeg.

> This noon Bagwell's wife was with me at the office and I did what I would, and at night came Mrs Burroughs, and appointed to meet upon the next holy day* and go abroad together.

Pepys met up with Doll Lane again on 26 November, but does not seem to have been allowed to complete the act:

> Thence to the Swan, having sent for some burnt claret, and there by and by comes Doll Lane, and she and I sat and drank and talked a great while, among other things about her sister being brought to bed, and I too to be the godfather to the girl. I did tumble Doll, and do almost what I would with her . . .

On 28 November Pepys's attention wandered even more brazenly. He enjoyed himself with Margaret 'Pegg' Penn, daughter of his neighbour Sir William Penn, and while her mother was on the premises:

> Thence home and there comes my Lady Pen, Pegg, and Mrs Turner and played at cards and supped with us, and were pretty merry. And Pegg with me in my closet a good while and did suffer me *a la besar mucho et tocar ses cosas* ['to kiss her much and touch her things'] upon her breast. Wherein I had great pleasure and so spent the evening and then broke up and I to bed, my mind mightily pleased with the day's entertainment.

Pegg was to marry the following year (15 February 1667, becoming Mrs Lowther). The wedding had already been arranged when the closet incident occurred.

Two days later, on 30 November, Pepys met up with Mrs Sarah Harmond (née Udall), the barmaid at the Swan, and made plans because of her new status. Sarah Udall's marriage is recorded as having occurred only twenty-six days earlier on 4 November 1666. Her new

---

* = 'holiday'.

marital status now made her eligible for Pepys to begin pursuing her more seriously. He had hoped to meet Mrs Burrows at Westminster Hall as arranged, but she did not appear:

> I did go drink at the Swan and there did meet with Sarah, who is now newly married, and there I did lay the beginnings of a future *amor con ella* which in time may come *para laisser me hazer alguna cosa con ella* ['a future affair with her, which in time may come for to let me do something with her']. Thence it being late, away; called at Mrs Burroughs' mother's door, and she come out to me, and I did *hazer* ['do'] whatever I would *con su mano tocando mi cosa* ['with her hand touching my thing'] and then parted and home and after some playing at cards with my wife, we to supper and to bed.

The entry is typical of Pepys's careless use of pronouns. It was Mrs Burrows who came out of her mother's door to accede to his wishes (she had been reluctantly prepared to engage with him in sexual activity, for some weeks now, see 28 October above) and not her mother, Mrs Crofts, in whom Pepys would have had no interest anyway.[16]

Making plans with Sarah and meeting Mrs Burrows later had therefore happened right at the end of a long day immediately before spending time with Elizabeth, who was unaware of Pepys's earlier activities.

On Sunday 2 December Pepys and Elizabeth attended the christening of Betty Martin's daughter Katherine where he was to be godfather (she was born on 24 November). On the way home, which involved a coach breakdown and repair, Betty Mitchell sat beside him:

> Betty Michell did sit at the same end with me and there *con su mano* under my *manteau*, I did pull off her *cheirotheca*[17] and did *tocar mi cosa con su mano* through my *chemise*, but yet so as to *hazer me hazer la grande cosa*. And she did let me *hazer le sin mucho trabaho* ['and there

> with my hand under her coat, I did pull off her glove and did touch my thing with her hand through my shirt, but yet so as to make myself do the big thing. And she did let me do it without much work']. Being very much pleased with this, we at last come home, and so to supper and thence sent them by boat home and we to bed.

'The big thing' of course was Pepys's euphemism for an orgasm, here specially emphasized. By 'without much work', Pepys meant he did not have to try very hard to force himself on her. The party must have taken a public hackney coach for this escapade, which was astonishing for Pepys's audacity and that his actions apparently went unnoticed by Elizabeth.

The very next day (3 December) Pepys was back with Mrs Burrows, whom he had decided to force himself on. Elizabeth was in bed, wracked with period pains:

> . . . away myself to Westminster hall by appointment and there found out Burroughs, and I took her by coach as far as the Lord Treasurers and called at the Cake house by Hales's, and there in the coach eat and drank and then carried her home with much ado making her to *tocar mi cosa*, she being endeed very averse *a alguna cosa* of that kind. However, time can *hazer la* the same as it hath *hecho* others ['with much ado making her to touch my thing, she being endeed very averse to something of that kind. However, time can make her the same as it hath made others'].

The occasion was unsuccessful, but the persistent Pepys was determined to keep up the pressure patiently, confident of eventual success.

Pepys was in the Bell tavern in Westminster on 14 December:

> . . . and thither comes Doll to me and *yo* did *tocar la cosa* of her as I pleased ['and I did touch her thing as I pleased'] and after an

> hour's stay away and stayed in Westminster hall till the rising of the house . . .

Four days later (18 December) Pepys visited Doll's sister Betty Martin who was looking forward to her childbed term ending the following day, but he experienced only frustration. She also told Pepys that the baby (a girl named Katherine)* must be his, but this does not seem to have bothered him, probably because she was married. He became her godfather (see 30 September 1667):

> I to see Mrs Martin who is very well and intends to go abroad tomorrow after her childbed. She doth tell me that this child did come *la même jour* that it ought to *hazer* after my *avoir été con elle* before her *marido* did *venir* home. And she would now have done anything *comigo*[18] and did endeavour but *su cosa stava mala*, which did *empescer*.[19] Thence to the Swan and there I sent for Sarah, and mighty merry we were but *contra* my will were very free from *hazer algo*. ['She doth tell me that this child did come the same day that it ought to do after my having been with her before her husband did come home. And she would now have done anything with me and did endeavour but her thing was afflicted, which did hurt. Thence to the Swan and there I sent for Sarah, and mighty merry we were but against my will were very free from doing something'.]

Unusually Pepys used an Italian word here, *stava* ('was'), but this enabled him to produce the rhyming phrase *cosa stava mala*. Pepys was probably describing Betty experiencing some postpartum bleeding and pain, which under normal conditions can last for four to six weeks after giving birth. It was still only twenty-four days since the baby had been born.

---

* The infant Katherine Martin's death was recorded at St Margaret's, Westminster on 6 May 1668.

On 21 December Pepys discovered his former neighbour Mrs Clerke of Greenwich had arrived to see him, bringing her daughter-in-law, Mrs Daniels, who wanted a favour for her naval officer husband Samuel Daniels. Pepys had encountered her on previous occasions, including 23 October 1665 when in his presence she refused to let Baron Rutherford touch her breasts:

> Lay long, and when up find Mrs Clerke of Greenwich and her daughter Daniel. Their business among other things was a request her daughter was to make so I took her into my chamber, and there it was to help her husband to the command of a little new pleasure boat building.* Which I promised to assist in. And here I had opportunity *para besar ella*, and *tocar ses mamelles* so as to make *mi mismo espender* ['to kiss her and touch her breasts so as to make me spend myself'] with great pleasure. Then to the office and there did a little business and then to the Change and did the like so home to dinner and spent all the afternoon in putting some things, pictures especially, in order and my Lady Castlemaynes print on a frame which I have made handsome and is a fine piece.

The use of the Spanish word *espender* (s.h. '*spender*') to refer to ejaculation was very unusual for Pepys but in the same entry he used the English form 'spent' to describe passing the afternoon. 'Spent' is a common word in the diary with several hundred usages and is easily formed in shorthand. Pepys was probably amusing himself here with the idea that he had 'spent' himself in two different ways, his second diversion involving Lady Castlemaine about whom he had had sexual fantasies in a dream (15 August 1665). The word *mamelles* followed here by *mi mismo* contributed more of his characteristic rhythmic alliteration in the polyglot.

On 23 December Betty Mitchell and her husband dined with

---

* i.e. 'now building', currently under construction.

Pepys on his own. Pepys took them back by coach to Whitehall. En route Pepys forced himself on Betty, even though her husband was with them:

> I did *prender su mano* with some little violence and so in every motion she seemed *para hazer contra su* will, but yet did *hazer* whatever I would. I did by degrees *poner mi cosa en su mano nudo* and did *hazer la, tener le, et fregar le, et tocar mi* thigh and so all the way home, and then did *doner ella su gans para* put on *encore*. She making many little endeavours *para ôter su mano* but yielded still. We came home, and there she did seem a little ill, but I did take several opportunities afterwards *para besar la*, and so goodnight. ['I did take her hand with some little violence and so in every motion she seemed to do against her will, but yet did do whatever I would. I did by degrees put my thing in her bare hand, and did do it, hold it, and rub it, and touch my thigh and so all the way home, and then did give her her gloves to put on again. She making many little endeavours to remove her hand but yielded still. We came home, and there she did seem a little ill, but I did take several opportunities afterwards to kiss her, and so goodnight'].
>
> They gone, I to my chamber and with my brother and wife did Number all my books in my closet, and took a list of their names, which pleases me mightily, and is a jobb I wanted much to have done.

Here Pepys used the word 'violence' (in shorthand 'vilense') to describe the force he applied to have his way with Betty. There is no question that he was referring to physical force, but in a coach and Betty's husband present it is difficult to envisage what that could have meant. The unedifying image is of the humiliation inflicted on Betty, coerced into masturbating her husband's patron, while the hapless Michael Mitchell sat by, unable or perhaps unwilling by virtue of his status and deference to do anything about the degrading spectacle.

Pepys was pleased to see a week later that Betty Mitchell was 'the same as ever', despite what he had done to her. He noted on New Year's Eve 'Thus ends this year of public wonder and mischief to this nation. And therefore generally wished by all people to have an end'. He did not bother with any vows or regrets about his behaviour, but bemoaned:

> A sad, vicious, negligent Court and all sober men there fearful of the ruin of the whole Kingdom this next year. From which good God deliver us.

But the acquisitive Pepys had a consoling thought to end 1666 with, which he crammed in as an afterthought at the bottom of the diary page:

> One thing I reckon remarkable in my own condition is that I am come to abound in good plate, so as at all entertainments to be served wholly with silver plates having two dozen and <a> half.

8

1667

My Mind Running On This Pretty Girl

In 1667 Pepys's 'dalliances' with a variety of other women increased apace. So did his recklessness. The most significant development was the arrival in the autumn of Deb Willet as his wife's companion.

Pepys started the New Year as he meant to continue. On 2 January:

So down to the hall and to the Rose tavern while Doll Lane come to me and we did *biber* a good deal *de vino et yo* did give *ella* 12 *solidos para comprar ella* some *gans* for a new *ano's* gift. I did *tocar et no mas su cosa* but in fit time and place *yo creo que je pouvais ferais* whatever I would *con ella* ['we did drink a good deal of wine and I did give her twelve sols* to buy her some gloves for a New Year's gift. I did touch and no more her thing, but in fit time and place I believe that I could do whatever I would with her'].

* Shillings.

Mrs Burrows was obliged to do Pepys's bidding on 10 January:

> This noon Mrs Burrows came to me about bus<iness> whom I did *bezar* and *hazer ella tocar mi chose* ['I did kiss and made her touch my thing'].

On 13 January 1667, after hearing about Peg Penn's wedding to Anthony Lowther, Pepys had plans to visit Betty Mitchell:

> . . . nor was there anybody at home at Michells where I thought to have sat with her. *Et peut être* obtain *algo de* her.[1] Which I did intend *para essayer* ['And perhaps obtain something from her. Which I did intend to try'].

He was more successful a week later (see below). Meanwhile, Pepys managed straight after lunch with Elizabeth to have a moment with Mrs Burrows on 15 January:

> At noon dined with my wife. And were pleasant, and then to the office, where I got Mrs Burroughs *sola comigo.*[2] And did *tocar ses mamelles* so as to *hazer me hazer* ['. . . where I got Mrs Burroughs alone with me. And did touch her breasts so as to make myself do'].

On Sunday 20 January Pepys went looking for Betty Mitchell again:

> . . . down to the Old Swan, there called on Michell and his wife, which in her night linen appeared as pretty almost as ever to my thinking I saw woman. Here I drank some burned brandy. And they showed me their house which, poor people, they have built and it is very pretty. I invited them to dine with me . . . I home, and there Michell and his wife, and we dined and mighty merry, I mightily taken, more and more, with her . . .

On 24 January Pepys enjoyed a musical day and evening with various friends at the office. The fun lasted until three in the morning until Mrs Knepp felt ill and Elizabeth took her home to bed. An indisposed woman was no obstacle to Pepys's inclinations, and nor was Elizabeth being on the premises:

> The company being all gone to their homes I up with Mrs Pierce to Knipp who was in bed and we waked her and there I handled her breasts and did *besar la* ['kiss her'] and sing a song lying by her on the bed and then left my wife to see Mrs Pierce in bed to her in our best chamber, and so to bed myself. My mind mightily satisfied with all this evening's work and thinking it to be one of the merriest enjoyment I must look for in the world . . .

On 27 January Pepys invited the Mitchells to join him and his cousin Roger and they took a boat on the Thames on an exceptionally warm winter's day:

> We home by water a fine moonshine and warm night, it having been also a very summer's day for warmth. I did get her hand to me under my cloak and did *ôter sa gans*, but *ella ne voudroit tocar mi cosa* today, whatever the matter was, and I was loath to *contraindre* her to *faire de peur qu'elle*[3] *faisait son mari prendre* notice thereof ['and did withdraw her gloves but she would not touch my thing today, whatever the matter was, and I was loath to force her to do so out of fear that she would make her husband take notice thereof']. So there we parted at their house . . .

By 1 February, Pepys was back with Mrs Bagwell in Deptford. His account of the meeting includes more detail compared to previous occasions:

> At noon home to dinner and after dinner down by water though it was a thick misty and raining day and walked to Deptford from

> Redriffe, and there to Bagwell's by appointment. Where the *moher erat* within expecting *mi venida*. And did *sensa alguna* difficulty *monter los degrés* and lie *como yo*[4] desired it upon *lo lectum* and there I did *la cosa con* much *voluptas*. *Je besa* also her *venter* and *coño*[5] and see the *poyle* thereof. She would seem *algunas vezes* very religious but yet did permit me to *hazer todo esto et quicquid amplius volebam*. ['Where the woman was within expecting my coming. And did sense some difficulty going up the stairs and lie as I desired it upon the bed and there I did the thing with much pleasure. I kissed also her belly and cony and see the hair thereof. She would seem sometimes very religious but yet did permit me to do all that and whatever more I wanted'].
>
> By and by *su marido* ['her husband'] came in and there without any notice taken by him we discoursed of our business of getting him the new ship building by Mr Deane which I shall do for him.

Pepys used the English 'by degrees' many times to describe the stages of progression to an outcome, as with wearing Mrs Bagwell down on 15 November 1664 (see previous chapter). Although in shorthand the English and French forms of 'degrees' cannot be distinguished, the context, *monter*, and the Spanish definite article *los* here instead of 'by', suggest P intended the French *degrés*, which can also mean steps or stairs.[6] If so, P was describing going upstairs on this occasion (he had expressly referred to the stairs in the Bagwell household on 13 June 1666, above). By 1670 William Bagwell and other members of his family were living in several houses in Flagon Row, a street demolished in 1896, a short distance west of the church of St Nicholas and leading to the north end of Deptford High St.[7] Photographs from the 1880s show various mostly small three-storied mid to late seventeenth-century timber houses, some with later brick facades.

The 'difficulty' was probably coercing Mrs Bagwell up to her bed. There may have been a pun intended: among meanings in Cotgrave (1611) for *monter* is 'to leap as the male upon the female'. Pepys also used here the Spanish *coño*, translated in Percivale's 1623 dictionary as 'a woman's privitie' but elsewhere he used the old English cony, for example on 25 October 1668. The longhand word *poyle* is *poil*, the French for hair, used with that spelling on 24 March 1667. Pepys of course meant pubic hair.

Pepys kept his side of the bargain. His retained copy of a letter dated 6 February 1667 that he gave to William Bagwell to take to Sir William Coventry, recommending him for a position as a ship's carpenter, has survived.[8]

Evidently in what he had once called a 'hot humour', Pepys was far from finished with women for the day (1 February). He headed back later to Westminster:

> . . . and find Doll Lane and *con ella* ['with her'] I went to the Bell tavern, and *ibi je* ['there I'] did do what I would *con ella* as well as I could, she *sedento sobra una* chair ['seated upon a chair'] and making some little resistance. But all with much content, and *yo tenia* ['I had'] much pleasure *cum ista* ['with her']. There parted and I by coach home and to the office, where pretty late doing business, and then home, and merry with my wife, and to supper.

He was now routinely touching other women even in his wife's presence. On 5 February he took Elizabeth and Betty Mitchell to the theatre:

> Thence by coach to the New Exchange and there laid out money and I did give Betty Michell 2 pair of gloves and a dressing-box. And so home in the dark over the ruins with a link. I was troubled with my pain having got a bruise on my right testicle I know not how. But this I did make good use of to make my wife shift sides with me and I did come to sit *avec* ['with'] Betty Michell and there had her *mano* ['hand'] which *ella* did give me very frankly now and did *hazer* whatever I *voudrais avec la*. Which did *plaisir* me *grandement* ['and did do whatever I would with her. Which did please me greatly']. And so set her at home with my

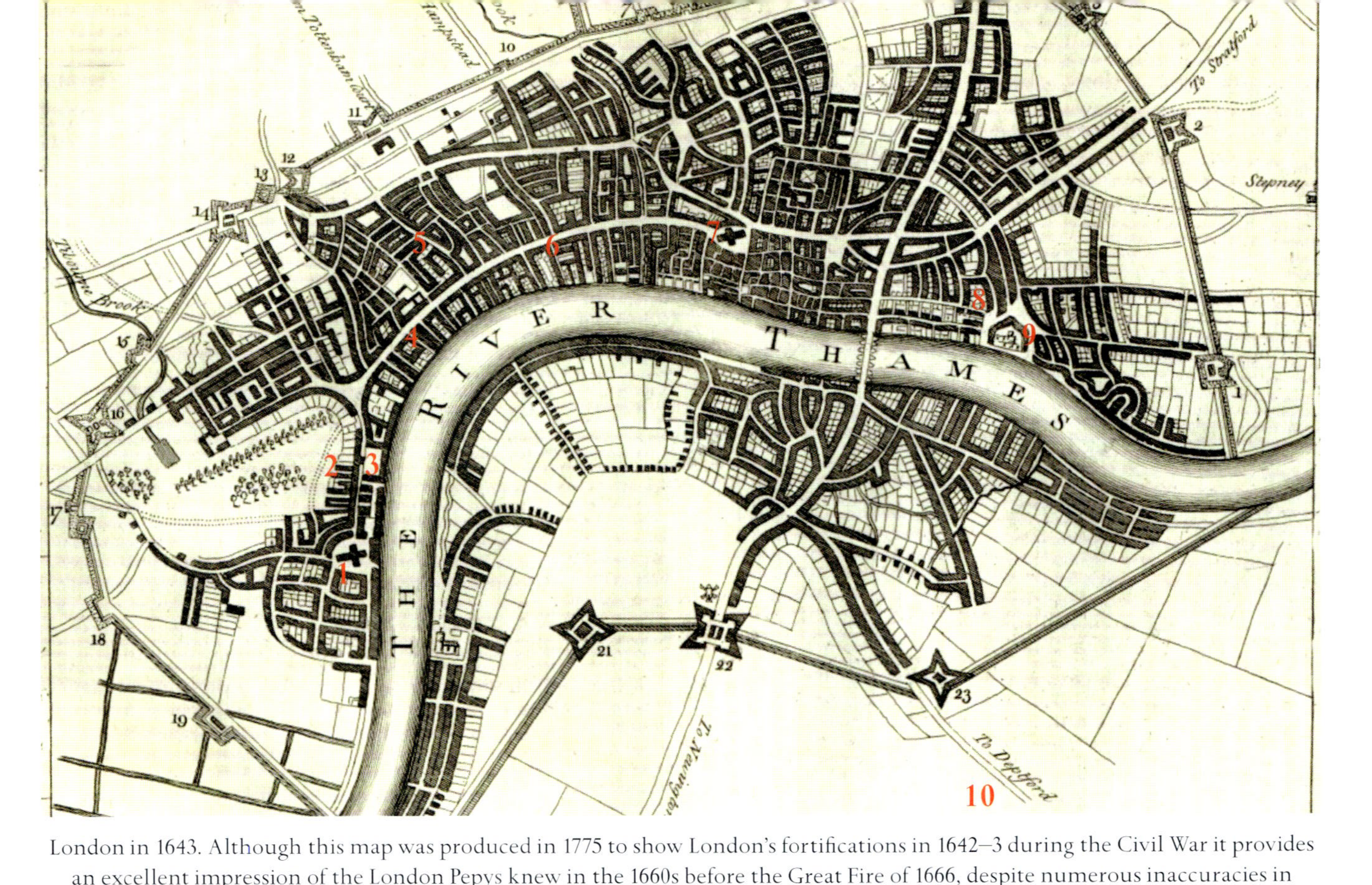

London in 1643. Although this map was produced in 1775 to show London's fortifications in 1642–3 during the Civil War it provides an excellent impression of the London Pepys knew in the 1660s before the Great Fire of 1666, despite numerous inaccuracies in detail. 1. Westminster Abbey. 2 Axe Yard. 3. Whitehall Palace. 4. The Strand. 5. Drury Lane. 6. Fleet Street. 7. St Paul's Cathedral. 8. Seething Lane and the Navy Office. 9. The Tower of London. 10. The road to Deptford.

Samuel (1633–1703), the diarist, and Elizabeth Pepys (1640–69), from portraits by John Hayls made between 1665 and 1666. She died in London, probably from typhoid, shortly after returning from a journey to Flanders with her husband. A colourized version of the engraving made by James Thompson for the 1825 edition of the diary from the original painting which was destroyed c. 1830 in the belief it depicted Elizabeth wearing an indecent dress.

The letters of the Alphabet.

a b c d e f g h i k l m n o p qu r s t v w x y z

Double consonants

To begin words: bl br cl cr dr dw fl fr gl gr kn pl pr sc sk sl sm sn sp st str tr tw

To end words: ld lk lm ln lp ls lst lt mp nd ng nk ns nst nt rd rk rl rm rn rp rs rst rt ch sh th wh

Prepositions for longe words.

Ab ob ac ad af all am an ap op as at circum com

Con cor col de di dis fall full for im liber mes miss per par

Pre pro re sub suff sup ser sur sal sol temp trans vn vp vt

Terminations for longe words.

Able ible ation ceiue dure fect ference fication fulness iect itude

ing lesse lent litie mer mar ment nesse ous cent sent

serue sion tion soeuer ternall ther tent ture ver

A composite image of three pages from Thomas Shelton's Tachygraphy (shorthand), the system used by Samuel Pepys to write his diary. These tables show the core signs for letters, double consonants, and common prefixes and suffixes for words. Pepys relied on these the most when making diary entries. Arbitrary individual symbols for certain words are not shown here but formed part of the rest of Shelton's handbook.

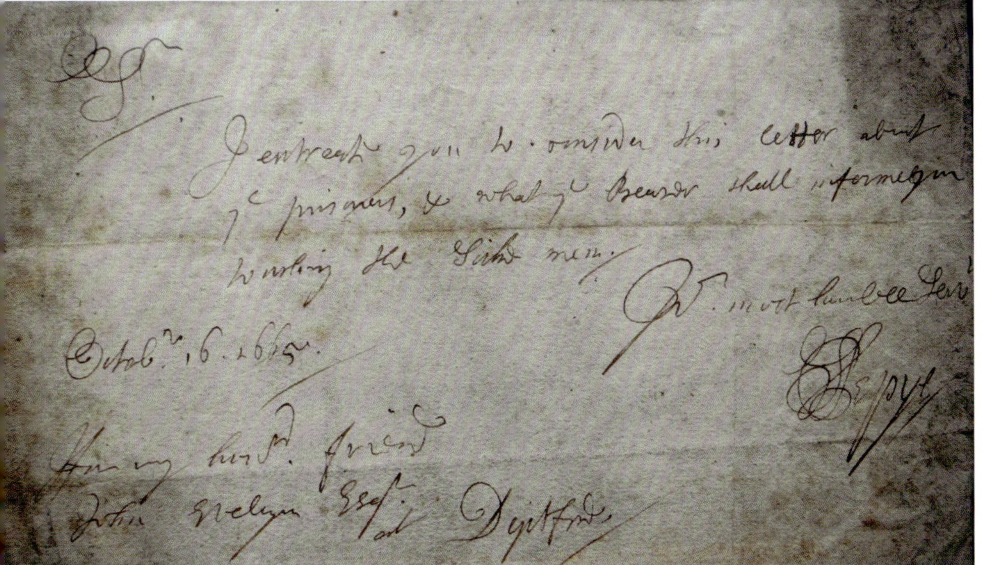

Sr

I entreate you to consider this Letter about ye prisoners, & what ye Bearer shall informe you touching the Sicke men.

Yr most humble Servt

S. Pepys

Octobr. 16. 1665

For my hond. friend John Evelyn Esq. at Deptford

Pepys was overwhelmed with administrative work during the Second Dutch War as the plague raged, while at the same time managing to see his mistresses. While working from Greenwich he wrote this note to John Evelyn in Deptford on 16 October 1665 concerning the sick men (see 5 October 1665 when he visited Mrs Bagwell before going on to Evelyn's house).

Left: Nell Gwyn (c. 1650–87), 'pretty witty Nell' (Pepys), who had two children by Charles II after the diary period. By Simon Verelst, c. 1670. Right: Barbara Palmer (née Villiers), Countess of Castlemaine and later 1st Duchess of Cleveland in her own right (1633–1709). Charles II's principal mistress of the 1660s and mother of at least five acknowledged children by him, among them Charles Fitzroy (1662–1730), shown here. Her voluptuous and sultry beauty caused Pepys to fantasize about her. Painted by Peter Lely in 1664 at the height of her power and influence.

Left: Engraving of a kitchen maid by Wenceslaus Hollar dated 1640. Unsurprisingly, no drawings or paintings of any of Pepys's maids or other ordinary women that he knew exist. Pepys usually targeted women of lower status to make sexual advances to. Right: portrait of an unknown woman 'of quality'. This English painting, made in the middle of the seventeenth century, must stand as a generic image for the women Pepys admired walking in London's parks or at the theatre and the others whom he knew socially.

The royal dockyard at Deptford (1770s), resembling what Pepys would have seen when approaching by boat, though he often walked there. Pepys frequently and surreptitiously visited Mrs Bagwell in her house in the vicinity. Virtually nothing survives from Pepys's time apart from the medieval tower of the church of St Nicholas (the nave was rebuilt in 1697 and the top of the tower in 1903–4), the right-hand church of the pair in the engraving. Pepys attended a service here on 13 January 1661 and walked out of a sermon during a funeral to visit Mrs Bagwell nearby on 29 March 1669.

The Pepys house at Brampton, Cambridgeshire, inherited by Pepys's father John from his brother Robert in 1661. Pepys knew the house as a child and visited during the diary period on family affairs, as did Elizabeth who came sometimes on her own. The garden was famously where she and John Pepys buried, and lost, the diarist's gold during the Dutch emergency in 1667.

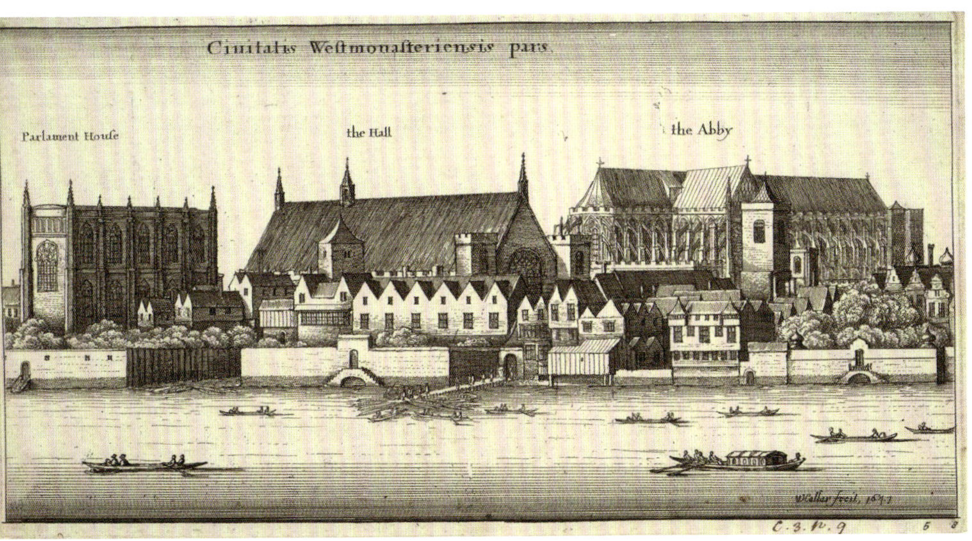

A view of Westminster Hall (centre), Parliament (left), and the Abbey (right) by Wenceslaus Hollar in 1641. It had not changed by the 1660s when Pepys frequented the area, often in search of Betty Mitchell (née Howlett), Betty Martin (née Lane), and her sister Doll.

Frances Stuart on the reverse of the silver so-called 'Breda' medal of 1667 which commemorated the Second Anglo-Dutch War, made from dies engraved by John Roettier. Pepys saw the medal on 25 February 1667 and was greatly impressed by the use of Frances Stuart as the model, 'a pretty thing it is that he should choose her face to represent Britannia by' (her portrait is enlarged at lower left). Diameter 55 mm.

Transcribing Pepys. Digital scans of microfilm and digital photographs have made it possible to study his diary in much greater detail than ever before. Work in progress for this book is shown here with an image of the diary text for 25 October 1668 enlarged on one screen, and the transcription and commentary in preparation on the other. A well-thumbed facsimile of Thomas Shelton's Tachygraphy and annotated copies of his most important tables provide the essential reference material.

Flagon Row (now demolished), Deptford. By 1670 William and Elizabeth Bagwell were living in this street, a few yards from St Nicholas and a short walk from the dockyard. They had probably done so for several years. This view of c. 1880 shows several three-storied small timber houses of the mid to late 1600s of the type where Pepys visited Mrs Bagwell and took her upstairs (for example 1 February 1667). The houses are likely to have been built by carpenters from the dockyard, using wood reclaimed from broken-up ships or siphoned off from dockyard stocks.

Charles II shilling (25 mm), struck in 1663 at the Tower Mint about 300 m (328 yards) from Pepys's home in Seething Lane. Pepys considered a shilling (about £8–9 today) a suitable gratuity for one of his maids after assaulting her (see, for example, 6 May 1668), and for a Shoe Lane prostitute's services (1 September 1668).

St Olave's, Hart Street, from Seething Lane. The mid-1400s church still stands close to the location of Pepys and Elizabeth's home in Seething Lane and the Navy Office. Samuel and Elizabeth Pepys remain buried there. The Navy Office had access to its own gallery via an entrance through the south aisle. The gate was erected in 1658 and was thus there in Pepys's time. Seething Lane was narrower than today. The brick section of the tower was added in 1732.

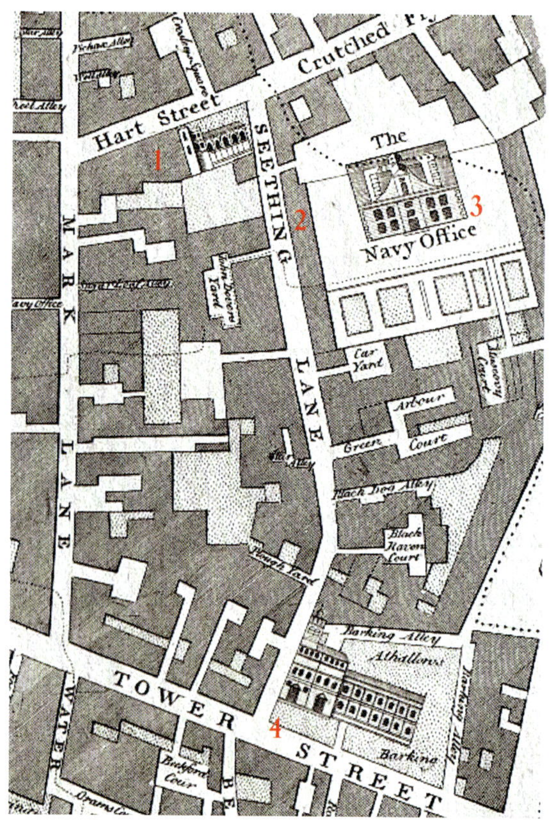

Pepys and Elizabeth's home throughout much of the diary period was in Seething Lane, visible in this mid-eighteenth-century map by Thomas Maitland (north at top). The Navy Office shown had been rebuilt after a fire in 1673. 1. St Olave's church. 2. Approximate location of Pepys's home, now commemorated by a small park. 3. The Navy Office (showing the new building of the 1670s). 4. All Hallows, where Deb Willet, then Mrs Jeremiah Wells, was buried in 1678. The location is now bisected east-west by Byward Street.

Elizabeth Pepys's memorial in St Olave's, Hart Street, commissioned by her grieving husband. Apart from the engraving of her lost portrait, this is the only surviving visual relic of her life. For her epitaph, see the Epilogue. The monument was placed on the north-east wall above the altar where Pepys could see it from the Navy Office gallery in the south aisle. Detail below. By John Bushnell c. 1670.

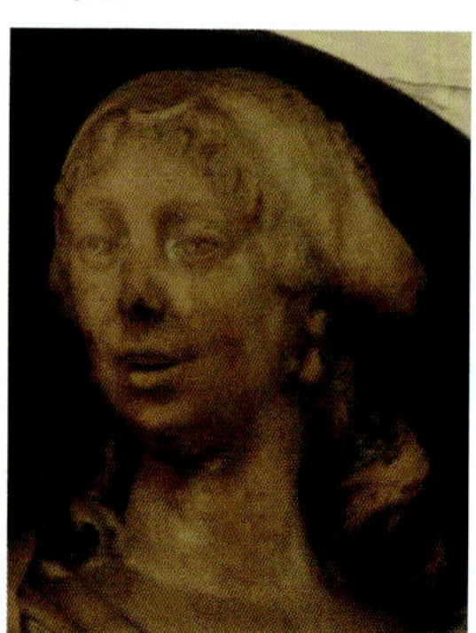

mind mighty glad of what I have prevailed for so far and so home and to the office . . .

On 6 February at Westminster Pepys found a way to contact Betty Mitchell again, by engineering a meeting with her mother and mother-in-law (Mrs Howlett and Mrs Mitchell):

> So down to the hall and there spied Betty Michell and so I sent for burnt wine to Mrs Michell's and there did drink with the 2 mothers, and by that means with Betty, poor girl, whom I love with all my heart. And God forgive me, it did make me stay longer and hover all the morning up and down the hall to *buscar* occasions *para ambulare con ella*. But *yo no podra* ['to seek occasions to walk with her. But I could not'].

On 11 February Pepys was at the New Exchange in a shop when Betty Mitchell arrived. They went shopping together, Pepys taking advantage of the opportunity to pretend to be Betty's husband and the father of her impending child, but the day descended into farce:

> . . . at the New Exchange where I stayed at Pottle's shop till Betty Michell come which she did about 5 a-clock and was surprised not to *trouver mi moher* ['find my wife'] there. But I did make an excuse good enough and so I took *ella* down and over the water to the Cabinet maker's and there bought a dressing-box for her for 20s but would require an hour's time to make fit. This I was glad of thinking to have got *ella* to *andar a la casa de biber* ['walk to the tavern'] but *ella* would not so I did not much press it but suffered *ella* to *andar a la casa de uno de sos hermanos* ['but suffered her to walk to the house of one her brothers'] and so I past my time walking up and down, and among other places to one Drumbelby, a maker of flagelettes, the best in town.
>
> He not within. My design to bespeak a pair of flagelettes of the same tune. Ordered him to come to me in a day or 2 and so I

back to the Cabinet makers and there stayed. And by and by Betty comes and here we stayed in the shop and above seeing the workmen work which was pretty and some exceeding good work and very pleasant to see them do it. Till it was late, quite dark. And the mistress of the shop took us into the kitchen and there talked and used us very prettily and took her for my wife which I owned and her big belly, and there very merry till my thing done, and then took coach and home in the way *tomando su mano* ['taking her hand'] and putting it where I used to do which *ella* did suffer but not *avec tant de* freedom ['with as much freedom'] as heretofore I perceiving plainly she had *algunas* ['some'] apprehensions *de* me, but I did offer *natha* ['nothing'][9] more then what I had often done.

But now comes our trouble I did begin to fear that *su marido* ['her husband'] might go to my house to enquire *por ella* and there *trovando mi moher* ['for her and there finding my wife'] at home would not only think himself but give my *femme* occasion to think strange things.

This did trouble me mightily so though *ella* would not seem to have me trouble myself about it yet did agree to the stopping the coach at the street's end, and *yo allais con ella* ['I went with her'] home and there presently hear by him that he had newly sent *su* ['his'] maid to my house to see for her mistress.

This doth much perplex me and I did go presently home (Betty whispering me behind the *tergo de* her *mari* ['behind her husband's back'] that if I would say that we did come home by water *ella* could make up *la cosa* well *satis* ['she could make up the thing well enough']) and there in a sweat did walk in the entry *antes* ['before'] my door thinking what I should say *a* my *femme* ['to my wife'] and as God would have it, while I was in this case (the worst in reference *a* my *femme* that ever I was in in my life) a little woman* comes stumbling to the entry steps in the dark whom asking who she was she enquired for my house so knowing her

* Presumably the Mitchell maid.

> voice, and telling her *su donna* ['her mistress'] is come home she went away. But Lord in what a trouble was I when she was gone to recollect whether this was not the second time of her coming but at last concluding that she had not been here before I did bless myself in my good fortune in getting home before her and do verily believe she had loitered some time by the way which was my great good fortune and so I in a-door and there find all well so my heart full of joy I to the office a little and then home and after supper and doing a little business in my chamber I to bed. After teaching Barker a little of my song.

This ludicrous escapade illustrates what a knife edge Pepys was now on. He had taken so many risks and engaged in such complicated arrangements he was now struggling to remember what he had said and done. He was on the cusp of being reassured on 13 February:

> . . . away by water home stopping at Michell's, where Mrs Martin was and I there drank with them and whispered with Betty who tells me all is well, but was prevented in something she would have said, her *marido venando* just then *a nos* ['her husband coming just then to us'] which did trouble me and so drank and parted . . .

Pepys had recovered by 16 February:

> I went to Mrs Martin's to thank her for her oysters and there *yo* did *hazer tout ce que je* would *con* her, and she grown *la plus* bold *moher* of the *orbis*. So that I was almost *defessus* of the pleasure *que ego* was used *para tener* with *ella* ['and there I did do all that I would with her, and she grown the boldest woman of the world. So that I was almost weary of the pleasure that I was used to having with her'].

Betty Mitchell, who was about seven months pregnant (see 23 April below), had distinctly cooled by 17 February. On an evening boat ride on the Thames:

I did to my trouble see all the way that *ella* did get as close *a su marido* as *ella* could and turn her *manos* away *quando yo* did endeavour to take one *de los* so that I had no pleasure at all *con ella ce* night. When we landed I did take occasion to send him back *a* the *bateau* while I did get *un besar* or 2 and would have taken *la* by *la* hand but *ella* did turn away, and *quand* I said 'shall I not *tocar te*?' answered '*yo no* love touching' in a slight *modo*.* I seemed† not to take notice of it but parted kindly *et su marido* did *andar* with me almost *a mi casa* and there we parted and so I home troubled at this, but I think I shall make good use of it and mind my business more. ['I did to my trouble see all the way that she did get as close to her husband as she could and turn her hands away when I did endeavour to take one of them so that I had no pleasure at all with her this night. When we landed I did take occasion to send him back to the boat while I did get a kiss or 2 and would have taken her by the hand but she did turn away, and when I said 'shall I not touch you?' answered 'I do not love touching', in a slight manner. I seemed not to take notice of it but parted kindly and her husband did walk with me almost to my house and there we parted and so I home troubled at this, but I think I shall make good use of it and mind my business more.']

Pepys made up for the disappointment the next day (18 February) in his office after dinner with Mrs Burrows:

. . . where *yo* had Mrs Burrows all *sola a* my closet and did there *besar and tocar su mamelles* as much as *yo quisere hasta a hazer me hazer*, but *ella* would not suffer that *yo* should *poner mi mano abaxo ses jupes* which *yo* endeavoured ['all alone in my closet and did there kiss and touch her breasts as much as I wanted until making myself do, but she would not suffer that I should put my hand below her skirts which

* 'Slight manner' here means in a dismissive, offhand way.

† Pretended.

I endeavoured']. Thence away, and with my wife by coach to the Duke of York's playhouse . . .

On 24 February Pepys learned from Elizabeth that Frances Tooker allegedly had contracted the 'clap',* for which Elizabeth confidently (and conveniently for Pepys) blamed her mother. But on 15 March (see below) it seemed less clear that this was true:

> Among other things my wife . . . tells me that little Miss Tooker hath got a clap as young as she is, being brought up loosely by her mother. Having been in bed with her mother when her mother hath had a man come into bed and lay with her.

The next day (25 February) Pepys and Elizabeth reminisced about their early married life. The day took an interesting turn when Pepys went to see his goldsmith and was shown a new medal made by John Roettier that commemorated the Second Dutch War, featuring Frances Stuart as a model:

> Lay long in bed talking with pleasure with my poor wife how she used to make coal fires, and wash my foul clothes with her own hand for me, poor wretch, in our little room at my Lord Sandwiches for which I ought for ever to love and admire her and do and persuade myself she would do the same thing again if God should reduce us to it . . . at my goldsmith's did observe the King's new Medall where in little there is Mrs Stewards face as well done as ever I saw anything in my whole life I think. And a pretty thing it is that he should choose her face to represent Brittania[10] by.

Pepys continued to find fault with Elizabeth. It must have been apparent that he had little interest in her company compared to that of

* Probably gonorrhoea, but the terms 'clap' and 'pox' were used indiscriminately in the 1600s.

his colourful female friends. He raged at her on 1 March, even though she was also suffering from her period pains again:

> So to the office till dinner, busy and then home to dinner and before dinner making my wife to sing, poor wretch her ear is so bad that it made me angry till the poor wretch cried to see me so vexed at her that I think I shall not discourage her so much again but will endeavour to make her understand sounds and do her good that way, for she hath a great mind to learn only to please me, and therefore I am mighty unjust to her in discouraging her so much. But we were good friends and to dinner and had she not been ill with those and that it were not Friday (on which in Lent there are no plays) I had carried her to a play. But she not being fit to go abroad I to the office . . .

Whether Elizabeth thought they were friends again is a moot point. She persevered with the music though. By 18 May Pepys could magnanimously comment that 'her growth in musique doth please me mightily'. Meanwhile, he was transfixed by the charismatic appearance of Nell Gwyn on the stage on 2 March in *The Maiden Queen*:

> . . . there is a comical part done by Nell which is Florimell that I never can hope ever to see the like done again by man or woman. The King and Duke of York were at the play, but so great performance of a comical part was never I believe in the world before as Nell doth this, both as a mad girle then most and best of all when she comes in like a young gallant and hath the notions and carriage of a spark the most that ever I saw any man have. It makes me, I confess, admire her.

By April 1668, Nell Gwyn was another of Charles II's mistresses.

On 4 March Pepys was back at Deptford. His polyglot phrase here was a direct translation of his conventional alliterative English phrase also deployed to record such occasions:

. . . and then to Bagwells where I befind[11] his wife washing and also I did *hazer tout que yo voudrais con* her ['also I did do all that I would with her'] and then sent for her husband and discoursed of his going to Harwich this week to his charge of the new ship building there which I have got him . . .

He was thwarted on 6 March at Deptford:

. . . then down by water to Redriffe and walked to Bagwell's where *la moher* was *dentro sed* ['the woman was within but'][12] would not have me *demorer* there *parce que* ['dally there because'] Mrs Batters and one of my *ancillas* ['maids'] I believe Jane (for she was gone abroad today) was in the town and coming thither so I away presently, esteeming it a great *escapar* ['escape'].[13]

On 13 March Pepys visited the Michell household:

. . . and there did *besar* ['kiss'] my Betty *que aegrotat* ['that is sick'][14] a little . . .

Evidently, being indisposed did not exempt Betty from Pepys's attentions. He moved on to Westminster Hall later:

. . . and thence to Martin's where he and she both within and with them the little widow[15] that was once there with her when I was there that dissembled so well to be grieved at hearing a tune that her late husband liked, but there being so much company I had no pleasure here and so away to the hall again and there met Doll Lane coming out and *per contract*[16] did *hazer* bargain *para andar* to the *cabaretto de vin* ['by agreement did make bargain to go to the wine-house'] called the Rose and *ibi* ['there'] I stayed 2 hours *sed* ['but'] she did not *venir, lequel* ['come, which'] troubled me . . .

There was more disappointment on 15 March, recounted in a disordered diary entry that jumbled up the day's events. After a morning's work and then dining at home:

> Then to Westminster Hall and spent an hour or 2 walking up and down, thinking *para aver* ['to have'] got out Doll Lane *sed yo no* could ['but I could not'] do it, having no opportunity *de hazer le, ainsi* lost the *todo* afternoon ['to do it, thus lost the whole afternoon'] and so away and called my wife . . .

Earlier that day:

> This noon come little Miss Tooker, who is grown a little woman, *ego* had opportunity *para besar* her and *tocar la abaxo con* my hand. She is pretty still but had no mind to be *vido*, being not *habillado*[17] as *ella* would be. My wife did tell me the other day that she heard she had had the *gran pacho*[18] but I hope no such thing. I *sum* certain that I should have been glad *para aver tempo* and *lugar* to have *hecho algo con* her ['I had opportunity to kiss her and touch her below with my hand. She is pretty still but had no mind to be seen, being not dressed as she would be. My wife did tell me the other day that she heard she had had the great pox but I hope no such thing. I am certain that I should have been glad to have the time and place to have done something with her'].

One explanation of this passage is that Elizabeth had deliberately sowed doubt in her husband's mind by suggesting she had 'the great pox', and that Frances also had the presence of mind to give Pepys the brush-off.[19]

On 20 March Pepys planned to visit Betty Martin in Westminster, but started with Frances Udall, Sarah's sister:

> Thence to Westminster and drank at the Swan and *besado* the *petite móça* ['kissed the little wench'] and so to Mrs Martins whom I find

> in *aposento* and *su hermana* rising.[20] So here I had opportunity *para tocar tout sobra su* body as I would and did *traher sus pernis*[21] out of the *lecto* and do *hazer* myself *hazer* ['whom I find in lodging and her sister rising. So here I had opportunity to touch all over her body as I would and did drag her legs out of the bed and do make myself do']. I sent for some burnt wine, and drank and then away, not pleased with my folly . . .

Pepys appears to have caught up with Betty at her lodgings where she was staying with her sister Doll (see 24 March below), though the passage is characteristically ambiguous. Doll was in the process of getting up, but Betty was still in bed where Pepys imposed himself on her. Pepys chose *pernis* with care to refer to her legs in a derogatory way. One of the Latin word's meanings is an animal thigh, as in a ham. He had called Betty's legs 'monstrous fat' on 29 June 1663.

That same day, Pepys visited Betty Mitchell's shop at Westminster Hall and bought a pair of gloves:

> . . . I *aime* her *de todo mi corazon*. Thence my mind wandered all this day upon my *mauvais amours* which *yo* be merry for ['I love her with all my heart. Thence my mind wandered all this day upon my lewd loves which I be merry for'].

Pepys drifted back to Westminster later after dropping Elizabeth at her tailor's:

> . . . only out of idleness and to get some little pleasure to my *mauvaises flammes* ['lewd loves'] but sped not and took up my wife . . .

He was unsuccessful; 'sped' was used here in its archaic meaning of 'succeed', thus 'but succeeded not'. The term *flammes* was used figuratively here as an equivalent to *amours*.

Two days later (22 March) Pepys briefly met Sarah Harmond (née Udall) and was later annoyed by Elizabeth's outfit:

> ... to Westminster to Herbert's ... and had a *besado* or 3 or 4 of Sarah whom *yo trouvais aqui* ['and had a kiss or 3 or 4 of Sarah whom I found there'] ... So home to dinner where my wife having dressed herself in a silly dress of a blue petticoat uppermost and a white satin waistcoat and white hood (though I think she did it because her gown is gone to the tailor's) did together with my being hungry (which always makes me peevish) make me angry. But when my belly was full were friends again ...

Pepys made progress with Mrs Burrows on 24 March, but only by tricking her:

> ... I to Martin's where I find her within and *su hermano*[22] and *la veuve* Burroughs. Here I did *demorer toda* the afternoon *bezando las* and drank and among other things did by a trick arrive at *tocando el poil de la* thing *de* the *veuve* abovesaid ['her within and her sister and the widow Burroughs. Here I did dally all the afternoon kissing them and drank and among other things did by a trick arrive at touching the hair of the thing of the widow abovesaid'].

The next day (25 March) Pepys learned that his mother's death was imminent. Margaret Pepys died that day. This does not seem to have overly distressed Pepys. On 31 March he dropped off Elizabeth's brother Balty at Whitehall and went straight to Betty Martin:

> and there *haze todo* ['did all'] which *yo* would *hazer con* ['I would do with'] her ...

On 1 April Pepys walked to and from Deptford:

> ... and pleased with a *jolie femme* ['pretty woman'] that I saw going and coming in the way, which *yo* could *aver sido* contented *para aver* stayed with if I could have *ganar* acquaintance *con ella* ['which I could have been contented to have stayed with if I could have gained

acquaintance with her'] but at such times as these I am at a great loss, having not confidence *ni alguno* ['nor some'] ready wit.

Confronted with a woman he did not know but was attracted to, Pepys believed he lacked the necessary skills to approach her.

On 9 April Pepys started out with hopes of progress with Elizabeth Knepp but discovered she was out. His plans thwarted, he had to move on to Frances Udall:

> . . . had a mind to have taken out Knepp and to have taken the ayre with her and to that end sent a porter in to her that she should take a coach and come to me to the piatz-a in Covent Garden where I waited for her but was doubtful* I might have done ill in doing it if we should be *visto ensemble, sed ella* ['seen together, but she'] was gone out and so was eased of that care therefore away to Westminster to the Swan and there did *bezar la* little *móça* and *hazer tocar* my thing through my *chemise con su mano* at which she was *enojado* but I did *donar ella algo* and so all well and drank and then by water to the Old Swan and there found Betty Michell sitting at the door, it being darkish. I stayed and talked a little with her but *no osa*[23] *bezar la* though she was to my thinking at this time *una de las plus* pretty *mohers* ever I did *ver* in my *vida*. And God forgive me my mind did run *sobre ella* all the *vespre* and night and *la* day *suivante*. ['. . . away to Westminster to the Swan and there did kiss the little wench and did touch my thing with her hand through my shirt at which she was angry but I did give her something and so all well and drank and then by water to the Old Swan and there found Betty Michell sitting at the door, it being darkish. I stayed and talked a little with her but dared not kiss her though she was to my thinking at this time one of the prettiest women that ever I did see in my life. And

* 'doubtful' was used here by P with its old meaning of 'fearful', i.e. he was fearful of a bad outcome if he had been seen with Elizabeth Knepp. He wrote 'piazza' as 'piatz-a' in longhand.

God forgive me my mind did run on her all the evening and night and the following day.']

Frances Udall's anger showed that acquiescence was not something that Pepys could take for granted, even if he used force. Throwing money at Frances was his way of taking back control. She would have to resist more fiercely next time (see 30 September below).

Luce, a 'very ugly and plain' cookmaid who had arrived on 12 June 1666, was on the receiving end of Pepys's anger on 12 April. This incident illustrates his impulsive use of violence to those who could not fight back, and his concern to hide his true nature from public view:

> Up and when ready and to my office to do a little business, and coming homeward again, saw my door and hatch open, left so by Luce our cookmaid, which so vexed me, that I did give her a kick in our entry, and offered a blow at her, and was seen doing so by Sir W. Penn's footboy, which did vex me to the heart because I know he will be telling their family of it, though I did put on presently a very pleasant face to the boy, and spoke kindly to him as one without passion, so as it may be he might not think I was angry, but yet I was troubled at it.

Luce walked out on 18 May after she was caught drunk. Pepys said he thought she was the 'dirtiest' servant he had ever had but regretted her leaving because of his 'love' for his staff.

On 13 April Pegg Lowther, Sir William Penn's recently married daughter, had become a better prospect:

> This afternoon come Mrs Lowther to me to the office, and there *yo* did *tocar ses mamelles* and did *bezar* them and *su boca* which she took *fort* willingly and perhaps *yo posse* in time a *hazer mas* to her ['I did touch her breasts and did kiss them and her mouth which she took most willingly and perhaps I can in time do more to her'].

On 23 April Elizabeth assisted in the delivery of Betty Mitchell's baby girl (who died on 24 June). He went to the office, dropped Elizabeth at her mother's and went straight on to Betty Martin:

> . . . to Mrs Martin's and there did *hazer* ['do'] what I would *con* ['with'] her and then called my wife and to little Michell's where we see the little child which I like mightily, being I allow very pretty and asked her how she did, being mighty glad of her doing well . . .

Pepys's behaviour illustrated how complicated and obsessive his pursuit of women was becoming. He had to abandon a meeting with Doll Lane on 1 May:

> To the hall and there walked a while it being term thence home to the Rose and there had Doll Lane *vener para* me but it was in a *lugar* mighty *ouvert* so as we no *poda hazer algo* ['there had Doll Lane come to me but it was in a mighty open place so as we could not do something'] so parted then met again at the Swan where for *la misma* reason we no *pode hazer* but put off to *rencontrar* anon ['for the same reason we could not do but put off to meet anon'] which I only used as a put-off . . .

Elizabeth's gynaecological problems continued to be an issue. On 3 May:

> . . . so home to dinner, where my wife hath *ceux là* ['those'][24] upon her and is very ill with them, so forced to go to bed.

This goes some way to explaining why Pepys might have had to keep his distance from Elizabeth. On 12 May another row broke out over Mrs Knepp, evidence of Elizabeth's increasing jealousy and rage at her husband's persistent preference for other women's company:

> Up and to my chamber to settle some accounts there and by and by down comes my wife to me in her night-gown and we begun calmly that upon having money to lace her gown for second mourning, she would promise to wear white locks no more in my sight, which I like a severe fool, thinking not enough, begun to except against, and made her fly out to very high terms and cry and in her heat told me of keeping company with Mrs Knipp, saying that if I would promise never to see her more (of whom she hath more reason to suspect then I had heretofore of Pembleton) she would never wear white locks more. This vexed me but I restrained myself from saying anything, but do think never to see this woman, at least to have her here more, but by and by I did give her money to buy lace, and she promised to wear no more white locks while I lived and so all very good friends as ever, and I to my business and she to dress herself.

On 20 May Pepys admired Betty Mitchell once again ('Lord, how pretty she is'), but later was with Betty Martin again after another near disaster with Frances Udall. Pepys's sexual encounters were now so frequent he could easily forget them:

> . . . by water to Westminster hall and there walked a while talking at random with Sir Wm. Doyly and so away to Mrs Martin's lodging, who was gone before expecting me, and there *yo haze* what *yo vellem cum* her ['I did what I would like with her'] and drank and so by coach home (but I have forgot that I did in the morning go to the Swan and there tumbling of *la* little *fille, son* uncle did *trouver* her *cum su* neckcloth off ['tumbling of the little girl, her uncle did find her with her neckcloth off'] which I was ashamed of but made no great matter of it, but let it pass with a laugh) and there spent the evening with my wife at our Flagelettes and so to supper and after a little reading to bed.

The ends of a woman or girl's neckcloth were normally tucked into the top of the dress above the bust. Its removal facilitated access for wandering hands.

Mrs Daniels returned to Pepys on 23 May seeking a position for her husband. Here Pepys exhibited his juxtaposition of demanding sex from a married woman with what he regarded as an honourable undertaking to reciprocate with a professional favour for her husband. The meeting provoked Elizabeth's suspicions:

> After dinner I to my chamber and my wife and father to talk and by and by they tell Mrs Daniel would speak with me so I down to the parlour to her, and sat down together and talked about getting her husband a place and here I did adventure *etsi* the *porta etait operta para*[25] put my *mano abajo su jupes* 2 or 3 *temps* et touch her *cosa con* great pleasure, *ella* resisting pretty much *sed* never the *minus* submitted ['and here I did adventure though the door was open to put my hand under her skirts 2 or 3 times and touch her thing with great pleasure, she resisting pretty much but nevertheless submitted'].
>
> I do promise and mean to do what kindness I can to her husband. After having been there *hasta yo* was ashamed *de peur* that my people *pensait* the *pragma*[26] *de* it ['until I was ashamed out of fear that my people supposed the thing (i.e. a sexual activity) from it'] or lest they might espy *nous* ['us'] through some trees, we parted and I to the office, and presently back home again and there was asked by my wife, I know not whether simply or with design, how I come to look as I did *car yo* ['because I'] was in much *calor et de* body and of *animi* ['much heat and of body and disposition'] which I put off with the heat of the season and so to other business, but I had some fear hung upon me lest *algo* had *sido decouvert* ['something had been discovered'].

That same day, Pepys enjoyed the attentions of Peg Lowther (née Penn) again in an almost identical manner to 13 April (see above), except that this time they were in her father's house:

> This afternoon I had opportunity *para jouer* with Mrs Pen *tocando* her *mamelles* and *besando ella* being *sola* in the *casa* of her *pater*. And she *fort* willing. ['This afternoon I had opportunity to play with Mrs Penn, touching her breasts and kissing her being alone in the house of her father. And she exceeding willing.']

On Sunday 26 May Pepys was back with Betty Martin heading to St Margaret's, Westminster. Betty told him she was going into the church for the sake of appearances, so Pepys did too. Betty then left so they could meet in private, but another farce ensued:

> . . . met with Mr Howlett* who offering me a pew in the gallery, I had no excuse but up with him I must go, and there much against my will stayed out the whole church in pain while she expected me at home but I did entertain myself with my perspective glass up and down the church by which I had the great pleasure of seeing and gazing a great many very fine women and what with that, and sleeping, I passed away the time till sermon was done and then to Mrs Martin, and there stayed with her an hour or 2 and there did what *yo* would do with her[27] . . .

In this entry, the last few words are written in shorthand as 'thalar dimid whanot *yoro* wolold wimith honor'. This was one of the first occasions that Pepys started inserting extraneous shorthand consonants into his words to confuse the meaning. He applied this technique principally only to English words in phrases and sentences that sometimes also included polyglot. Apart from a very few exceptions he did not apply the extra consonants to the polyglot.[28] The idea must have come from the published ideas of John Wilkins (1614–72) whom Pepys knew through the Royal Society and mentioned several times in the diary (see Introduction).

---

* Betty Mitchell's father. L&M suggest a John Howlett, recorded as assessed for tax in 1663.

Pepys was at the Foxhall pleasure gardens on 28 May. He was disturbed by an incident he witnessed, but is more memorable for his lack of self-awareness about his own conduct:

> Among others there were 2 pretty women alone that walked a great while, which discovered by some idle gentlemen, they would needs take them up but to see the poor ladies how they were put to it to run from them, and they after them, and sometimes the ladies put themselves along with other company then the other drew back at last, the last did get off out of the house and took boat and away. I was troubled to see them abused so and could have found my heart,* as little desire of fighting as I have, to have protected the ladies.

More rage at Elizabeth's chosen outfit followed on 29 May:

> Anon comes down my wife dress<ed> in her second mourning with her black moyre waistcoat and short petticoat laced with silver lace so basely that I could not endure to see her, and with laced lining which is too soon, so that I was horrid angry and went out of doors to the office and there stayed, and would not go to our intended meeting which vexed me to the blood, and my wife sent twice or thrice to me to direct her any way to dress her, but to put on her cloth gown which she would not venture, which made me mad . . .

Pepys regarded storming off to get his accounts done made up for the row. He was disappointed by a tryst with Mrs Daniels on 31 May. On this occasion he recorded the event in English and continued the use of extraneous consonants which he had started a few days before (see 26 May above):

---

* Courage.

> Up and there came young Mrs Daniel in the morning as I expected about business of her husband's, I took her into the office to discourse with her about getting some imployment for him. And there I did put my hand to her belly, so as to make myself do, but she is so lean that I had no great pleasure with her. So parted and I by water to White hall.

The key words were written 'but sherer ilis so leanen that I had no grearet plealesur with hunur'. For obvious reasons only selected further examples are supplied here for subsequent passages. Three weeks later (22 June, below), he had a more satisfactory experience with Mrs Daniels.

By early June Pepys was not so preoccupied by the humiliating debacle when the Dutch sailed up the Medway, destroying or capturing thirteen ships, that he overlooked meeting up with Betty Martin on Sunday 9 June:

> . . . after church time to Mrs Martin's and there *haze* what *yo* ['did what I'] would with her.[29]

On 12 June as the Dutch emergency began Pepys had panicked and sent Elizabeth and his father to the family house at Brampton to bury some of his money (see 19 June below, and colour plate section).

With Elizabeth away, Pepys turned his attention elsewhere. The notes here give what Pepys originally wrote in shorthand with the extra consonants. On 16 June he 'did show some dalliance to my maid Nell',[30] but the next day he ruminated on his behaviour:

> I have lately played the fool much with our Nell in playing with her breasts.[31]

The following morning (18 June), guilt followed another assault on Nell:

> Up and did this morning dally with Nell and touch her thing[32] which I was afterward troubled for.

He had set his guilt aside by the afternoon and planned a tryst with Peg Lowther at his home but was thwarted by her having arrived with company.

On 19 June Elizabeth was able to explain to Pepys how she and his father had hidden the money (on 12 June):

> . . . I and my wife to talk who did give me so bad an account of her and my father's method in burying of our gold, that made me mad and she herself is not pleased with it, she believing that my sister knows of it. My father and she did it on Sunday, when they were gone to church in open daylight in the midst of the garden where for aught they knew, many eyes might see them which put me into such trouble that I was almost mad about it, and presently cast about how to have it back again to secure it here, the times being a little better now . . .

A farcical recovery attempt was to follow on 10–11 October. Neither Elizabeth nor John Pepys could remember where they had buried the money. A despairing Pepys had to give up on around twenty to thirty of the coins.

Mrs Daniel visited Pepys on 22 June at the office again. Pepys noted how easily he was roused to orgasm merely by touching her, unlike their last encounter on 31 May:

> Up and to my office where busy and there came Mrs Daniel and it is strange how merely the putting of my hand to her belly through her coats did make me do.

The incident was so casual that he carried on working immediately afterwards. Two days later (24 June) Michael and Betty Mitchell ('poor woman') came to tell Pepys that their little girl, born in April, had died.

An ex-soldier, 'pensioner of the King's Guard', called Edward Coleman had been in the coach that Elizabeth and John Pepys had travelled south in after burying the coins. Elizabeth appears to have been taken by him and he by her, much to Pepys's jealous fury on 29 June:

> After having done my business at the office I home and there I find Coleman come again to my house and with my wife in our great chamber, which vexed me there being a bed therein. I stayed there awhile and then to my study vexed, showing no civility to the man. But he comes on a compliment to receive my wife's commands into the country, whither he is going, and it being Saturday my wife told me there was no other room for her to bring him in, and so much is truth. But I stayed vexed in my closet . . .

Pepys was to be told on 23 December 1667 by Creed that Coleman was 'as very a rogue for women as in any in the world'. Pepys called his late brother Thomas (see above, April 1664) a rogue, but never considered whether it might have applied to him too.

On his visit to the Medway and the Medway towns on 30 June to inspect the aftermath of the Dutch raid, Pepys found a local distraction in Rochester, but managed to exercise restraint:

> . . . back to our inn and bespoke supper, and so back to the fields and into the Cherry garden, where we had them fresh gathered, and here met with a young, plain, silly shopkeeper and his wife, a pretty young woman, the man's name Hawkins, and I did kiss her, and we talked (and the woman of the house, one May, is a very talking bawdy jade) and eat cherries together, and then to walk in the fields till it was late and did kiss her, and I believe had I had a fit time and place I might have done what I would with her.

On 2 July Pepys accosted Nell again:

I to my chamber and there dallied a little with my maid Nell to touch her thing[33] but nothing more.

A pregnancy scare followed on 3 July when Pepys visited Betty Martin who told him her period had not started. Pepys wondered whether to try and recall her naval purser husband Samuel to provide a cover story. However, before hearing Betty's revelation he was thwarted by Michael Mitchell:

> . . . by water to White hall (calling at Michell's in my way, but the rogue would not invite me in, I having a mind *para ver* ['for to see'] his wife)[34] . . . I to Mrs Martins and there she was gone in before but when I come, contrary to my expectation, I find her all in trouble, and what was it for but that I have got her with child for those do not *venir* ['come'] upon her as they should have done and is in exceeding grief and swears that the child is mine which I do not believe, but yet do comfort her that either it can<not> be so or if it be that I will take care to send for her husband,[35] though I do hardly see how I can be sure of that, the ship being at sea and as far as Scotland, but however I must do it and shall find some way or other of doing it though it do trouble me not a little.

Calling Michael Mitchell a 'rogue' for denying him access to Betty illustrated Pepys's belief in the entitlement afforded by his status and influence. The term had connotations of treachery, dishonesty, and a lack of principles (see Edward Coleman, 29 June above). The outraged Pepys expected to be treated with deference and compliance by his social inferiors.

On 6 July Pepys was in Westminster on business, and went to Betty Martin's lodgings, the landlady being a Mrs 'Cragg' (probably Crake):

> . . . where I met with the good news *que elsta*[36] *no es con* child ['that she is not with child'] (she having *de estos* ['those'] upon her), the fear of which she did give me the other day had troubled me

> much. My joy in this made me send for wine, and thither come her sister and Mrs Cragg, and I stayed a good while there. But here happened the best instance of a woman's falseness in the world, that her sister Doll, who went for a bottle of wine, did come home all blubbering and swearing against one Captain van den A<nker?>, a Dutchman of the Rhenish wine house, that pulled her into a stable by the Dog tavern and there did tumble her and toss her, calling him all the rogues and toads in the world when she knows that *ella* hath suffered me to do anything with her 100 times.[37]

'100 times' here was obviously metaphorical but implies that Pepys recorded only a fraction of the sexual encounters he had had, not only with Doll but also with others. This incident also showed that Pepys expected a woman to acquiesce in the face of male sexual violence: Doll had been prepared to subject herself to his demands on numerous occasions, and thus had no business complaining about another man assaulting her.

Another furious row with Elizabeth occurred on 12 July, this time because of Pepys's absence from home, Pepys again showing how easily he became violent when it came to easy targets (see 28 May above when he referred to his 'little desire of fighting'):

> . . . so home, and there find my wife in a dogged humour for my not dining at home, and I did give her a pull by the nose and some ill words, which she provoked me to by something she spoke, that we fell extraordinarily out, insomuch that I going to the office to avoid further anger, she fallowed me in a devilish manner thither and with much ado I got her into the garden out of hearing to prevent shame, and so home, and by degrees I found it necessary to calm her and did, and then to the office, where pretty late and then to walk with her in the garden, and so to supper and pretty good friends, and so to bed. With my mind very quiet.

On 1 August Elizabeth was 'out of humour, as she always is' when Elizabeth Knepp was with them. She was still seething the following day (2 August). Pepys applied a tactic he had used before, which was to say nothing (on 24 August he decided not to tell his wife if he had seen Elizabeth Knepp):

> Up but before I rose my wife fell into angry discourse of my kindness yesterday to Mrs Knip, and leading her and sitting in the coach hand-in-hand and my arm about her middle, and in some bad words reproached me with it. I was troubled, but having much business in my head and desirous of peace rose and did not provoke her. So she up and come to me and added more, and spoke basely of my father, who I perceive did do something in the country, at her last being there, that did not like her, but I would not enquire into anything, but let her talk, and when ready away to the office I went.

The entry appears to allude to the possibility that Pepys's father had made some sort of advance to Elizabeth, or perhaps had admonished her. There was another reason for her anger directly linked, though she was unaware, to Pepys's increasingly extensive adulteries. Later the same day she confronted him with news that her period had started, and from this we learn that she and her husband had effectively ceased to have sexual relations:

> This noon my wife comes to me alone and tells me she had those upon her and bid me remember it. I asked her why and she said she had a reason. I do think by something too she said today, that she took notice that I had not lain with her this ½ year that she thinks that I have some doubt that she might be with child by somebody else. Which God knows never entered into my head, or whether my father observed anything at Brampton with Coleman I know not. But I do not do well to let these beginnings of discontents take so much root between us.

By 6 August Elizabeth had sacked Nell Payne, blaming her for being a gossip and apparently unaware of what Pepys had been up to. Although Pepys professed not to be sorry about this, he did not lose interest in Nell (see 30 April 1668 below). Betty Martin and Elizabeth Burrows also turned up earlier the same day at Pepys's office, much to his alarm:

> I to the office (only, met at the door with Mrs Martin and Mrs Burroughs, who I took in and drank with but was afraid my wife should see them, they being, especially the first, a twattling* gossip and so after drinking with them parted, and I to the office . . .

On 12 August Pepys calculated that it was only three months since he and Elizabeth had last slept together:

> My wife waked betimes to call up her people to washing and so to bed again, whom I then hugged it being cold now in the mornings and then did *la otra cosa con* ['the other thing with'] her which I had not done *con ella* for these *tres meses* ['with her for these three months'] past, which I do believe is a great matter towards the making her of late so indifferent towards me and with good reason but now she had much pleasure and so to sleep again.

If it seemed that Pepys was prepared to work to restore their relationship it did not preclude any more adventures. On Sunday 18 August he ventured into St Dunstan-in-the-West in Fleet Street:

> . . . where I heard an able sermon of the Minister of the place. And stood by a pretty, modest maid, whom I did labour to take by the hand and the body but she would not, but got further and further

* 'Twattle' is a rare word, but related to 'twaddle', i.e. pretentious silly nonsense.

from me and at last I could perceive her to take pins out of her pocket to prick me if I should touch her again which seeing I did forbear, and was glad I did espy her design. And then I fell to gaze upon another pretty maid in a pew close to me and she on me and I did go about to take her by the hand, which she suffered a little and then withdrew. So the sermon ended, and the church broke up and my amours ended also, and so took coach and home and there took up my wife, and to Islington with her, our old road.

Pepys was thus able to move from one woman or girl to another in pursuit of gratification before going home to his wife, apparently unconcerned that he might be spotted.

Three days later (21 August) Pepys had to back down to avoid more trouble with Elizabeth, despite starting out by standing up against her:

Up and my wife and I fell out about the pair of cuffs which she hath a mind to have to go to see the ladies dancing tomorrow at Betty Turner's school and doth vex me so that I am resolve<d> to deny them her. However, by and by a way was found that she had them, and I well satisfied, being unwilling to let our difference grow higher upon so small an occasion and frowardness of mine.

Even so, Pepys managed to meet later that day with Betty Martin and her sister Doll, one of several other such fleeting occasions recorded over the next few weeks:

So to Westminster hall and there stayed a while and thence to Mrs Martin's and there did take a little pleasure both with her and her sister. Here sat and talked and it is a strange thing to see the impudence of the woman that desires by all means to have her *marido* ['husband'] come home only that she might be at liberty to have me *para tocar* her ['to touch her'] which is a thing I do not so much desire.

Pepys's moral compass allowed him to be outraged that Betty Martin only wanted her own husband home so that she could continue sexual activity with Pepys without fear of a pregnancy that could not be passed off as her husband's. He was equally offended that she applied such a condition to her dalliances with him.

On Sunday 25 August, Pepys went to St Margaret's, Westminster, and nearly made a fool of himself again:

> ... thinking to see Betty Michell and did stay an hour in the crowd, think<ing> by the end of a nose that I saw that it had been her but at last the head turned toward me and it was her mother. Which vexed me and so I back to my boat ...

On 17 September Pepys kissed Betty Mitchell. He was perturbed by her lack of enthusiasm but was prepared to play the long game, as he had with Mrs Bagwell. In the meantime, he returned to Betty Martin:

> I walked to the Old Swan, the way mighty dirty, and there called at Michell's and there had opportunity *para* kiss *su moher* ['to kiss his wife'] but *ella* did receive it with a great deal of seeming regret which did vex me. But however I do not doubt overcoming her as I did the *moher* of the *menusier* ['wife of the carpenter']* at Deptford ... and so to Mrs Martin's to pay for my cuffs and drink with her and did *hazer la cosa* ['do the thing'] with her.[38]

Five days later (22 September), Pepys was irritated that his pleasure-seeking meant he had no time or energy left to start picking holes in Elizabeth's domestic accounts:

> This night I did even my accounts of the house which I have (to my great shame) omitted now above 2 months or more and therefore

* Mrs Bagwell.

> am content to take my wife's and maids' accounts as they give them, being not able to correct them, which vexes me but the fault being my own, contrary to my wife's frequent desires, I cannot find fault, but am resolved never to let them come to that pass again. The truth is I have indulged myself more in pleasure for these last 2 months then ever I did in my life before, since I come to be a person concerned in business. And I doubt* when I come to make up my accounts I shall find it so by the expense.

However, a new appointment to the household was unexpectedly to change everything for Pepys and Elizabeth. On 24 September:

> This evening my wife tells me that W. Batelier hath been here today and brought with him the pretty girl he speaks of to come to serve my wife as a woman, out of the School at Bow. My wife says she is extraordinary handsome and enclines to have her and I am glad of it. At least that if we must have one, she should be handsome. But I am leav<ing> it wholly to my wife to do what she will therein.

The girl, Deborah Willet, arrived three days later (27th) for another preliminary meeting. She was the daughter of a Bristol merchant called Robert Willet and his wife Elizabeth, and the third of seven children. Whether or not her parents were dead by 1667 is unknown, though one possibility is that they had moved to Ireland; her family, apart from an aunt, goes unmentioned in the diary.[39] Pepys was unsettled and transfixed immediately:

> While I was busy at the office my wife sends for me to come home and what was it but to see the pretty girl which she is taking to wait upon her? And though she seems not altogether so great a beauty as she had before told me, yet endeed she is mi<ghty>

---

* The usage of 'doubt' at this time was in the sense of the modern 'do not doubt'.

> pretty and so pretty that I find I shall be too much pleased with it, and therefore could be contented as to my judgement though not to my passion, that she might not come lest I may be found too much minding her to the discontent of my wife. She is to come next week. She seems by her discourse to be grave beyond her bigness and age, and exceeding well bred as to her deportment having been a scholar in a school at Bow these 7 or 8 years. To the office again, my <mind>[40] running on this pretty girl . . .

Deborah Willet, always referred to by Pepys as Deb, or to begin with 'Willet', was sixteen when she joined the Pepys household.

On 30 September Pepys was back at the Swan in Westminster and tried again with Frances Udall (see above, 9 April 1667):

> So to Westminster where to the Swan, and there I did fling down the *fille* ['girl'] there upon the chair and did *tocar* ['touch'] her thigh with my hand at which she begin to cry out, so I left off and drank and away to the hall, and thence to Mrs Martin's to bespeak some linen and there *yo* did *hazer algo* with *ella* ['I did do something with her'] and drank and away having first promised my god-daughter a new coat, her first coat.

Pepys here graphically recounted the force he had used, and thereby his sense of entitlement, but was compelled to back off by Frances's vocal protestation in a public place. Yet he had taken the chance in the first place. Presumably aroused but frustrated, Pepys had resorted to Betty Martin for relief but was relaxed enough to fulfil the social niceties of a godfather's obligations (the child was dead by 5 May 1668). Deb Willet arrived the same day:

> So by coach home and there find our pretty girl Willet come, brought by Mr Batelier and she is very pretty and so grave as I never saw little thing in my life. Endeed I think her a little good for our family and so well carriaged as I hardly ever saw.

Perhaps Deb's fresh-faced and youthful appearance appealed to Pepys, but her dignified seriousness may have had more to do with it given his negative comments about Elizabeth's personality. On 5 October his views about Nell Gwyn and Elizabeth Knepp's use of cosmetics on stage provide us with more information about his preference for natural-looking young women:

> But Lord to see how they were both painted would make a man mad. And did make me loath them. And what base company of men comes among them, and how lewdly they talk. And how poor the men are in clothes and yet what a shew they make on the stage by candlelight, is very observable.

From the outset, Deb's presence was close. On a family visit to Cambridgeshire earlier in the month she came too, sleeping in a pull-out trundle bed beside them in their bedchamber (9 October). By 12 October alarm bells were ringing for Elizabeth:

> . . . (who I perceive is already a little jealous of my being fond of Willett, but I will avoid giving her any cause to continue in that mind, as much as possible) . . .

The next day (13th) Pepys was with his other favourite Sunday afternoon companions:

> And thence only walked to Mrs Martin's and there sat with her and her sister and Burroughs and did *tocar la primera* ['touch the first'][41] and there drank and talked and away by water home . . .

On 14 October Pepys was worried that Betty Mitchell's mother Mrs Howlett was about to confront him. They met by arrangement at Betty Martin's home:

> Thence I to Mrs Martin's where by appointment comes to me Mrs Howlett which I was afeared was to have told me something of my freedom with her daughter but it was not so but only to complain to me of her son-in-law, how he abuses and makes a slave of her and his mother is one that encourages him in it so they are at this time upon very bad terms one with another and desires that I would take a time to advise him and tell him what becomes him to do, which office I am very glad of for some end of my own also *con su filia* ['with her daughter'].

A few days later (15th) at the theatre:

> But here before the play begun my wife begun to complain to me of Willetts confidence in sitting cheek by jowl by us which was a poor thing but I perceive she is already jealous of my kindness* to her, so that I begin to fear this girl is not likely to stay long with us.

Pepys was bothered that Elizabeth's jealousy would result in Deb being sacked just like some of her predecessors. Deb would be, but not under circumstances Elizabeth had yet envisaged. Nevertheless, future theatre visits usually involved the three of them going together until Pepys tried on 13 November to renew his vows to keep away from theatres. Pepys was still visiting Betty Martin, his mentions of sex with her now barely incidental, such as on 23 October (which was also Elizabeth's birthday, as usual unmentioned):

> Thence to Mrs Martins, and there stayed till 2 a-clock and drank and talked, and did give her 3£ to buy my god-daughter her first new gowne. And I did *hazer algo con* ['do something with'] her . . .

* The word 'kindness' in this context means P's evident sexual interest in Deb.

These abbreviated references may have been linked to struggling with his eyesight as a result of any close work, which he was increasingly referring to (among these 'my eyes were ready to fall out of my head', 18 November, and 'my eyes aching, having overwrought them today reading so much shorthand', 29 November). He had visited a spectacle-maker on 4 November.

However, Pepys also mentioned fewer sexual episodes in the latter part of 1667 though he managed some social contact. For example, Betty Mitchell and her husband came to dine at Pepys's house on 10 November. Either his habits had changed, or he was choosing no longer to write about them.

Pepys did let his guard down on 4 December, first with a prostitute, and next with Mrs Burrows, but to no avail. He had dropped Elizabeth and Deb at Charing Cross earlier before heading to the House of Commons:

> . . . and there spied a pretty woman with spots on her face, well clad, who was enquiring for the guard chamber. I fallowed her and there she went up and turned into the turning towards the Chapel and I after her and upon the stairs there met her coming up again and there kissed her twice, and her business was to enquire for Sir Edwd Bishop, one of the sergeants-at-armes. I believe she was a woman of pleasure but was shy enough to me, and so I saw her go out afterwards, and I took a hackney coach, and away. I to Westminster hall and there walked, and thence towards White hall by coach and spying Mrs Burroughs in a shop did stop and light and speak to her and so to White hall, where I light and went and met her coming towards White hall but was upon business and I could not get her to go anywhither* and so parted, and I home with my wife and girl . . .

* To anywhere.

On 7 December, Deb's aunt, a Mrs Hunt with whom Deb had been living, arrived to visit her and Elizabeth. She had an unusual conversation topic:

> And while we were at dinner comes Willett's aunt to see her and my wife. She is a very fine widow and pretty handsome but extraordinary well-carriaged and speaks very handsomely and with extraordinary understanding so as I spent the whole afternoon in her company with my wife, she understanding all the things of note touching plays and fashions and Court and everything and speaks rarely, which pleases me mightily, and seems to love her niece very well and was so glad (which was pretty odde) to see that since she came hither her breasts* begin to swell, she being afeard before that she would have none. Which was a pretty kind of content she gave herself.

Despite Mrs Hunt's dignified deportment and well-informed conversation, the possibility must be that drawing attention to her niece's developing physical form was targeted at Pepys in the knowledge that he would be interested, which might benefit Deb. The extent to which Pepys was played by some of the families of the women he pursued is very hard to gauge, but undoubtedly a factor.

As Christmas 1667 approached, Elizabeth was suffering from toothache and was confined to bed. Pepys, who had made only perfunctory references to Deb since her arrival, was developing the interest in her that he had feared and now made his first move. On 22 December:

> Up and my wife, poor wretch still in pain, and then to dress myself and down to my chamber to settle some papers, and thither come to me Willet with an errand from her mistress, and this time I first did give her a little kiss, she being a very pretty humoured girl, and so one that I doth love mightily.

---

* Deb's breasts.

On Christmas Eve 1667 Pepys visited the Swan and 'did *besar* ['kiss'] a little Frank' (Frances Udall).[42] Later, Pepys resorted to hands-free masturbation again (he had managed this feat before on 16 December 1665), this time in the Queen's Chapel at St James's Palace during an epic Catholic high mass that lasted five hours and required 'a great deal of patience':

> The Queen was there and some ladies. But Lord what an odde thing it was for me to be in a crowd of people, here a footman, there a beggar, here a fine lady, there a zealous poor papist, and here a Protestant, 2 or 3 together, come to see the show. I was afeared of my pocket being picked very much. But here I did make myself to do *la cosa* ['the thing'] by mere imagination *mirando* a *jolie móça* ['looking on a pretty wench'] and with my eyes open which I never did before. And God forgive me for it, it being in the chapel.

The polyglot here provided Pepys with an opportunity for rhyming. He also incorporated alliteration based on 'm' and composed the sentence in a form of metre:

> But here I did make myself to do *la cosa*
> By mere imagination *mirando a jolie móça* . . .

The metrical need for 'to' and 'mere', which are otherwise superfluous, thereby becomes obvious. These characteristics of Pepys's polyglot composition have escaped notice up till now but his musical inclinations and his habit of collecting ballads make them unsurprising.[43] Whether Pepys realized what he was doing is less clear; he perhaps could not help himself, but examples like this suggest he spent time enjoying composing these lines, probably while he sat out the service.

On 30 December Pepys made the mistake of telling Elizabeth he had spent time earlier with Knepp, while Will Hewer and Deb had to listen:

> . . . but she was as mad as a devil and nothing but ill words between us all the evening while we sat at Cards, W. Hewer and the girl by, even to gross ill words which I was troubled for but do see that I must use policy to keep her spirit down and to give her no offence by my being with Knipp and Pierce. Of which, though she will not own it, yet she is heartily jealous. At last it ended in few words and my silence (which for fear of growing higher between us I did forbear) and so to supper and to bed without word one to another.

The year ending badly this way, Pepys was back to Betty Martin on 31 December, dropping off Elizabeth on the way at her tailor's and considerately picking her up afterwards:

> After dinner with my wife and girl to Unthankes and there left her and I to Westminster, and there to Mrs Martin's and did *hazer con ella* ['do with her'] what I desired and there did drink with her and find fault with her husband's wearing of too fine clothes, by which I perceive he will be a beggar. And so after a little talking I away and took up my wife again and so home and to the office . . .

Pepys still claimed as he finished his entry for the day that 1667 was ending 'with great happiness to myself and family as to health and good condition in the world, blessed be God for it'.

9

1668

Very Great Sorrow With My Wife By My Folly

By 1668 Pepys was routinely exploiting any opportunity to philander at will while deceiving Elizabeth as well as exploiting her absences. He resented her attempts to assert herself, but the critical moment came on 25 October when Elizabeth caught Pepys with Deb.

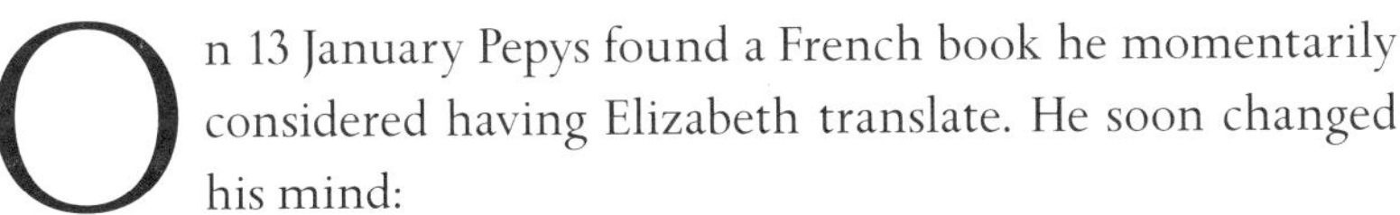

On 13 January Pepys found a French book he momentarily considered having Elizabeth translate. He soon changed his mind:

> Thence homeward by coach and stopped at Martin's, my bookseller, where I saw the French book which I did think to have had for my wife to translate called *L'escholle des Filles*, but when I come to look into it, it is the most bawdy, lewd book that ever I see rather worse then *putana errante*. So that I was ashamed of reading in it . . .

The first book (known in England as *The School of Venus*) was about a virgin learning from a sexually experienced woman. The second,

'*The Wandering Whore*', which Pepys considered less offensive, is self-explanatory. He was not put off though (see 9 February below).

Pepys came to terms with Elizabeth's limited singing talents on 22 January:

> So home and there to cards with my wife, Deb, and Betty Turner, and Batelier, and after supper late to sing but Lord how did I please myself to make Betty Turner sing to see what a beast she is as to singing, not knowing how to sing one note in tune but, only for the experiment, I would not for 40s hear her sing a tune. Worse then my wife 1000 times, so that it doth a little reconcile me to her.

Pepys, despite his disapproval, had purchased a copy of *L'escholle des Filles*. On 9 February he read it, tortuously justifying this as 'not amiss for a sober man once to read over to inform himself in the villainy of the world'. That evening he settled down for a closer look:

> I to my chamber where I did read through *L'escholle des Filles*, a lewd book, but what do me no wrong once to read for information sake (but it did *hazer* my prick[1] *para* stand all the while and *una vez* to *decharger* ['once to spend']) and after I had done it I burned it, that it might not be among my books to my shame and so at night to supper and then to bed.

After a period of relatively fewer references to encounters with other women, they resumed. On 18 February:

> I stepped to the Dog Tavern, and thither come to me Doll Lane and there we did drink together, and she tells me she is my valentine and there I did *tocar sa cosa* ['touch her thing'] and might have done whatever else *yo voudrais* ['I would'] but there was nothing but only chairs in the room and so we were unable *para hazer algo* ['to do something'].

This followed the last time he had slept with Elizabeth by only one day. He had to wait another week because she was ill (25 February):

Up having lain the last night the first night that I have lain with my wife since she was last ill which is about 8 days.

The other side of Pepys was the way in which he could be transported to ecstasy by music. On 27 February:

. . . thence with my wife and Deb to the King's House to see *The Virgin Martyr*, the first time it hath been acted a great while and it is mighty pleasant not that the play is worth much but it is finely Acted by Becke Marshall. But that which did please me beyond anything in the whole world was the wind musique when the Angell comes down which is so sweet that it ravished me and endeed in a word did wrap up my soul so that it made me really sick, just as I have formerly been when in love with my wife that neither then nor all the evening going home, and at home, I was able to think of anything, but remained all night transported so as I could not believe that ever any music hath that real command over the soul of a man as this did upon me and makes me resolve to practice wind music and to make my wife do the like.

Pepys thereby used his experience of loving Elizabeth to the point of feeling sick as an analogy. However, a few days later Pepys was back with Betty Martin on 1 March, observing that he had not been with her for some time:

Thence to Mr<s> Martin's where I have not been also a good while, and with great difficulty, company being there, did get an opportunity to *hazer* what I would *con* her ['do what I would with her']. And here I was mightily taken with a starling which she hath, that was the King's, which he kept in his bedchamber and

> doth whistle and talk the most and best that ever I heard anything in my life.

On 5 March Pepys gave a speech lasting around three hours to the House of Commons defending the Navy Board and its officers from long-running accusations of corruption. It was one of his finest moments, and in public life perhaps the finest, but it followed much preoccupation and worry. His speech was greeted with a gale of enthusiasm and compliments, even though by his own admission some of those present had 'gone out to dinner and come in again ½ drunk'. On 15 March:

> I to Mrs Martin's and there spent the afternoon and did *hazer con ella* ['did do <what I would> with her'], and here was her sister and Mrs Burrows, and so in the evening got a coach and home . . .

The omitted part of the key phrase probably resulted from the increasingly incidental nature and brevity of these records, Pepys dashing them off hurriedly and with increasing difficulty as he struggled with his failing eyesight.

On 18 March, by when the ructions following Pepys's triumphant speech were continuing, Doll Lane obliged Pepys again, the pair finding a solution to the furniture issue that had caused problems a month before:

> . . . met Doll Lane at the Dog tavern and there *yo* did *hazer* ['I did do'] what I did desire with her and did it backward, not having convenience to do it the other way. And I did give her as being my valentine 20s to buy what *ella* would.

Pepys managed the same technique with Doll's sister Betty Martin three days later on 21 March. In both entries he wrote 'backward' in shorthand as 'balak wamard':

> . . . here *yo* did *hazer la cosa* ['I did do the thing'] with Mrs Martin backward . . .

On 24 and 25 March 1668 the Bawdy House riots erupted. Armed apprentices, angered by Charles II's prohibition of lay gatherings in private houses, attacked brothels, which the King tolerated but they regarded as symbolic of the court's decadence. Pepys's 25 March description provides more background on the conspicuous level of prostitution in Restoration times and its links to the Navy, and the alleged origin of the protests among men who had served in Cromwell's army:

> Some blood hath been spilt but a great many houses pulled down and, among others, <the> Duke of York was mighty merry at that of Damaris Page's, the great bawd[2] of the seamen. And <the> Duke of York complained merrily that he hath lost two tenants by their houses being pulled down who paid him for their wine licenses 15£ a year. But here it was said how these idle fellows have had the confidence to say that they did ill in contenting themselves in pulling down the little bawdy houses and did not go and pull down the great bawdy house at White hall. And some of them have the last night had a word among them, and it was 'Reformation and Reducement.' This doth make the courtiers ill at ease to see this spirit among people though they think this matter will not come to much but it speaks people's minds. And then they do say that there are men of understanding among them, that have been of Cromwell's army but how true that is, I know not.

Just over a year later on 11 June 1669, Pepys recorded in his Navy White Book how the madam Damaris Page, 'the most famous bawd in town', was considered by the naval commander Sir Edward Spragge to be an exceptionally useful source of naval recruits because she allowed press gangs to operate at her brothel. Pepys also mentioned the 'great affliction' John Evelyn had felt on hearing this.[3]

Once home on 25 March, Pepys encountered Mrs Daniels close to his home in Seething Lane. Pepys initially planned to take her off somewhere else but then remembered he did not have time:

> I took her into the coach and was going to the other end of the town with her, thinking to have taken her abroad, but remembering that I was to go out with my wife this afternoon, I only did *hazer* her *para tocar* my prick *con* her hand which did *hazer me hazer* ['I only did make her touch my prick with her hand, which did make myself do'] and so to a milliner at the corner shop going into Bishopsgate and Leadenhall street and there did give her 8 pair of gloves and so dismissed her . . .

Saying that he 'dismissed' Mrs Daniels after she had masturbated him to orgasm, paid for by the gloves shortly afterwards, reflected Pepys's transactional approach to these liaisons.

Pepys and Elizabeth had a 'small squabble' on 27 March, Pepys trying to avoid saying anything when she was in a bad temper. Although he had already kissed Frances Udall at the Swan earlier in the day, with Elizabeth placated he dropped her off at her mercer's to buy linen:

> I to White hall but did nothing, but then to Westminster hall and took a turn, and so to Mrs Martins and there did sit a little and talk and drink, and did *hazer con* ['do <something> with'] her and so took coach and called my wife at Unthankes . . .

On 31 March Pepys was unable to restrain himself with Deb. This followed an aborted attempt to take Mrs Burrows out that afternoon:

> . . . but *ella* being in the shop, *ego* did speak *con* her, but she could not then go *foras* ['abroad/out of doors'],[4] and so I took coach and

away to Unthankes, and there took up my wife and Deb, and to the parke where, being in a Hackny and they undressed, was ashamed to go into the Tour but went round the park, and so with pleasure home, where Mr Pelling come and sat and talked late with us, and he being gone, I called Deb to take pen, ink, and paper and write down what things come into my head for my wife to do in order to her going into the country and the girl writing not so well as she would do, cried, and her mistress construed it to be sullenness and so was angry with her too, and I seemed angry with her too but going to be, she undressed me, and there I did give her good advice and *beso la, ella* weeping still and *yo* did take her, the first time in my life, *sobra mi genouil*[5] and did *poner mi mano sub* her *jupes* and *tocar su* thigh which did *hazer* me great pleasure and so did more, but *besando la* went to my bed ['and there I did give her good advice and kissed her, she weeping still and I did take her, the first time in my life, on my knee and did put my hand under her skirts and touched her thigh, which did do me great pleasure and so did more, but kissing her went to my bed'].

Pepys took advantage of Deb coming to dress him the following morning (1 April).

Up, and to dress myself and called as I use Deb to brush and dress me and there I did again as I did the last night *con mi mano* ['with my hand'] but would have *tocado su* ['touched her'] thing but *ella* endeavoured to prevent me *con* much modesty by putting *su* hand there about, which I was well pleased with and would not do too much, and so *con* great kindness dismissed *la* ['and so with great kindness dismissed her'] . . .

Next day (2 April) Elizabeth and Deb, along with Betty Turner and Jane the maid, set out.

With Elizabeth away, Pepys was soon looking for female company.

On 7 April he went to the theatre, enjoying the privileged spectacle after the performance of being allowed to watch Elizabeth Knepp changing, but was repelled by her cosmetics:

> Here I see a wonderful pretty maid of her own that come to undress her and one so pretty that she says she intends for fear of her being undone in her service by coming to the playhouse . . . I took her then up into a coach and away to the park which is now very fine after some rain. But the company was going away most and so I took her to the Lodge* and there treated her and had a deal of good talk and now and then did *besar la* ['kiss her'] and that was all and that as much or more then I had much mind to because of her paint.

By 9 April he was back to Mrs Burrows and a more promising occasion:

> I to the New Exchange, there to meet Mrs Burroughs and did *tomar* ['take'] her in a carosse† and carry *ella* towards the park kissing her and *tocando su* ['touching her'] breast so as to make myself do but did not go into any house,‡ but come back and set her down at White hall . . .

Elizabeth Burrows thereafter disappears from Pepys's story. An 'Elizabeth Burroughs' was buried on 10 June 1687 in Middlesex. There is no means of verifying her identity as the woman Pepys knew.

From 10 to 19 April, the diary exists only in the form of Pepys's shorthand notes which he had never written up. On 16 April he recorded that he had spent a shilling on Betty Martin:

---

* A shop in Hyde Park where dairy products were sold.

† A carriage.

‡ Tavern or inn, i.e. to find a private room.

> . . . thence to Mrs Martin and there did what I would, she troubled for want of imploy for her husband, spent on her 0–1–0*

This example suggests that those other frequent brief references to his meetings with her and Doll, among others, were unelaborated transcriptions of the notes, which he had normally later destroyed after writing them up in the diary with partial conversion to polyglot or the extraneous consonant method.

Pepys made progress with Elizabeth Knepp on 21 April, after collecting her following a visit to the theatre with Mrs Turner:

> . . . home and dark about 9 a'clock or more and in my coming had the opportunity the first time in my life to be bold with Knepp by putting my hand *abaxo de* her coats and *tocar su* thighs and *venter* ['underneath her coats and touched her thighs and belly'] and a little of the other thing, *ella* but a little opposing me, *su* skin very *douce* ['her skin very soft'] and I mighty pleased with this and so left her at home, and so Mrs Turner and I home to my letters and to bed.

Emboldened, Pepys was out with Mrs Knepp and other female friends two days later (23 April) at Foxhall gardens:

> . . . there she and I drank and *yo* did *tocar* her *corps* all over and *besar sans fin* her ['I did touch her body all over and endlessly kissed her']. But did not offer *algo mas* ['something more'] and so back and led her home, it being now 10 at night . . .

On 24 April Pepys tried to make contact with a bookseller's wife he had kissed on 10 April but had not '*la* confidence *para hablar a ella*' ['the confidence to speak to her']. She was Mary Shrewsbury, wife of William. He went to see Betty Mitchell the same day but:

---

* In full this would have read: £0–1s–0d.

> . . . that was all, for either she is shy or foolish and *su marido* hath no mind *para laisser* me see *su moher* ['and her husband hath no mind to let me see his wife'].

With Elizabeth still away, Pepys applied himself to other opportunities on 30 April:

> This evening, coming home in the dusk I saw and spoke to our Nell, Pain's daughter, and had I not been very cold I should have taken her to Tower hill *para* talk together *et tocar* her ['to talk together and touch her'].

Pepys reached orgasm on Sunday 3 May, in church while ogling at a young woman:

> After dinner to church again where I did please myself *con mes ojos* shut in *futuere*[6] in conceit ['with my eyes shut in fucking in conceit'] the hook-nosed young lady, a merchant's daughter, in the upper pew in the church under the pulpit.

By 'fucking in conceit', Pepys meant generating in his imagination an image of the girl with his eyes closed. The phrase, which begins with *con* and ends with conceit, is unique in the polyglot and the diary.

On 6 May, the day after Pepys heard that his goddaughter Katherine Martin had died, he managed to make the missed opportunity good, slipping Nell money to keep her quiet, but only after he had molested Elizabeth Knepp while she was asleep:

> . . . to the King's playhouse and there see *The Virgin Martyr.* And heard the music that I like so well and entended to have seen Knipp but I let her alone and having there done went to Mrs Pierce's back again where she was and there I found her on a pallet in the dark where *yo* did *poner mi manos* under her *jupe* and *tocar su cosa* ['I did put my hands under her skirt and touched her thing'] and

> waked her, that is, Knipp. And so to talk and by and by did eat some Curds and cream and thence away home and it being night, I did walk in the dusk up and down round through our garden, over Tower hill, and so through Crutched Friars, 3 or 4 times, and once did meet Mercer and another pretty lady but being surprised I could say little to them though I had an opportunity of pleasing myself with them, but left them and then I did see our Nell, Payne's daughter, and her *yo* did *diser*[7] *venga* after *migo* ['and her I did tell "come after me"'] and so *ella* did *seque* ['she did follow'] me to Tower hill to our back entry there that comes upon the *degrés entrant* into *nostra* garden ['the steps leading into our garden'] and there, *ponendo* the key in the door, *yo tocar sus mamelles con*[8] *mi mano* and *su cosa* with *mi cosa et yo* did *dar la* a shilling ['putting the key in the door, I touched her breasts with my hand and her thing with my thing and I did give her a shilling'] and so parted, and *yo* home to put up things against tomorrow's carrier for my wife . . .

Once more the rhymes and alliteration in the polyglot are in evidence. Nell seems to have ended up working for the Bagwells (see 4 March 1669). The following day (7 May) Pepys tried a similar approach to Elizabeth Knepp after she had come off stage:

> . . . and so home by moonshine I all the way having *mi mano abaxo la jupe de* Knepp[9] *con* much *plaisir*[10] and freedom ['my hand underneath Knepp's skirt with much pleasure and freedom'] but endeavouring afterward to *tocar* her *con mi cosa, ella* ['touch her with my thing, she'] did strive against that but yet I do not think that she did find much fault with it, but I was a little moved at my offering it and not having it. And so set Mrs Knepp at her lodging . . .

Pepys referred to this incident on 30 May with some relief at the discovery that Elizabeth Knepp was not angry with him. On 10 May Pepys was out with Peg Lowther and others. Peg's shoes were soaked by the rain so:

> . . . we did send for a pair of old shoes for Mrs Lowther and there I did pull the others off and put them on and did endeavour *para tocar su* ['to touch her'] thigh but *ella* had drawers on but *yo* did *besar la* and *tocar sus mamelles, ella* being *poco* shy ['I did kiss her and touch her breasts, she being a little shy'] but doth speak *con* ['with'] mighty kindness to me that she would desire me *por su marido* ['for her husband'] if it were to be done . . .

This could not have been a planned assignation and therefore serves as an example of Pepys's impulsive opportunism, as well as Peg's (apparent) ready compliance. Betty Mitchell might have been similarly willing to participate on 13 May, but her husband proved an obstacle:

> . . . there to Michells and did see her and drink there but he being there *yo no podo besar la* ['I could not kiss her'].

On 16 May at Elizabeth Knepp's house, Pepys widened his scope to her staff:

> . . .here *yo* did *besar* her *ancilla* which is so mighty *belle* ['and here I did kiss her maid which is so mighty pretty'].

Two days later (18 May) he speculated about an otherwise unknown woman called Mrs Horsfield whom he had met:

> But I find Mrs Horsfield one of the veriest citizen's wifes in the world so full of little silly talk and now and then a little sillily bawdy, that I believe if you had her *sola* a man might *hazer algo* ['if you had her alone a man might do something'] with her.

A routine meeting with Betty Martin followed on 21 May:

> . . . so to Westminster, and there to walk a little in the hall and so to Mrs Martin's, and there did *hazer ce que yo voudrais mit*[11] her ['did do

> that I would with her']. And drank and sat most of the afternoon with her and her sister . . .

He followed this with a more innocent evening out in Mile End with Mrs Turner and Mercer, spending his time in as much female company as possible while Elizabeth was away.

Pepys barely mentioned Elizabeth during this period but was due to set off to see her on 23 May, arriving at Brampton early in the morning of Sunday 24 May. Despite his exertions of recent weeks, Pepys still had the energy to resume relations with Elizabeth the following morning (25 May):

> Waked betimes and lay long *hazendo doz vezes con mi moher con grande* pleasure to me and *ella* ['doing twice with my wife with great pleasure to me and her'] and there fell to talking and by and by rose, it being the first fair day and yet not quite fair, that we have had some time . . .

They returned home the following day. On 28 May Pepys snatched a kiss from a woman who had come to the office on behalf of another woman who needed a Navy ticket paid. Pepys said nothing about honouring the ticket in return for the kiss.

Even though Pepys had been so delighted to sleep with Elizabeth a few days before, by 29 May he had arranged to meet Mrs Bagwell. He was prevented:

> This night *yo* had agreed *para andar* <*a*>[12] Deptford, there *para aver*[13] lain *con* the *moher de* Bagwell, but this company did hinder me ['This night I had agreed to go to Deptford, there to have lain with the wife of Bagwell, but this company did hinder me'].

A few weeks earlier (7 May above) Pepys had tried unsuccessfully to have Elizabeth Knepp touch his penis. He was relieved on 30 May to discover she did not seem to resent him:

> Thence to Mr Pierces and there see Knepp also . . . Here I was freed from a fear that Knepp was angry or might take advantage, did *parler* that *esto* that *yo* did the *otra* day *quand yo* was *con* her in *ponendo* her *mano* upon *mi cosa* ['did declare that this thing that I did the other day when I was with her in putting her hand upon my thing'].[14] But I see no such thing but as pleased as ever and I believe she can bear with any such thing.

Pepys was back with Betty Martin and her landlady on 1 June, also witnessing Richard Newport (1644–1723), the future MP and 2nd Earl of Bradford, treating women as he did:

> I to Westminster and to Mrs Martin's and did *hazer* what *yo* would *con* her and did *aussi tocar la* thigh *de su* landlady ['and did do what I would with her and did also touch the thigh of her landlady'] and thence all alone to Fox hall and walked and see young Newport and 2 more rogues of the town seize on 2 ladies who walked with them an hour with their masks on, perhaps civil ladies and there I left them, and so home . . .

Pepys made it to Deptford on 2 June:

> . . . so by water, it being now about 9 a-clock, down to Deptford where I have not been many a day and there it being dark I did by agreement *andar a la* ['walk/go to the'] house *de* Bagwell, and there after a little playing and *besando* ['kissing'] we did go up in the dark *a su cama* ['to her bed'] and there *facero*[15] *la grand cosa* ['I did the great thing'] upon the bed and that being *hecho* ['done'] did go away and to my boat again, and against the tide home, got there by 12 a-clock and to bed . . .

Between 5 and 17 June Pepys took Elizabeth, Deb, Will Hewer, and Betty Turner on a trip to Oxford and other places, including Stonehenge, the thermal baths at Bath, and Bristol from where Deb had come and was greeted by people who knew her. This part of the diary survives only as his rudimentary notes. On their way home on 17 June, Pepys confided in these notes about what he really thought of Elizabeth:

> Somewhat out of humour all day reflecting on my wife's neglect of things and impertinent humour got by this liberty of being from me, which she is never to be trusted with for she is a fool.

The comment reads like a verdict which Pepys had privately resigned himself to but usually did not acknowledge. The following day (18 June), Pepys was confronted by a distraught Elizabeth who had heard what Pepys had been up to (a clue also that it is implausible his sexual exploits had gone unnoticed by their wider circle of acquaintances):

> At noon home to dinner where my wife still in a melancholy fusty humour and crying, and do not tell me plainly what it is but I by little words find that she hath heard of my going to plays and carrying people abroad every day, in her absence and that I cannot help but the storm will break out I know in a little time . . . At night home where supped Mr Turner, his wife, and Betty, and Mercer as merry as the ill melancholy that my wife was in would let us which vexed me but took no notice of it, thinking that will be the best way and that it would wear away itself.
>
> . . . my wife troubled all night and about one a-clock goes out of the bed to the girl's bed, which did trouble me, she crying and sobbing without telling the cause. By and by she comes back to me and still crying, I then rose and would have sat up all night, but she would have me come to bed again. And being pretty well pacified we to sleep . . .

Elizabeth was conveniently out of the way on 22 June:

> . . . I away home to dinner alone, my wife being at her tailor's, and after dinner comes Creed, whom I hate, to speak with me, and before him comes Mrs Daniel about business and *yo* did *tocar su cosa* with *mi mano* ['I did touch her thing with my hand'].

By late June Pepys felt he was 'able to do nothing by candlelight, my eyes being now constantly so bad that I must take present advice or be blind' (20 June). The diary manuscript was increasingly messy, with deletions and uneven lines, and the shorthand written larger. The lengthy entries of 1667 had also given way in 1668 to shorter ones. In daylight, Pepys had no problems with his eyesight when it came to spotting prospective women. On 27 July he sought out Mary Shrewsbury, the bookseller's wife:

> At noon dined and then I out of doors to my bookseller in Duck lane but *su moher* ['his wife'] not at home. And it was pretty here to see a pretty woman pass by with a little wanton look and *yo* did *sequi* ['I did follow'] her round about the street from Duck lane to Newgate market and then *ella* did turn back and *yo* did lose her.

Later the same day, Pepys visited Spring Gardens, now marked by a cul-de-sac between Whitehall and The Mall close to Trafalgar Square, with Elizabeth, Deb, and Mercer. Ever quick to condemn the immorality of others, he was disgusted by how 'some of the young gallants' forced women who were on their own in any of the arbors to go with them.

On 6 August Pepys turned his attention back to Deb, this time in the coach on a journey to Surrey where they spent two nights. Elizabeth was in the coach with them:

> This day *yo* did first with my hand *tocar la cosa de* ['touch the thing of'][16] our Deb in the coach. *Ella* being troubled at it. But yet did give way to it. To bed.

Pepys apparently achieved this without Elizabeth noticing, Deb presumably being unable to stop him and perhaps also fearful of the consequences of audibly and visibly protesting. By 18 August Pepys had drawn her in to greater complicity:

> This night *yo* did *hazer* Deb *tocar mi* thing with her hand after *yo* was in *lecto*. ['This night I did make Deb touch my thing with her hand after I was in bed.'] With great pleasure.

Pepys made comparatively few references to Deb around this time but given the nature of these two incidents, it is very unlikely they were the only ones. He was probably making these acts part of his daily routine, steadily familiarizing Deb with his expectations. Pepys was practised at this (for example, 3 December 1666). The boundaries had always been opaque because Elizabeth's companions helped dress Pepys, slept in the same room with him and Elizabeth, and routinely socialized with them.

Pepys had a busy day on 1 September at Bartholomew's Fair where a psychic horse appeared to know who Pepys was (its owner had presumably been prompted):

> Up and all the morning at the office busy. And after dinner to the office again busy till about 4, and then I abroad (my wife being gone to Hales's about drawing her hand new in her picture) and I to see Betty Michell, which I did, but *su marido* was *dentro* ['her husband was within']. And no pleasure. So to the Fair, and there saw several sights, among others, a Mare that tells* money, and saw many things to admiration, and, among others, came to me, when she was bid to go to him of the company that most loved a pretty wench in a corner. And this did cost me 12d to the horse which I had flung him before, and did give me occasion to *besar* a mighty *belle fille* ['kiss a mighty comely

* i.e. 'counts money'.

> girl'] that was in the house that was exceeding plain but *fort belle* ['exceeding comely'].
>
> At night going home I went to my bookseller's in Ducke lane, and find her weeping in the shop, so as *yo* could not have any discourse *con* ['with'] her nor ask the reason, so departed and took coach home, and taking coach was set on by a wench that was naught,* and would have gone along with me to her lodging in Shoe lane, but *yo* did *donner* her a shilling and *hazer* her *tocar mi cosa* ['I did give her a shilling and make her touch my thing'] and left her, and home where after supper, W. Batelier with us, we to bed. This day Mrs Martin come to see us and dined with us.

The polyglot here translates simply into his stock phrase 'make her touch my thing'. This was possibly a euphemism for hand stimulation to orgasm since it is hard to see why else Pepys would have bothered. The same probably applies to some of his other similar cryptic references, though of course on other occasions he specified that he had ejaculated. The shilling he handed over was around the equivalent of £9 today.

The association between money and sex came up in a different way on 15 September. Pepys would not lend Mrs Daniel money because it was not possible to have sex with her:

> So home to the office where Mrs Daniel come and stayed talking to little purpose with me to borrow money but I did not lend her any, having not opportunity *para hazer* anything *mit* her ['to do anything with her'].[17]

Regardless of his growing interest in Deb, Pepys had not diverted his attention from other prospects. Increasingly asserting his patriarchal role as head of a household mainly consisting of women,

* The word 'naught', written in s.h. as 'not' = behaving in a sexually reprehensible way.

he made an advance towards the long-serving maid Jane Birch on 16 September (she had returned to his employment in 1666 after a second break). She was now about twenty-four years old:

> Up and dressing myself I did begin *para tocar* ['to touch'] the breasts of my maid Jane which *ella* did give way to more then usual heretofore, so as I have a design to try more when[18] I can bring it to.

Pepys had obviously been touching Jane's breasts for some time; he had certainly considered forcing himself on her on previous occasions (for example, 1 and 6 August 1662). He only bothered to mention this instance because she was unusually compliant, though it is more probable that she had gradually given up trying to resist. Moreover, her impending marriage to Thomas Edwards made her potentially a safer prospect for trying to go further.[19]

On 20 September Pepys made progress with 'Mrs Turner', Elizabeth, the wife of Thomas Turner,* as well, but did not go as far as he subsequently realized he might have:

> Mrs Turner stayed an hour talking with me and *yo* did now the first time *tocar* her *cosa* ['touch her thing'] with my hand and did make her do the like *con su* ['with her'] hand to my thing, whereto neither did she show any averseness really but a merry kind of opposition, but *yo* did do both and *yo* do believe I might have *hecho la cosa* too *mit* her ['I might have done the thing too with her'].

Pepys repeated the occasion, this time in the garden, but with no further progress, on 22 September:

> Mrs Turner and I to walk in the garden, and there *yo* did the 2[d] part of Sunday night last, *tocando su cosa* and making her *tocar mi* thing,

---

* Storekeeper at Deptford dockyard from 1668, who held other naval administrative positions before that.

> but no *mas* ['touching her thing and making her touch my thing, but no more'] which she did bear with very merrily but with a seeming remorse.

Pepys claimed Mrs Turner acted 'very merrily' but also with 'remorse'. This suggests that Betty Turner was discomfited by a situation she tried to laugh off but had lost control of.

A visit to Westminster on 26 September provides a clue to how Pepys operated when he wanted to organize a meeting with a mistress:

> I at noon to Westminster hall and there stayed a little, and at the Swan also, thinking to have got Doll Lane thither, but *ella* did not understand my signs and so I away and walked to Charing cross . . .

By 13 October Pepys was veering ever closer to disaster. Here he had to add in Deb's name later, having originally written the entry as if Elizabeth had both read to him and combed his head:

> . . . to the office to finish my letters and so home and did get my wife to read to me and then Deb to comb my head and here I had the pleasure *para* touch the *cosa* ['to touch the thing'] of her and all about with a little opposition, and so to bed.

The most significant moment in the diary for Pepys's personal life occurred on 25 October 1668. Deb had barely been mentioned in recent weeks other than indirectly, compounded by there being a gap in the diary for the first ten days of October. It is likely that he had been making regular sexual contact for some time with Deb, regardless of whether she wanted him to, just as he had with other servants like Jane but had not mentioned it in his daily entries. This time was different only because Elizabeth caught him:

> . . . after supper, to have my head combed by Deb, which occasioned the greatest sorrow to me that ever I knew in this world for my wife coming up suddenly did find me imbracing the girl *con* my hand *sub su* ['under her'] coats and endeed I was with my *main* ['hand'] in her cony. I was at a wonderful loss upon it, and the girl also and I endeavoured to put it off, but my wife was struck mute and grew angry, and so her voice[20] come to her, grew quite out of order, and I to say little but to bed and my wife said little also but could not sleep all night but about 2 in the morning waked me and cried and fell to tell me as a great secret that she was a Roman Catholique and had received the Holy Sacrament, which troubled me, but I took no notice of it, but she went on from one thing to another till at last it appeared plainly her trouble was at what she saw, but yet I did not know how much she saw and therefore said nothing to her. But after her much crying and reproaching me with inconstancy and preferring a sorry girl before her, I did give her no provocation but did promise all fair usage to her and love and foreswore any hurt that I did with her. Till at last she seemed to be at ease again and so toward morning a little sleep and so I with some little repose and rest . . .

Pepys used his extraneous consonants to write the incriminating line which in shorthand reads 'the girl *con* my helend *sub su* comits and endeed, I was with mili *min* in heler ciloni'. Latham and Matthews read 'cunny' but the shorthand does not say that; Pepys wrote the shorthand for 'cony' (still current in the seventeenth century), adding the 'l' to confuse. 'Coats' is more of a problem in the shorthand, but other references make it certain that was what he meant.[21] To represent the hard 'c' in 'comits' and 'ciloni', Pepys as usual employed the shorthand sign for 'k', so strictly speaking they read 'komits' and 'kiloni'. One biographer of Pepys limited his description of the occasion to 'Elizabeth . . . found them embracing', surely one of the most disingenuous references to Pepys's private conduct in print.[22]

Elizabeth's threat to become a Roman Catholic, which she never followed through, was because she knew her conversion would be professionally destructive to Pepys in an era when Catholics were considered a threat to the state. However, in a letter to Pepys of 8 February 1674, her brother Balty assured him that she had said, 'I have now a man to my husband so wise, and so religious in the Protestant religion (joined with my riper years which gives me more understanding) to ever suffer my thought to bend that way anymore'. This is also a rare possible instance of Elizabeth's reported speech, though Balty's obsequious and florid hyperbole made him an unreliable witness.[23]

The following morning (26th) the storm had not abated. It had only just begun:

> ... rose, and up and by water to White hall, but with my mind mightily troubled for the poor girl whom I fear I have undone by this, my <wife> telling me that she would turn her out of doors.

Pepys had to deal with the day's business, but inevitably had to face Elizabeth that evening:

> Thence by coach home and to dinner finding my wife mightily discontented and the girl sad and no words from my wife to her. So after dinner they out with me about 2 or 3 things and so home again, I all the evening busy and my wife full of trouble in her looks, and anon to bed. Where about midnight she wakes me and there falls foul of me again, affirming that she saw me hug and kiss the girl.[24] The latter I denied and truly, the other I confessed and no more. And upon her pressing me did offer to give her under my hand that I would never see Mrs Pierce more nor Knepp but did promise her perticular demonstrations of my true love to her, owning some indiscretions in what I did, but that there was no harm in it. She at last upon these promises was quiet, and very kind we were, and so to sleep ...

Pepys's admission of 'some indiscretions' but which were 'no harm' came because he had been cornered. By conceding some of his faults, but insisting they were harmless, merely added to the litany of lies he had been telling Elizabeth for years. She was still furious on the 27th and had by then realized she could threaten Pepys with a public denunciation:

> ... and in the morning up but with my mind troubled for the poor girl with whom I could not get opportunity to speak, but to the office my mind mighty full of sorrow for her ... my wife did towards bedtime begin to be in a mighty rage from some new matter that she had got in her head and did most part of the night in bed rant at me in most high terms of threats of publishing my shame, and when I offered to rise would have rose too, and caused a candle to be lit to burn by her all night in the chimney while she ranted, while that <I> know myself to have given some grounds for it, did make it my business to appease her all I could possibly and by good words and fair promises did make her very quiet and so rested all night and rose with perfect good peace ...

The matter seemed to have settled down temporarily, but by 30 October Pepys had still not had an opportunity to say anything to Deb:

> ... my wife and I at good peace, but my heart troubled and her mind not at ease, I perceive, she against and I for the girl to whom I have not said anything these 3 days but resolve to be mighty strange in appearance to her.

Pepys was also, for the first time, properly filled with remorse as he recorded on 31 October, but he did not want to let Deb go:

> So ends this month with some quiet to my mind though not perfect, after the greatest falling out with my poor wife, and through

> my folly with the girl, that ever I had and I have reason to be sorry and ashamed of it and more to be troubled for the poor girl's sake, whom I fear I shall by this means prove the ruin of. Though I shall think myself concerned both to love and be a friend to her.

By 3 November the atmosphere in Seething Lane was more tense than it had ever been:

> So home and there to supper and I observed my wife to eye my eyes whether I did ever look upon Deb which I could not, but do now and then (and to my grief did see the poor wretch look on me and see me look on her and then let drop a tear or 2 which doth make my heart relent at this minute that I am writing this with great trouble of mind, for she is endeed my sacrifice, poor girl) and my wife did tell me in bed by the by of my looking on other people and that the only way is to put things out of sight, and this I know she means by Deb, for she tells me that her aunt was here on Monday, and she did tell her of her desire of parting with Deb, but in such kind terms on both sides that my wife is mightily taken with her. I see it will be, and it is but necessary, and therefore though it cannot but grieve me, yet I must bring my mind to give way to it.

Unsurprisingly, the debacle brought a hiatus in Pepys's recorded casual philandering. The tension continued on Sunday 8 November, witnessed by a visiting apothecary called Pelling:

> Up and at my chamber all the morning setting papers to rights, with my boy. And so to dinner at noon, the girl with us but my wife troubled thereat to see her and do tell me so, which troubles me, for I love the girl. At my chamber again to work all the afternoon till night when Pelling comes who wonders to find my wife so dull and melancholy but God knows she hath too much cause. However, as pleasant as we can, we supped together and so made

the boy read to me, the poor girl not appearing at supper, but hid herself in her chamber. So that I could wish in that respect that she was out of the house, for our peace is broke to all of us while she is here. And so to bed where my wife mighty unquiet all night, so as my bed is become burdensome to me.

The following day (9th) even Deb had turned against Pepys. After all, she stood to lose her livelihood:

Up and I did by a little note which I flung to Deb advise her that I did continue to deny that ever I kissed her and so she might govern herself. The truth <is> that I did adventure upon God's pardoning me this lie, knowing how heavy a thing it would be for me to the ruin of the poor girl, and next knowing that if my wife should know all it were impossible ever for her to be at peace with me again. And so our whole lives would be uncomfortable. The girl read, and as I bid her returned me the note, flinging it to me in passing by.

On 10 November Elizabeth continued to make Pepys pay for his behaviour. She had also interrogated Deb:

Up and my wife still every day as ill as she is all night, will rise to see me out doors, telling me plainly that she dares not let me see the girl, and so I out to the office, where all the morning and so home to dinner, where I found my wife mightily troubled again, more then ever and she tells me that it is from her examining the girl and getting a confession now from her of all even to the very *tocando su* ['touching her'] thing with my hand, which doth mightily trouble me, as not being able to foresee the consequences of it as to our future peace together. So my wife would not go down to dinner but I would dine in her chamber with her, and there after mollifying her as much as I could we were pretty quiet and eat . . .

On 13 November 1668 Pepys said that he had a 'great mind' to have Deb's virginity. For this entry his unusually complicated use of extraneous consonants has been retained to show further how he tried to disguise his thoughts:

> Thence I home, and there to talk with great pleasure all the evening with my wife who tells me that Deb hath been abroad today and is come home and says she hath got a pla<ce> to go to, so as she will be gone tomorrow morning. This troubled me and the truth is I have a great mind to have the maladimen hered of thilis gimerl which I should not doubt to have if *yo* could gemet time *para* be *con* heler ['to have the maidenhead of this girl which I should not doubt to have if I could get time to be with her']. Bulot ['But'] she will be gone and I nomot knoro whither ['not know whither']. Before we went to bed my wife told me she would not have me to see her or give her her wages and so I did give my wife 10£ for her year and ½ a ¼ wages which she went into her chamber and paid her and so to bed and there, blessed be God, we did sleep well and with peace which I had not done now in almost 20 nights together.

The contrition Pepys had shown to Elizabeth was humbug. He had no intention of losing Deb; he was bent on taking her virginity. Yet on 18 November 1664 (see above) he had expressed disgust at Lord Craven's reference to the ambition of having a girl's virginity.

Another row followed on 14 November, but Pepys was troubled that he was not going to be able to forget Deb, who was about to leave. Pepys's careless use of pronouns here, which require editorial clarification, was a mark of the stress he was under while writing this:

> Up and had a mighty mind to have seen or given a note to Deb or to have given her a little money to which purpose I wrapt up 40s in a paper, thinking to have given her but my wife rose

> presently, and would not let me be out of her sight and went down before me into the kitchen and come up and told me that she* was in the kitchen, and therefore would have me go round the other way which she repeating and I vexed at it, answered her a little angrily upon which she instantly flew out into a rage, calling me dog and rogue, and that I had a rotten heart, all which, knowing that I deserved it, I bore with, and word being brought presently up that she was gone away by coach with her things, my wife was friends and so all quiet and I to the office with my heart sad, and find that I cannot forget the girl, and vexed I know not where to look for her. And more troubled to see how my wife is by this means likely for ever to have her hand over me, that I shall for ever be a slave to her, that is to say, only in matters of pleasure, but in other things she will make her business, I know, to please me and to keep me right to her. Which I will labour to be endeed, for she deserves it of me, though it will be I fear a little time before I shall be able to wear Deb out of my mind.

Interestingly, it appears that a by-product had been to heal the marriage. That night they slept together:

> . . . my mind being free of all troubles I thank God, but only for my thoughts of this girl, which hang after her. And so at night home to supper and then did sleep with great content with my wife. I must here remember that I have lain with my *moher* ['wife'] as a husband more times since this falling-out then in I believe 12 months before. And with more pleasure to her then I think in all the time of our marriage before.

Elizabeth claimed on 16 November to have news about Deb, which distressed Pepys. Deb had supposedly gone to Whetstone Park, a

---

* Deb.

narrow lane lined with brothels south of High Holborn near Lincoln's Inn Fields,* and sought refuge with the mysterious Dr Allbon:

> I away to Holborn, about Whetstones park where I never was in my life before, where I understand by my wife's discourse that Deb is gone, which doth trouble me mightily that the poor girl should be in a desperate condition forced to go thereabouts, and there not hearing of any such man as Allbon, with whom my wife said she now was, I to the Strand, and there by sending Drumbleby's boy, my flagelette-maker, to Eagle court where my wife also by discourse lately let fall that he did lately live, I find that this Dr Allbon is a kind of poor broken fellow that dare not shew his head nor be known where he is gone, but to Lincoln's Inn fields I went to Mr Povy's, but missed him, and so hearing only that this Allbon is gone to Fleet street . . .

Pepys abandoned the chase for the afternoon but was desperate to contact Deb 'without trouble or the knowledge of my wife' (17 November). He was not helped by Elizabeth making it clear the next day she did not want him going out. Pretending to be looking for Dr Allbon and recognizing 'I could not be commanded by my reason', Pepys managed to track him and therefore Deb down (18 November). In a spectacular twist he managed to combine forcing her to masturbate him while groping her breasts with giving her advice about how to protect her honour. He then went home to lie to Elizabeth once again:

> . . . she come into the coach to me and *yo* did *besar* ['I did kiss'] her and *tocar* ['touch'] her thing but *ella* was against it and laboured with much earnestness such as I believed to be real and yet at last *yo* did make her *tener mi cosa* in her *mano* while *mi mano* was *sobra* her *pectus* and so did *hazer* with *grand* delight ['I did make her hold my

* Whetstone Park exists today, and remains a narrow alleyway now lined with office buildings, but including parts of much older brick buildings.

> thing in her hand while my hand was over her chest and so did do with great delight'].[25] I did nevertheless give her the best counsel I could to have a care of her honour, and to fear God and suffer no man *para aver* to do *con* her ['to have to do with her']. As *yo* have done. Which she promised. *Yo* did give her 20s and directions *para laisser* ['to leave'] sealed in paper at any time the name of the place of her being at Herringman's, my bookseller in the Change.[26] By which I might go *para* ['to'] her.
>
> And so bid her good night with much content to my mind and resolution to look after her no more till I heard from her. And so home, and there told my wife a fair tale, God knows, how I spent the whole day with which the poor wretch was satisfied, or at least seemed so and so to supper and to bed . . .

Pepys was trying to soft-soap Elizabeth while doing everything possible to ensure he could remain in contact with Deb. He lacked the ability or will to imagine life without either Elizabeth or Deb, while also trying to circumvent the paradox that the relationships were incompatible.

Elizabeth's explosive reaction troubled Pepys. He had commented on the Queen's stoical behaviour in the face of the King's flaunting of his mistresses and had been ashamed by the Earl of Sandwich's blatant keeping of a mistress.[27] The dignity which royal and noblewomen exhibited, knowing that to have reacted otherwise would have been publicly to humiliate themselves and simultaneously shame and diminish their husbands, thereby buried the men's hypocrisy. Elizabeth's bourgeois fury risked public shame for Pepys, and at the price of advertising how easily she had been humiliated. Pepys had placed Elizabeth in an impossible position.

By the following day, 19 November, Elizabeth had discovered where Pepys had been:

> . . . she begun to call me all the false, rotten-hearted rogues in the world, letting me understand that I was with Deb yesterday,

> which, thinking it impossible for her ever to understand, I did a while deny, but at last did, for the ease of my mind and hers, and for ever to discharge my heart of this wicked business, I did confess all, and above stairs in our bed chamber there I did endure the sorrow of her threats and vows[28] and curses all the afternoon, and, what was worse, she swore by all that was good that she would slit the nose of this girl, and be gone herself this very night from me, and did there demand 3 or 400£ of me to buy my peace, that she might be gone without making any noise, or else protested that she would make all the world know of it. So with most perfect confusion of face and heart and sorrow and shame, in the greatest agony in the world I did pass this afternoon, fearing that it will never have an end but at last I did call for W. Hewers, who I was forced to make privy now to all, and the poor fellow did cry like a child, <and> obtained what I could not, that she would be pacified upon condition that I would give it under my hand never to see or speak with Deb . . .

By 20 November, Elizabeth had co-opted Will Hewer to act as her husband's chaperone, but Pepys had already decided to use him as a conciliation service:

> This morning up with mighty kind words between my poor wife and I and so to White hall by water, W. Hewer with me, who is to go with me everywhere, until my wife be in condition to go out along with me herself for she doth plainly declare that she dares not trust me out alone, and therefore made it a piece of our league that I should always take somebody with me or her herself, which I am mighty willing to, being by the grace of God resolved never to do her wrong more.
>
> . . . He is I think, so honest and true a servant to us both and one that loves us, that I was not much troubled at his being privy to all this, but rejoiced in my heart that I had him to assist in the making us friends, which he did truly and heartily and with

good success. For I did get him to go to Deb to tell her that I had told my wife all of my being with her the other night, that so if my wife should send, she might not make the business worse by denying it. While I was at White hall with the Duke of York, doing our ordinary business with him, here being also the first time the new Treasurers, W. Hewer did go to her and come back again, and so I took him into St. James's park and there he did tell me he had been with her, and found what I said about my manner of being with her true, and had given her advice as I desired. I did there enter into more talk about my wife and myself, and he did give me great assurance of several perticular cases to which my wife had from time to time made him privy of her loyalty and truth to me after many and great temptations, and I believe them truly. I did also discourse the unfitness of my leaving of my imployment now in many respects to go into the country, as my wife desires. But that I would labour to fit myself for it, which he thoroughly understands and doth agree with me in it . . .

But when I come home hoping for a further degree of peace and quiet, I find my wife upon her bed in a horrible rage afresh, calling me all the bitter names and rising, did fall to revile me in the bitterest manner in the world, and could not refrain to strike me and pull my hair which I resolved to bear with, and had good reason to bear it. So I by silence and weeping did prevail with her a little to be quiet, and she would not eat her dinner without me but yet by and by into a raging fit she fell again, worse then before, that she would slit the girl's nose, and at last W. Hewer come in and come up, who did allay her fury, I flinging myself in a sad desperate condition upon the bed in the blue room and there lay while they spoke together and at last it come to this, that if I would call Deb 'whore' under my hand and write to her that I hated her and would never see her more, she would believe me and trust in me. Which I did agree to, only as to the name of 'whore' I would have excused and therefore wrote to her sparing that word, which my wife thereupon tore it and would not be satisfied till, W. Hewer winking upon me, I did write so with the name of a whore as that I did fear she might too probably have been prevailed upon to have been a whore by her carriage to me and therefore as such I did resolve never to see her more. This pleased my wife, and she gives it W. Hewer to carry to her with a sharp message from her. So from that minute my wife begun to be kind to me and we to kiss and be friends . . .

On 21 November, Will Hewer reported good news to Pepys:

Up with great joy to my wife and me and to the office where W. Hewer did most honestly bring me back the part of my letter under my hand to Deb wherein I called her 'whore', assuring me that he did not show it her. And that he did only give her to understand that wherein I did declare my desire never to see her and did give her the best Christian counsel he could which was mighty well done of him. But by the grace of God, though I love the poor girl and wish her well, as having gone too far toward the undoing her, yet I will never enquire after or think of her more. My peace being certainly to do right to my wife.

By Sunday 29 November Elizabeth appeared reconciled. Pepys could not do anything now that would arouse suspicion. Elizabeth would have assumed he was off looking for Deb. He could not stop thinking about her, despite what he had written only eight days earlier:

Lay long in bed with pleasure <with my wife>* with whom I have now a great deal of content and my mind is in other things also mightily more at ease and I do mind my business better then ever and am more at peace, and trust in God I shall ever be so though I cannot yet get my mind off from thinking now and then of Deb . . .

---

* An unusual instance of missing words. There is no obvious reason for this in the diary manuscript.

Elizabeth remained vigilant for any suggestion that Deb was on Pepys's mind, even at night. They woke up on 5 December:

> Up after a little talk with my wife which troubled me, she being ever since our late difference mighty watchful of sleep and dreams, and will not be persuaded but I do dream of Deb and doth tell me that I speak in my dreams and that this night I did cry 'Huzzy', and it must be she. And now and then I start otherwise then I used to do, she says, which I know not, for I do not know that I dream of her more then usual, though I cannot deny that my thoughts waking doth run now and then against my will and judgment upon her, for that only is wanting to undo me being now in every other thing as to my mind most happy. And may still be so but for my own fault, if I be ketched[29] loving anybody but my wife again.

By chance, two days later (7 December), Pepys caught sight of Deb:

> This afternoon passing through Queen's street,* I saw pass by our coach on foot Deb, which, God forgive me, did put me into some new thoughts of her and for her, but durst not shew them and I think my wife did not see her, but I did get my thoughts free of her soon as I could.

Pepys no longer felt free to admire other women (9 December):

> So took out coach and home, having now little pleasure to look about me to see the fine faces for fear of displeasing my wife, whom I take great comfort now, more then ever, in pleasing. And it is a real joy to me.

Nonetheless, on 18 December he had to pacify Elizabeth again:

---

* A north-south road built after the Great Fire from the Thames to Cheapside where it ran into King St which continued to the Guildhall.

> . . . and so home. Where I have a new fight to fight with my wife who is under new trouble by some news she hath heard of Deb's being mighty fine and gives out that she hath a friend that gives her money, and this my wife believes to be me, and poor wretch I cannot blame her. And therefore she run into mi<ghty> extremes but I did pacify all and were mighty good friends, and to bed and I hope it will be our last struggle from this business, for I am resolved never to give any new occasion. And great peace I find in my mind by it.

Pepys closed the year much more briefly than he had in the past, it being now two years since he had drawn up his annual accounts (31 December):

> And blessed be God the year ends after some late very great sorrow with my wife by my folly, yet ends I say, with great mutual peace and content. And likely to last so by my care, who am resolved to enjoy the sweet[30] of it which I now possess, by never giving her like cause of trouble.

10

1669

Now My Amours To Deb Are Past

The last five months of Pepys's diary were characterized by his contrition and confusion. He continued to pursue Deb and gradually resumed contact with his other mistresses. The diary ends abruptly, with matters unresolved.

Any hint of one of her husband's favourite women could unsettle Elizabeth Pepys. He avoided seeing Mrs Knepp, other than on the stage. By 3 January he had agreed to an annual allowance of £30 (around £5,000 today) for all his wife's expenses. Pepys trod on eggshells every day, such as on Sunday 10 January:

> Accidentally talking of our maids before we rose, I said a little word that did give occasion to my wife to fall out and she did most vexatiously almost all the morning but ended most perfect good friends but the thoughts of the unquiet which her ripping up of old faults will give me, did make me melancholy all day long.

Elizabeth now suspected Pepys was up to no good every time he left home. On 12 January, she had worked herself up into an explosive and potentially violent frame of mind:

> This evening I observed my wife mighty dull and I myself was not mighty fond because of some hard words she did give me at noon out of a jealousy at my being abroad this morning which, God knows, it was upon the business of the office unexpectedly but I to bed, not thinking but she would come after me but waking by and by out of a slumber, which I usually fall into presently after my coming into the bed, I found she did not prepare to come to bed but got fresh candles and more wood for her fire, it being mighty cold, too.
>
> At this being troubled I after a while prayed her to come to bed all my people being gone to bed; so after an hour or 2 she silent and I now and then praying her to come to bed, she fell out into a fury that I was a rogue and false to her. But yet I did perceive that she was to seek what to say only she invented, I believe, a business that I was seen in a hackney coach with the glasses up with Deb, but could not tell the time, nor was sure I was he. I did, as I might truly, deny it and was mightily troubled, but all would not serve.
>
> At last, about one a-clock she come to my side of the bed and drew my curtaine open and with the tongs red hot at the ends, made as if she did design to pinch me with them at which, in dismay, I rose up, and with a few words she laid them down and did by little and little, very sillily, let all the discourse fall and about 2, but with much seeming difficulty, come to bed and there lay well all night, and long in bed talking together, with much pleasure, it being I know nothing but her doubt of my going out yesterday, without telling her of my going, which did vex her, poor wretch, last night and I cannot blame her jealousy, though it doth vex me to the heart.

Pepys still thought little of Elizabeth's judgement. On 29 January he went to look at a picture she had recommended:

> I and my wife and aunt to see Mr Cole but he nor his wife was within, but we looked upon his picture of Cleopatra which I went principally to see, being so much commended by my wife and aunt, but I find it a base copy of a good originall that vexed me to hear so much commended.

By Sunday 7 February Elizabeth had transferred her preoccupations to Jane, convinced she was a threat too, but this eruption had an unexpected outcome. In this transcription the lack of original punctuation has been largely retained to preserve the pace and tone of how Pepys wrote on this occasion:

> My wife mighty peevish in the morning about my lying unquietly a-nights and she will have it that it is a late practice from my evil thoughts in my dreams and I do often find that in my dreams she doth lay her hand upon my cockerel[1] to observe what she can. And mightily she is troubled about it but all blew over and I up and to church and so home to dinner where she in a worse fit which lasted all the afternoon and shut herself up in her closet and I mightily grieved and vexed and could not get her to tell me what ayled her or to let me into her closet but at last she did where I found her crying on the ground and I could not please her but I did at last find that she did plainly expound it to me it was that she did believe me false to her with Jane and did rip up 3 or 4 most silly circumstances of her not rising till I come out of my chamber and her letting me thereby see her dressing herself and that I must needs go into her chamber and was naught* with her which was so silly and so far from truth that I could not be troubled at it though I could not wonder at her being troubled if she had these thoughts. And therefore she would lie from me and caused sheets to be put on in the blue room, and would have Jane to lie with her lest I should come to her.

* Badly behaved sexually.

> At last I did give her such satisfaction that we were mighty good friends and went to bed betimes where *yo* did *hazer* very well *con* her ['I did do very well with her'] and did this night by chance the first time *poner* my *digito en* ['put my finger in'] her thing which did do her much pleasure but I pray God that *ella* do not think that *yo* did know before.[2] Or get a trick of liking it. So *para* ['to'] sleep.

Pepys's concern that Elizabeth might wonder how he had learned to stimulate a woman that way, a technique unmentioned previously, is another indication of the detail and probable extent omitted from his previous references to sexual encounters.

For the first time in their marriage perhaps Elizabeth now believed she was in control. One possibility is that this was Elizabeth's subconscious intention all along, enticing Pepys to entrap him with Deb.[3] Elizabeth's scheming is a possibility, but there is very little (if any) evidence in the diary to suggest she had an organized strategy. Pepys's activities were, however, undoubtedly heavily restricted (see 19 April below).

Danger followed on 4 March when Pepys escaped company and walked to Deptford for the first time he had recorded doing so for months. Here he found more company at the Treasurer's house, including the Duke and Duchess of York, together with several other great ladies and Maids of Honour from court. He moved on later:

> . . . while I slunk out to Bagwell's and there see her and her mother and our late maid Nell who cried for joy to see me, but I had no time for pleasure there nor could stay but after drinking I back to the yard, having a month's mind *para* ['to'] have had a bout with Nell, which I believe I could have had. And may another time.

Back home, Elizabeth erupted in the belief that Pepys had been off with Mrs Pierce and Elizabeth Knepp, but without any evidence to support a specific allegation against her husband.

On 11 March Elizabeth made her husband squirm. She told Pepys about her plan to hire a new maid, and what a risk she was taking, given the girl's looks:

> ... then home tired to supper with content with my wife, and so to bed. She pleasing me, though I dare not own it, that she hath hired a chambermaid but she after many commendations told me that she had one great fault and that was that she was very handsome, at which I made nothing but let her go on but many times tonight she took occasion to discourse of her handsomeness and the danger she was in by taking her, and that she did doubt yet whether it would be fit for her to take her. But I did assure her of my resolutions to have nothing to do with her maids, but in myself I was glad to have the content to have a handsome one to look on.

The girl concerned was the one referred to only ever as 'Matt'. She started on 29 March (see below) when it became apparent, to Pepys at least, that Elizabeth's concerns might have some basis.

By 12 March Elizabeth had heard more about Deb. Pepys swore that he knew nothing of her:

> ... and so home where thinking to meet my wife with content, after my pains all this day I find her in her closet, alone in the dark, in a hot fit of railing against me, upon some news she hath this day heard of Deb's living very fine and with black spots* and speaking ill words of her mistress, which with good reason might vex her and the baggage is to blame but, God knows, I know nothing of her nor what she doth, nor what becomes of her, though God knows that my devil that is within me doth wish that I could. Yet God I hope will prevent me therein. For I dare not trust myself with it if I should know it. But what with my high words and slighting it and then serious, I did at last bring her to very good and kind terms, poor heart, and I was heartily glad of <it> for I

* A fashionable cosmetic facial embellishment used by women.

> doth see there is no man can be happier then myself if I will with her. But in her fit she did tell me what vexed me all the night, that this had put her upon putting off her handsome maid and hiring another that was full of the small pox. Which did mightily vex me though I said nothing, and doth still.

On 17 March Pepys had surprising news about Doll Lane (see 9 April below for more on this revelation):

> Thence to Westminster by water and to the hall, where Mrs Michell doth surprize me with the news that Doll Lane is suddenly brought to bed at her sister's lodging and gives it out that she is married, but there is no such thing certainly, she never mentioning it before, but I have cause to rejoice that I have not seen her a great while, she having several times desired my company, but I doubt* to an evil end.

The reason for rejoicing was that it was impossible the child was Pepys's.

Inevitably, it was only a matter of time before Pepys succumbed to temptation elsewhere. On 24 March Pepys made a naval business trip to Maidstone and the Medway towns in Kent. Here he encountered Rebecca Jowles, the married (since 1662) daughter of John Allen, Clerk of the Ropeyard at Chatham dockyard. She was at least in her mid to late twenties. The flirting soon started. Pepys had known and admired her since 1661 (see 10 April 1661). The circumstances limited the opportunity. Pepys noted that he had not needed to use force with her, suggesting that he was generally accustomed to using some physical coercion:

> . . . there comes to us Mrs Jowles who is a very fine, proper lady as most I know. And well dressed. Here was also a gentleman,

* In the archaic sense of 'fear', i.e. 'but I fear to an evil end'.

> one Major Manly and his wife, neighbours and here we stayed, and drank, and talked, and set Cony and him to play while Mrs Jowles and I to talk, and there had all our old stories up, and there I had the liberty to salute her often, and pull off her glove, where her hand mighty moist and she mighty free in kindness to me, and *yo* do not at all doubt that I might have had that that I would have desired *de ella* ['of her'] had I had time to have carried her to Cobham as she, upon <my> proposing it, was very willing to go, for *ella* is a whore, that is certain, but a very brave and comely one. Here was a pretty cousin of hers come into supper also of a great fortune, daughter-in-law[4] to this Manly but had now such a cold she could not speak. Here mightily pleased with Mrs Jowles and did get her to the street door in the dark and there *tocar su* breasts, and *besar* her ['touch her breasts and kiss her'] without any force and *creo* that I might have *hecho algo* else ['I believe that I might have had something else'] but it was not time nor place.

On 29 March Pepys was back in Deptford with the convenient cover of attending the funeral service of an associate of Captain Cocke's in the company of John Evelyn and Evelyn's father-in-law Sir Richard Browne at the church of St Nicholas:

> I with Sir Rd. Browne and Mr Eveling in their coach to the church where Mr Plume preached but I in the midst of the sermon did go out and walked all alone round to Deptford thinking *para* ['to'] have seen the wife of Bagwell which I did at her door but could not conveniently go into her house and so lost my labour.

Given the admiration Pepys had for Evelyn, disappearing from church mid-service apparently on an impulse to meet up with a mistress was an extraordinary act. There can be no doubt that Pepys would have betrayed Elizabeth again, had he been able to. He did not mention whether he bothered to return to the church, which was barely one or two minutes' walk from and in sight of the Bagwell residence in Flagon Row (where they were in 1670).

There was some compensation back home. Jane Birch had just married Pepys's clerk Tom Edwards, leaving a vacancy in the Pepys household. The new chambermaid was called 'Matt', probably short for Matilda. Pepys was so taken by her he went to bed and masturbated:

> The new maid's name is Matt, a proper and very comely maid so as when I was in bed the thoughts de *ella* did make me *para hazer in mi mano* ['the thoughts of her did make me do in my hand'].

The same day the cookmaid Bridget left. It turned out as she went that she was a thief. Pepys and Elizabeth had to borrow a replacement, as he explained on 5 April:

> . . . for a cookmaid, we have, ever since Bridget went, used a black moore of Mr Batelier's (Doll) who dresses our meat mighty well and we mightily pleased with her.

Pepys had seen Doll dancing with another black servant of his neighbour and friend William Batelier's at a musical evening he had laid on at the Navy Office on 2 March. She was not owned by Pepys though it has been suggested she was.[5] Whereas Pepys was excited by Matt, he said nothing similar about Doll. Since Doll was on loan to him it would have been an act of folly to commit an indiscretion that was bound to get back to the Bateliers. Doll and her dancing partner were presumably slaves.

By 9 April he was in Westminster and with Betty Martin again (he had tried earlier in the day but missed her), this time managing the act even though she was menstruating. Betty, who was now almost thirty-three, appears to have given birth to a daughter called Elizabeth who was christened at Maidstone, not far from the Chatham dockyard, on 2 February 1669.[6] She had probably been in lodgings there while her husband was at sea, explaining her absence from Pepys's attention. He made a point of recording how absurd he believed both Betty and her sister Doll were, especially the latter's cover story about her baby:

> . . . I took occasion to make a stop to Mrs Martins, the first time I have been with her since her husband went last to sea which is I think a year since but *yo* did now *hazer con ella* ['do with her'] what I would though she had *ellos* ['those'] upon her but *yo* did *algo* ['I did something'].
>
> But Lord, to hear how sillily she tells the story of her sister Doll's being a widow and lately brought to bed and her husband, one Rowland Powell drowned, that was at sea with her husband, but by chance dead at sea cast away. When God knows she hath played the whore and is sillily forced at this time after she was brought to bed to forge this story.

Doll's promiscuity had resulted in a pregnancy (see 17 March above) and she had come up with a preposterous explanation, now being circulated by Betty to protect her younger sister. Doll claimed that she was in fact married but her 'husband' had drowned at sea, meaning she could try and pass off the birth as legitimate. The name 'Rowland Powell' is attested in contemporary birth records but whether Doll knew a Rowland Powell cannot be unravelled. He may have been one of her lovers and a genuine maritime casualty whose death she conveniently utilized for her pregnancy cover story, or she simply invented him.[7]

However idiotic Pepys thought Doll was, he was back with her ten days later (below, 19 April). She was twenty-three.

On 13 April Pepys was in Whitehall:

> . . . as God would have it, I spied Deb which made my heart and head to work and I presently could not refrain but sent W. Hewer away to look for Mr Wren (W. Hewer I perceive did see her but

whether he did see me see her I know not or suspect me sending him away, I know not) but my heart could not hinder me. And I run after her and 2 women and a man, more ordinary people and she in her old clothes and after hunting a little, find them in the lobby of the chapel below stairs, there I observed she endeavoured to avoid me, but I did speak to her and she to me, and did get her *para dizer*[8] me *ou* she *demeures* now ['to tell me where she dwells now']. And did charge her *para* ['to'] say nothing of me that I had *vu ella* ['seen her']. Which she did promise, and so with my heart full of surprise and disorder I away and meeting with Sir Henry Cholmley walked into the park with him and back again looking to see if I could spy her again in the park but I could not.

... so home to my wife who is come home from Deptford. But, God forgive me, I hardly know how to put on confidence enough to speak as innocent, having had this passage today with Deb, though only, God knows, by accident. But my great pain is lest God Almighty shall suffer me to find out this girl, whom endeed I love and with a bad *amour*, but I will pray to God to give me grace to forbear it.

So home to supper where very sparing in my discourse, not giving occasion of any enquiry where I have been today or what I have done, and so without any trouble tonight more then my fear, we to bed.

Two days later (15 April), Pepys tried to meet up with Deb and also had his last meeting with Mrs Bagwell recorded in the diary (but see the Epilogue):

... I by Deb's direction did know whither in Jewen street to direct my hackney coachman, while I stayed in the coach in Ald<ers>gate street to go thither first to enquire whether Mrs Hunt, her aunt, was in town, who brought me word she was not. I thought this was as much as I could do at once, and therefore went away troubled though that I could do no more but to the

> office I must go and did, and there all the morning, but coming thither I find Bagwell's wife who did give me a little note into my hand, wherein I find her *para* ['to'] invite me *para* meet her in Moor fields this noon, where I might speak with her, and so after the office was up, my wife being gone before by invitation to my cousin Turner's to dine, I to the place, and there after walking up and down by the windmills, I did find her and talk with her, but it being holiday and the place full of people, we parted, leaving further discourse and doing to another time, thence I away, and through Jewen street, my mind, God knows, running that way, but stopped not, but going down Holburn hill by the Conduit, I did see Deb on foot going up the hill. I saw her and she me, but she made no stop, but seemed unwilling to speak to me so I away on, but then stopped and light and after her and overtook her at the end of Hosier lane in Smithfield, and without standing in the street desired her to follow me, and I led her into a little blind alehouse within the walls, and there she and I alone fell to talk and *besar la* and *tocar su mamelles* ['kiss her and touch her breasts'] but she mighty coy and I ought[9] modest but however, though with great force, did *hazer ella con su* hand *para tocar mi* thing, but *ella* was in great pain *para* be brought *para* it ['make her with her hand touch my thing, but she was in great pain to be brought to it']. I did give her in a paper 20s, and we did agree *para* meet again in the hall at Westminster on Monday next and so giving me great hopes by her carriage that she continues modest and honest, we did there part, she going home and I to Mrs Turner's . . .

Untroubled by the physical force he had used, on 19 April Pepys eagerly set off to meet Deb, as arranged:

> I to Westminster hall and there walked from 10 a-clock to past 12, expecting to have met Deb but whether she had been there before and missing me went away or is prevented in coming, and hath no mind to come to me (the last whereof as being most pleasing, as

> shewing most modesty, I should be most glad of) I know not, but she not then appearing, I being tired with walking went home . . .

Despite his professed admiration for Deb's modesty, Pepys found time the same day after the best part of a year to head back to Westminster Hall in search of someone less protective of her honour:

> . . . and there did beckon to Doll Lane, now Mrs Powell as she would have herself called, and went to her sister Martin's lodgings, the first time I have been there these 8 or 10 months I think, and her sister being gone to Portsmouth to her husband, I did stay and talk and drink with Doll and *hazer ella para tocar mi* thing ['and made her touch my thing'] and *yo* did the like *para* ['to'] her but not the thing itself having not opportunity enough and so away, and to White hall and there took my own coach which was now come, and so away home, and there to do business, and my wife being come home we to talk and to sup, there having been nothing yet like discovery in my wife of what hath lately passed with me about Deb, and so with great content to bed.

It is worth noting that while this drama was being played out, Pepys remained immersed in naval business which was meticulously recorded in his Navy White Book. The entry there for 24 April 1669 shows his concern to have a detailed record of 'all the ships that his Majesty hath at any time had since *anno* 1660 and hath at this day'.[10]

Elizabeth did not notice on 26 April when Pepys saw Deb while they were out near the Temple where Fleet Street becomes the Strand:

> . . . and just at the Temple gate I spied Deb with another gentlewoman and Deb winked on me and smiled, but undiscovered and I was glad to see her.

By 4 May Pepys was still actively pursuing Deb:

> Up and to the office and then my wife being gone with the coach to see her mother at Deptford, I before the office sat went to the Excise Office, and thence being alone stepped into Duck lane and thence tried to have sent a porter to Deb's but durst not trust him, and therefore having bought a book to satisfy the bookseller for my stay there, a 12d book, Andronicus of Tom Fuller,[11] I took coach, and at the end of Jewen street next Red Cross street I cause[12] the coachman to her lodging, and understand she is gone for Greenwich to one Marys's,[13] a tanner's, at which I was glad, hoping to have opportunity to find her out. And so, in great fear of being seen, I to the office, and there all the morning. Dined at home, and presently after dinner comes home my wife, who I believe is jealous of my spending the day, and I had very good fortune in being at home, for if Deb had been to have been found it is 40 to one but I had been abroad. God forgive me.

'Marys's' was Henry Maris (d.1677), tanner of East Greenwich. Pepys must have been familiar with Maris's establishment, but this was the only time he mentioned him. Deb had apparently gone there to lodge, but her connection to Maris is unknown.

Both Pepys and Elizabeth were on a knife edge, with Elizabeth alert to the slightest possibility that her husband could still not be trusted, as on 7 May:

> So to the Treasury chamber and then walked home round by the Excise Office, having by private vows last night in prayer to God Almighty cleared my mind for the present of the thoughts of going to Deb at Greenwich, which I did long after . . .
>
> Thence with my wife abroad with our coach, most pleasant weather, and to Hackny and into the marshes, where I never was before, and thence round about to Old ford and Bow and coming through the latter home, there being some young gentlewomen at a door and I seeming* not to know who they were, my wife's

* Pretending.

jealousy told me presently that I knew well enough it was that damned place where Deb dwelt, which made me swear very angrily that it was false, as it was, and I carried <her> back again to see the place, and it proved not it, so I continued out of humour a good while at it, she being willing to be friends, so I was by and by, saying no more of it.

On 9 May Pepys spotted Betty Mitchell in St Margaret's, Westminster, but was disappointed by her appearance.

And here at distance I saw Betty Michell but she is become much a plainer woman then she was a girl.

This did not stop him seeking her out on 31 May (below). Betty Mitchell was now about twenty-three years old.

On 10 May Pepys was out looking for Betty and Doll, but he appears to have been unlucky:

. . . took boat to Westminster, and to Mrs Martins who is not come to town from her husband at Portsmouth so drank only at Cragg's with her and Doll and so to the Swan and there *besared* ['kissed'] a fat new maid that is there, and so to White hall . . . [14]

Pepys meant here that he had drunk with Betty's landlady, a Mrs 'Cragg', thought to be a Mrs Alice or Mrs Susanna Crake, and Doll (there is no explanation for the whereabouts of Doll's baby). Despite writing out Mrs Martin, Cragg's and Doll in longhand, he still resorted to writing 'malad' in shorthand for 'maid'. Doll was not mentioned again. Pepys had his last recorded meeting with Betty on 12 May, and sneered at her:

. . . so to Mrs Martin's lodging, who come to town last night, and there *yo* did *hazer* her ['I did do her'], she having been a month I

> think at Portsmouth with her husband newly come home from the Streights.* But lord, how silly the woman talks of her great entertainment[15] there and how all the gentry come to visit her, and she believes her husband is worth 6 or 700£ which nevertheless I am glad of but I doubt† they will spend it as fast.

Elizabeth sacked the maid Matt on 20 May. Pepys suggests they had fallen out but did not interfere; the real reason was probably that Elizabeth wanted to dispose of any other temptations for her husband. He was planning a trip to France and the Low Countries with Elizabeth, hoping this meant they could hire a new maid who spoke French.

Pepys was now thirty-six years old, more influential and better off than he had ever been. On 31 May Pepys had his last recorded meeting with Betty Mitchell. That day he ended his diary. The main reason he gave was his terror of going blind, but it is no less likely that trying to record his complex personal life had taken a toll. He was probably developing long-sightedness (hypermetropia), normal for his age but exacerbated by long hours working by candlelight. His private life was disintegrating, and it was soon to become much worse (see Epilogue for Elizabeth Pepys's death in November 1669).

> Dined at home and home that afternoon by water to White hall at Michell's where I have not been many a day till just[16] the other day and now I met her mother there and know her husband to be out of town and here *yo* did *besar ella* ['I did kiss her'] but have not opportunity to *para hazer mas* ['to do more'] with her if *yo* had had it . . .
>
> And thus ends all that I doubt I shall ever be able to do with

---

* 'Streights' = Straits. Usually applied to the Mediterranean and derived from 'The Straits of Gibraltar', a descriptor found on old maps, and the other straits found in that sea.

† By 'doubt' P meant 'fear'. Samuel Martin was to end up in prison a debtor, dying in 1678.

my own eyes in the keeping of my journall, I being not able to do it any longer having done now so long as to undo my eyes almost every time that I take a pen in my hand. And, therefore, whatever comes of it, I must forbear and therefore resolve from this time forward, to have it kept by my people in long-hand,[17] and must therefore be contented to set down no more then is fit for them and all the world to know or if there be anything, (which cannot be much, now my amours to Deb[18] are past, and my eyes hindering me in almost all other pleasures) I must endeavour to keep a margin in my book open to add here and there a note in short-hand with my own hand. And so I betake myself to that course which <is> almost as much as to see myself go into my grave. For which and all the discomforts that will accompany my being blind the good God prepare me! May.31.1669. SP

EPILOGUE

When Samuel Pepys closed his diary on 31 May 1669, he was just over halfway through his life. Although he kept other shorthand journals, for example the account of his voyage to Tangier in 1683, he never again wrote anything so personal. He had, however, left enough to establish himself in perpetuity as a source of fascination. 'Pepys's nature was singularly contradictory', said Henry Wheatley in 1880, resigning himself to having to itemize Pepys's bad points before turning to the good ones as a 'set-off'.[1]

Pepys was a bully, a vain and philandering hypocrite, and a domineering and mean-minded husband. He was capable of sexual violence as well as being coercive, deceitful, and manipulative. He groomed his female targets into submission and disregarded their feelings. He was also easily manipulated by others who spotted his inclinations. Some of his conduct was not exceptional for his own time or since but his candid diary ensured that sordid and discomfiting aspects of his private life would be preserved among the record of his other daily activities. Pepys probably also suffered from a behavioural addiction manifested in the compulsive pursuit of subversive extramarital sex. This also added to his sense of entitlement. Secrecy was part of the thrill.

Pepys's professional corruption challenged even what was considered acceptable at the time. For example, on 3 May 1664 he condemned Sir William Batten's 'many rogueries' in expecting bribes such as a 'piece of sattin and cabinetts and other things' but greedily enumerated the money and gifts in kind he received himself. On 18 May 1664 Pepys accepted a 'pretty cabinet' and gave it to Elizabeth. It was typical of his personality that he could condemn another's conduct while being at ease with his own, just as he condemned sexual decadence at court and was disgusted by prostitution. That side of his life has been generally beyond the scope of this book, but some of his adulterous activity, the Bagwell affair being the most obvious example, was another way of profiting from his position.

The best one can say is that Pepys was conscious of a transactional obligation in some of these instances. He expected to reciprocate, whether in commissioning a service for the Navy in return for 'a pair of the noblest flagons that ever I saw' (21 July 1664) or finding William Bagwell and Samuel Martin positions in return for sexual relations with their wives.

Samuel Pepys was equally capable of generosity, compassion, and love. His enduring loyalty was one of his most edifying characteristics. He constructed a system of patronage which, despite being muddied by the sexual services he demanded from the wives of some of the men he helped forward, he diligently maintained long afterwards. He was meticulous, exceptionally well-organized and a superb administrator. He had a form of high intelligence, had an overwhelming if credulous curiosity about life, and a well-developed appreciation of art and music.[2] He was an invigorating individual and was manifestly held in great esteem by many of his contemporaries, which he enthusiastically recorded at every opportunity, though he also made enemies.

Pepys realized that even by the standards of the time his sexual conduct was reprehensible. The question is whether he sought to compensate for his behaviour by seeking to be the 'very worthy, industrious and curious person' John Evelyn described him as. The phenomenon of the figure assiduously cultivating a positive public reputation to cancel out a secret dark side, and thereby to hide in plain sight, is a familiar one.

The story was not all one-sided. Betty Martin was already an established draper and single woman in Westminster in her late twenties when she was first recorded willingly consorting with Pepys, prior to her marriage in 1664. Later joined by her much younger sister Doll, the pair proved to be his most reliable mistresses, even though he constantly disparaged them. But their friend Mrs Elizabeth Burrows, the naval widow and mother of several children, illustrated the powerlessness of women in need at the time. She was obliged to use the only commodity at her disposal to secure some financial security. Betty Martin's behaviour was also partly motivated by seeking naval posts for her husband.

The tragedy is that the women in Pepys's story have no voices. Without the diary we would know little or nothing about them at all. To read Elizabeth Pepys's and Deb Willet's private papers, or those of the naval carpenter's wife Elizabeth Bagwell whose unhappy forced submission to Pepys was recorded by him in painful detail, would be a revelation if, at least, they had set some of their thoughts down and they had survived. The absence of any such notes or letters passed between him and his wife suggests that, after she died, Pepys either systematically destroyed anything that remained or took no steps to ensure their preservation.

ELIZABETH PEPYS

Of all the women and girls described we learn most about Elizabeth Pepys, but only from the diary. She was a victim of her era and of the disregard Pepys so often exhibited for her feelings. She was in her own way difficult to live with, exhibited by her explosive and legitimately jealous rage recorded throughout the diary and especially in the last few months. This is a trepidatious path to tread because Pepys predictably chose to portray and treat her as irrational, unreasonable, volatile, and foolish in contrast to himself. He persistently infantilized Elizabeth, depicting himself as the medium through which she might hope to become an educated and edifying companion for him. All the methods by which she could improve herself in his eyes were described as in his gift. Today we would call that gaslighting. Her gynaecological health was poor and at the mercy of contemporary medical ignorance, undoubtedly affecting her composure. Unfortunately, it is now impossible to form reliable diagnoses or judgements of her physical and mental health.

Elizabeth fell sick as she and her husband arrived home following a journey to Holland, Flanders, and Paris over the summer of 1669. She died aged twenty-nine of probable typhoid fever on 10 November 1669 and was buried three days later. Pepys commissioned a marble memorial to Elizabeth which remains in St Olave's church today on the north wall of the chancel overlooking where she was buried. Her bust is accompanied by a Latin inscription which in translation reads:

> Wife of Samuel Pepys, Clerk of the Acts of the Royal Navy, she was educated first in a convent, and then in a seminary of France. In both she was distinguished by excellence, gifted together with beauty, accomplishments, and languages. She bore no offspring, for she could not have borne her equal. To this she bid a gentle farewell, a journey completed through the lovelier sights of Europe. Returned, she better departed to a more enlightened world.

It is unlikely that the habits Pepys had developed were abruptly curtailed. The very small amount of evidence that has survived, in marked contrast to the earlier graphic detail of the diary, suggests they had not abated. Despite being caught with Deb, he had not only continued to pursue her but also resumed his visits to mistresses in the last few months of the diary. Pepys's long-term relationship with Mary Skynner, which started during the 1670s, was the most conspicuous case in point, and had clearly both troubled and embarrassed her family (see below).

DEB WILLET

In 2006 the scholar Kate Loveman traced Deb Willet. On 27 January 1670 in Chelmsford Deb married Jeremiah Wells, a client of Pepys's.[3] Wells was a scholar, born close to Pepys's house in Seething Lane, and the couple continued to live nearby. By early 1671 Wells sought Pepys's help for employment. As Loveman has observed, this is reminiscent of how Pepys's patronage had become entwined previously with other married women, such as Elizabeth Bagwell. There is no means of knowing now whether Deb Willet resumed physical relations with Pepys in return, but with Elizabeth Pepys deceased this would have been far easier than beforehand.

It is also possible that Deb had not been wholly unwelcoming of Pepys's advances, if she was prepared to remain nearby and in contact. She might have believed maintaining contact was essential to ensure her husband's (and her own) security and future. However, the sudden death of his wife may have been enough to shock Pepys out of continuing as he had been, at least temporarily. He was certainly capable of seeing her loss as a punishment.

Pepys found Wells a Navy chaplaincy. Jeremiah and Deb, who had at least two children (Deborah born in 1670 and Elizabeth in 1672, the latter an interesting link to the deceased Mrs Pepys, but it was also Deb's mother's name), were helped by other members of Pepys's immediate circle, including Will Hewer, and even Betty Martin's purser husband Samuel.[4] Pepys continued to advance Jeremiah's career. However, Deb died of unknown causes and was buried nearby at All Hallows Barking on 30 March 1678. 'Jeremy Wells curate' died and was buried there on 24 August 1679, having briefly remarried after Deb's death. The fate of their daughters is unknown. The support Pepys had given the couple was a good example of his interesting sense of obligation and loyalty. Had they lived, there is good reason to believe that Pepys would have continued to assist them.

ELIZABETH AND WILLIAM BAGWELL

At Alverstoke (Hampshire), very close to the major naval dockyard at Portsmouth, a boy called William Bagwell was christened on 29 December 1671. His parents were William and Elizabeth Bagwell, the birthplace probably because she was staying there, having followed her husband. At the Chatham church of St Mary near the naval dockyard on 20 July 1673, a John Bagwell, whose parents were also William and Elizabeth Bagwell, was christened. These form the earliest evidence for Mrs Bagwell's first name and have hitherto gone unnoticed, but her name is also confirmed by her and her husband's wills (see below). It is also impossible to know if these children were genuinely her husband's, especially if the couple had also become entangled with other naval officials in the interests of William's career. Perhaps significantly, there is no record of her bearing any children during the 1660s, either in Pepys's diary or birth registers.

By 1673 William Bagwell was working at Chatham as a shipwright, arranged by Pepys who had extensive dealings with the dockyard. A decade earlier, his wife Elizabeth had been treated in the contemporary manner as a chattel by both her husband and his parents who used her as a honeytrap to entice Pepys. She probably expected to benefit as a result from the advancement of her husband through Pepys's patronage. Nonetheless, the demands made of her were remarkable even by the standards of the time, when for a woman to have extra-marital sex usually resulted in her irremediable shame and ruin. Her frantic but futile resistance when Pepys first raped her on 20 December 1664 suggests she had not until then anticipated the risks she was being obliged to take.

Nevertheless, in the years that followed both Elizabeth and William Bagwell continued to regard Pepys as their benefactor. In January 1687 and over twenty years since their first meetings, Elizabeth Bagwell was still going to the expense of visiting the exalted Pepys's London office to make representations on her husband's behalf. On 7 January Pepys wrote sternly to William Bagwell as 'your friend and always have and will be so'. He had advised Mrs Bagwell it was a waste of time and money to make follow-up visits to his office, and told William to abandon 'the apprehension you seem to be under of my backwardness to do you kindness on occasion of the late vacancies of a Master Shipwright's and Assistant's place which you shall have no cause ever to doubt'. In early 1689 Pepys recommended Bagwell for another post at Chatham.[5]

When William Bagwell died in late 1697, he was Master Shipwright at the dockyard in Portsmouth. His extended family was closely involved in shipbuilding and remained so. His nephew, William Sutherland (1668–1740), grandson of Owen Bagwell, wrote a long-lasting book called *The Ship-builder's Assistant; or Marine Architecture* in 1711.[6] It seems that the promotion of the family's interests, for which Elizabeth Bagwell had paid a price, resonated down into the eighteenth century. Under William Bagwell's will, made on 22 September 1697 and proved on 26 January 1698, his widow was to inherit his estate but if she married half the estate would pass to his cousins and his nephews and nieces. He and Elizabeth were apparently by then childless.

The 9 July 1702 will of 'Elizabeth Bagwell of the parish of Deptford' (by then she lived in Back Lane, which led to the dockyard's south entrance) contained provision for a significant number of her own and her husband's kinsmen and kinswomen, among them members of the Sutherland family, of money, silver, and other property (see Glossary of People and Places). Much of the silverware probably originated in gifts and inducements to her late husband during his employment. She made no mention of any siblings of her own and died about a month later, probably in her late fifties. She was buried at St Nicholas, Deptford, on 14 August.[7] Elizabeth Bagwell ended her life a woman of some means. Perhaps it was a small consolation that the indignities she had suffered as a young woman at Pepys's hands on behalf of her husband's career had brought her some security in later life, incomprehensible though that may seem today.

BETTY MARTIN AND DOLL LANE

Betty Martin was widowed in 1678 when her husband Samuel died in Dartmouth after being imprisoned for debt, unfortunately living down to Pepys's low opinion of him. What appears to be her modest will was drawn up in April 1686 and proved in June after her death. Only two siblings and her daughter Elizabeth born in 1669 appear to have survived her.[8] The death of Betty's younger sister Doll could not be traced (see Glossary of People and Places).

MARY SKYNNER

During the early 1670s Pepys had become embroiled with Mary Skynner (or Skinner), who eventually became his common-law wife. She was the same age as Deb and may have supplanted her in Pepys's eyes. Mary had come into Pepys's life as the daughter of neighbours soon after Elizabeth's death, probably in some household capacity.[9]

On 5 July 1676 Pepys received a letter written in Latin (probably tactfully, given the contents) by Mary's brother Daniel. In it he explained how 'I have often wept for my loss, and it is painful to recall, they say, the loss and inconvenience (only to be judged by my parents) from this commerce which took place between you and my sister and was not a small one. But whether these things are square in you, or whether you can engage in what parents are most ready to object to in this case, it is certainly not mine to look into or to care.'[10]

Pepys had evidently imposed himself on a young woman once again, but this time there was a happier outcome even if the Skynner family had to bury their shame. However, Mary was probably obliged to stay with Pepys once it was known she had been the subject of his attentions. They did not apparently share a household until later in life, but Mary was treated by Pepys's friends as if she was his wife. By 1699 she was writing out Pepys's letters to his dictation, apparently badly. She was left an annuity of £200 in his will and other verbal bequests.[11]

PEPYS'S LATTER DAYS

By 1673 Pepys was Secretary of the Admiralty and soon afterwards elected MP for Castle Rising. He fell from grace in the 'Popish Plot' scare of 1679 when his innocent clerk Samuel Atkins was mischievously implicated in the murder of Sir Edmund Berry Godfrey, leading to accusations of Pepys's corruption and for having Catholic sympathies and affiliations. The case collapsed. Pepys, who had been temporarily imprisoned in the Tower in the summer of 1679, escaped further risk of prosecution. Nonetheless, his critics and enemies had mocked his lowly origins as a tailor's son and his pretensions in office.[12] Pepys was not restored to the Secretaryship until 1684, when he was also elected President of the Royal Society.

Pepys enjoyed favour under the Catholic James II (1685–8), to whom he had been so loyal since the Second Dutch War, but he was doomed in 1689 after James fled at the end of 1688. William III and Mary II's Protestant constitutional monarchy ended many careers and started others. Pepys resigned and was twice more sent to the Tower, in 1689 and 1690. In 1690 he published his only book, *Memoires Relating to the State of the Royal Navy of England, For Ten Years, Determin'd December 1688*. Typically Pepysian in its listing of detail and finances, it fell far short of the great naval history John Evelyn had expected him to write. Pepys never remarried, but during the 1690s he retreated into retirement with Mary Skynner, eventually moving in with the wealthy Will Hewer in Clapham by 1701.[13]

PEPYS'S DEATH AND LATER JUDGEMENTS

Samuel Pepys died in Clapham on 26 May 1703. In his diary Evelyn, who had last visited Pepys on 14 May, recalled Pepys as 'a very worthy, industrious and curious person' whose 'library and other collections of curiosities was one of the most considerable', and had been for 'near forty years, so my particular friend'.[14] Pepys was buried according to his wishes alongside Elizabeth in St Olave's across the road from their house by the Navy Office. They rest there still, their monuments surviving the devastation caused to the church during the Blitz in 1941.

Pepys had invested all his hopes for the future in his nephew John Jackson (1673–1723), son of his sister Paulina ('Pall'), to whom he bequeathed charge of his library and some of his papers. His will specified that his library (which included the six diary volumes) and his book presses, would go after Jackson's death preferably to Magdalene College, where they arrived in 1724 and remain.[15] The rest of Pepys's surviving archives have been more widely dispersed. Some, like most of the Pepys-Cockerell papers, are in private ownership or have found their way to the Bodleian Library in Oxford and the National Maritime Museum at Greenwich, among other places.

The diary passages concerning Pepys's sexual activity troubled all his early editors and biographers. In different ways they falsified his witnessing of his own life, while at the same time tantalizing their readers with vague allusions to the excised filth. They usually omitted what they classed as offensive phrases or words, or whole sections. In his 1848–9 edition, Braybrooke said 'no-one with a well-regulated mind will regret their loss'.

In the 1870s Mynors Bright left out what he considered 'unfit for publication' and invited readers to be 'a little blind' to Pepys's faults. In his 1890s edition Henry Wheatley, who increased the amount of Bright's transcription in print, explained that he had omitted 'a few passages which cannot possibly be printed'. He asked his readers 'to have faith in the judgement of the editor'. Elsewhere, Wheatley commented on the women, among whom in his view Betty Martin was 'the most objectionable of all' with 'no evidence she had any virtue to lose, and her conduct throughout is very revolting'. He found Mrs Bagwell 'less objectionable', describing her seduction by Pepys as 'to his discredit'.[16]

In a short biography of Pepys published in 1925, J. R. Tanner explained that he had omitted references to 'the more squalid aspects of his amours' but defended them as 'flirtations, pursued in the strenuous manner of the 17th century, but innocent enough for all that'. He commended Pepys for preserving 'a kind of fundamental decency' and for having 'a wholesome distaste for the lower forms of vice', and generally avoided mentioning any of the women by name. However, he conceded that a 'suppressed passage' threw a different light on the catastrophic incident with Deb on 25 October 1668.[17] Tanner saved his readers from more. Thirty-four years later, John Wilson blamed Pepys's 'love of beauty and pleasure' and the 'easy-going, loose-moraled society' overseen by a 'libertine King and Court', as well as Elizabeth's failure 'to yield "due benevolence" to her husband', for his libidinous indulgences.[18]

Latham and Matthews called Pepys's escapades 'sexual adventures' and 'amorous encounters' as if they had been harmless recreational capers (see the Introduction for how they included the polyglot passages and those they called 'garbled shorthand' but simultaneously distanced themselves and the reader from them). The relationship with Betty Martin was a 'casual liaison'. They described how Pepys's 'successful siege of Deb Willet's virtue' resulted in 'the degradation that slowly came upon' her in a drama worthy of a 'sentimental novelette', as if she was lethargically culpable and he deserved a round of applause.[19] The Bagwells passed virtually without comment. These and other examples served to massage further Pepys's posthumous reputation, helping to avoid confronting the evidence that he was a rapist alongside his other characteristics.[20]

In their examination of Pepys's health, Latham and Matthews included 'A Psychoanalyst's View'. This explored Pepys's sexual behaviour only in the context of a man who lived in a precarious and dangerous era. It was suggested that Pepys used sex as a 'mode of reassurance' to achieve a 'psychological victory over death'. His own testimony of his grooming, coercion, and violence, as well as the compulsive nature of his behaviour, was ignored along with the effect on his victims, who were barely mentioned. Only the impact on Elizabeth was fleetingly considered, Pepys being defended as 'faithful in his fashion'.[21] Claire Tomalin is one biographer who has been prepared to confront Pepys's self-confessed reality, as has the Pepysian scholar Kate Loveman (see Further Reading).

The site of the Navy Office is marked by a bust of Pepys in a small park just across Seething Lane from St Olave's. The house where he and Elizabeth lived was nearby. Some places Pepys knew well remain, like St Margaret's in Westminster, Westminster Abbey, and Westminster Hall. Victoria Embankment Gardens is home to York Stairs, built in 1626, one of the last of the old watergates that Pepys used when he went 'by water' up and down the Thames. The royal dockyard at Deptford is long gone but John Evelyn's adjacent lost gardens at Sayes Court, which Pepys visited and admired,[22] are commemorated with a small park.

The miracle of written words, in this case those represented by Shelton's Tachygraphy, can recreate all the colour, sound, and emotion of dramas played out centuries ago. To read Pepys's shorthand is an unmatched experience and privilege as his world and the people he knew emerge from the characters he inscribed laboriously with his pen by the flickering and spitting light of thousands of candles.

Exactly why Pepys chose to write such an incriminating private account of his life in the 1660s, despite the precautions he took to obscure but not conceal his diary's contents beyond recovery, will probably never be wholly explained. However, his most intimate private revelations and the fascinating ways in which they were composed can now properly be treated as integral features of his diary's famously unmatched introspection and commentary on his times.

Had the diary emerged during his life, Pepys would have risked professional and financial ruin, despite his undoubted virtues, skills, and public standing in other areas. How well or badly this remarkable man emerges from a more complete picture of the person he really was and deliberately recorded himself as, by the standards of his own time and in retrospect, is for the reader to decide.

PRINCIPAL DATES

1633	23 Feb	Born at Salisbury Court near St Bride's, London
1644		Starts at Huntingdon Grammar School
1646–50		Attended St Paul's School, London
1650	Jun	Enters Trinity College, Cambridge
	Oct	Transfers to Magdalene College, Cambridge
1654	Mar	Takes his BA degree at Cambridge
1655	1 Dec	Marries Elizabeth St Michel at St Margaret's, Westminster
1656	11 Mar	Employed as Mountagu's steward
		Clerkship to the Exchequer
1658	26 Mar	Operated on for a bladder stone, celebrated annually thereafter
	3 Sep	Death of Cromwell
1659		Pepys and Elizabeth resident in Axe Yard
1660	1 Jan	Begins the diary

1660	22 Mar	Appointed Secretary to the Generals of the Fleet
	29 Jun	Appointed Clerk of the Acts
1663	9 Jan	Burns Elizabeth's letters and papers in front of her
	9 Jul	First mention of Mrs Bagwell
1664	15 Mar	Death of his brother Tom
	18 Dec	Pepys strikes Elizabeth over the eye (night of 18/19th)
1665	15 Feb	Elected Fellow of the Royal Society
	22 Feb	Second Dutch War begins
	20 Mar	Appointed Treasurer for Tangier
	5 Jul	Moves household to Greenwich to escape the plague
	27 Oct	Made Surveyor-General of the Victualling (until July 1667)
1666	2 Sep	Great Fire of London begins
1667	25 Mar	Death of his mother at Brampton
	31 Jul	End of the Second Dutch War
	27 Sep	Deb Willet arrives to live with the Pepyses
1668	5 Mar	Defends the Navy Office in a speech to the House of Commons
	25 Oct	Pepys caught with Deb Willet by Elizabeth
1669	31 May	Ends the diary

1669	Jun–Oct	Travels in northern France and the Low Countries
	10 Nov	Death of Elizabeth Pepys
1672	24 Jan	Made Elder Brother of Trinity House
	Mar	Third Dutch War begins
	7 Jun	Sandwich killed at Battle of Solebay
1673	29 Jan	Navy Office destroyed by fire. Moves to Winchester Street
	18 Jun	Appointed Secretary of the Admiralty
	4 Nov	Elected MP for Castle Rising (colleague: Sir John Trevor)
1674	Jan	Moves to Admiralty Office at Derby House
	Feb	End of Third Dutch War
1676	1 Feb	Made Governor of Christ's Hospital
	22 May	Master of Trinity House
1679	Feb	Samuel Atkins, P's clerk, accused of being an accessory in the murder of Sir Edmund Berry Godfrey. Acquitted 11 Feb
	Mar	Elected MP for Harwich
	21 May	Forced to resign Secretaryship. Imprisoned in the Tower
	Jul	Released on bail. Moves in with Will Hewer
1680	Feb	Released from bail
	Jun	Case against P dropped

1682	May	Accompanies Duke of York north and witnesses shipwreck
1683	30 Jul	To Tangier for supervision of evacuation. Second diary begins
	1 Dec	Second diary ends
	Dec	Visits Spain (until March 1684)
1684	10 Jun	Reappointed Secretary of the Admiralty
	1 Dec	Elected President of the Royal Society
1685	6 Feb	Charles II dies. Accession of James II
	Apr	Elected MP for Harwich and Sandwich
	Jul	Master of Trinity House for the second time
1686	Mar	Special Commission for Navy begins
1687	Jan	Instructs William Bagwell to stop his wife bothering him
1688	1 Nov	William of Orange lands at Torbay
	23 Dec	James II leaves for France
1689	Jan	Loses seat at Harwich
	20 Feb	Resigns Secretaryship
	26 Aug	Resigns from Trinity House
1690	25 Jun	Reimprisoned in the Tower, released 30 Jun
	Dec	Publishes *Memoirs of the Royal Navy*
1693	29 Sep	Robbed by highwaymen
1697	Apr	Seriously ill

1701	Jun	Moves permanently to Hewer's Clapham house
1702	Aug	Death of Mrs Elizabeth Bagwell
1703	26 May	Death of Samuel Pepys
	4 Jun	Burial at St Olave's
1724		Pepys's library passed to Magdalene College, Cambridge
1825		Braybrooke (first) edition of the diary (Smith's transcription) published
1841		Smith's edition of letters and the 'second diary' (Tangier) published
1875–9		Mynors Bright publishes his transcription of the diary
1893–9		Wheatley's edition of Bright's transcription published
1971–83		Latham and Matthews's diary edition published

GLOSSARY OF PEPYS'S POLYGLOT

The following are most of the foreign words used by Pepys, principally in the polyglot passages. Translations based on contemporary dictionaries have been preferred along with Pepys's normal English usage when he was clearly using a polyglot synonym. Some basic words like *ego/yo*, possessive pronouns such as *su*, conjunctions, and prepositions are not included. Note that Pepys's polyglot words often reflected contemporary spellings and his phonetic attempts to represent them in shorthand, which have confused some transcribers and biographers. Pepys did not spell or use these words consistently or accurately. Some words appear repeatedly, others only occasionally or just once or twice. Forms found in Cotgrave (French 1611) and Percivale (Spanish 1623), both books Pepys knew, have been preferred where readings are in doubt. Greek words were either written in Greek characters in longhand or transliterated into English characters in shorthand. There was huge variation in how Pepys used the polyglot. Some of the more complex and ungrammatical polyglot phrases made up from both French and other languages suggest that Pepys may have composed them in French first. However, because French is more difficult to write in Shelton's Tachygraphy, as he wrote them out in shorthand he substituted selected words in (mainly) Spanish and Latin. These were easier to represent with the shorthand symbols and helped disguise the text further.

(C) = Catalan, (F) French, (Ge) German, (Gk) Greek, (I) Italian, (L) Latin, (P) Portuguese, (S) Spanish.

abaxo = (S) 'below', i.e. below a woman's clothing to reach her genitals

aegrotat = (L) 'is sick'

alguna/o = (S) 'some', for example *alguna cosa*, 'something'; sometimes feminine plural *algunas*

ἀλλῳ = (Gk) l.h. 'another'

amours = (F) 'loves'

amplius = (L) 'more'

ancilla = (L) 'maidservant'

andar = (S) 'go/walk'

animi = (L) 'disposition/mood'

aposento = (S) 'lodging'

aqui = (S) 'here'

aussi = (F) 'also'

belle = (F) 'beautiful/comely'

besar = (S) 'kiss', also *bezar, besado/besando*

biber = (F) 'drink', adapted from *biberon* (Cotgrave), 'a tippler/quaffer'

cabaret = (F) 'tavern'; in common parlance and not really polyglot

calor = (L) 'flushed'

cama = (S) 'bed'

casa = (S) 'house', or 'tavern' (*casa de biber*)

ceux là = (F) 'those', i.e. a woman's period

chair = (F) 'flesh'

cheirotheca = (Gk) 'glove', literally 'hand sheath', P's version of χειρώθηκά(ρια) (plural). See also χειρώ below

chemise = (F) 'shirt'

chose = (F) 'thing', indiscriminately used for any sex act, nipples, or male/female genitals

clos? = (F) 'enclosed space', hence the old French *lit/littée clos* 'box/closed bed'. Uncertain

comprar = (F) 'buy'

con ella = (S) 'with her'

coño = (S) 'privitie' or 'cony', an old English word for female genitals also used by Pepys

contentment = (F) 'full satisfaction/contentment'

contraindre = (F) 'to compel/force'

corazon = (S) 'heart'

cosa = (S) 'thing', indiscriminately used for any sex act, nipples, or male/female genitals

decouvert = (F) 'discovered'

dedans = (F) 'within'

defessus = (L) 'weary/worn out/exhausted'

degrés = (F) physical 'steps/stairs', or 'degrees/stages' (the latter normally in English)[1]

delante = (S) 'before/forward' in association with 'backward', sexual positions

demeures = (F) 'dally/linger/dwells', also *demeurais*

demorado = (P) 'remained/delayed'

dentro = (S) 'within'

digito = (L) 'finger', from *digitus*

dizer/diser = (P) 'say/tell' (old Spanish was *dezir*, but P's s.h. makes the Portuguese certain)

donner = (F) 'give'

douce = (F) 'soft/gentle'

empescér = (S) 'hurt' (contemporary variant of *empecér*, not to be confused with *empeçar*)

enojado = (S) 'angry'

ensemble = (F) 'together', with *visto* (q.v.)

escaper = (S) 'escape'

espender = (S) 'spend', i.e. ejaculate

estos = (S) 'those', i.e. a woman's period

etsi = (L) 'though'

facero = (L) 'do'

faciebam = (L) 'did', e.g. 'did the thing'

faire = (F) 'do/make', 'ejaculate/orgasm'. Numerous forms of the verb were used, and cannot always be distinguished

femme = (F) 'wife/woman'

fille = (F) 'girl', used normally for maids or serving girls

flammes = (F) literally 'flames/fires' but figuratively 'loves' as in *amours*

foras = (L) 'abroad/out of doors'

force = (F) 'resistance/strength'

formosa = (S) 'beautifully formed'

fort = (F) 'very much/exceeding/exceedingly'

foutée = (F) 'fucked', see also *futuere* (q.v.)

fregar = (S) 'rub'

futuere = (L) 'fuck', Pepys's abbreviated s.h. phonetic version being *futer*

ganar = (S) 'gain'

gans = (F) 'gloves', *gans* being a variant spelling of *gants*[2]

genouil = (F) 'knee', s.h. *genol*. An old French form, also meaning a knee-shaped ship timber

gunaica = (Gk) 'woman/wife', Pepys's s.h. transliteration of γυναίκα

habillado = (S) 'dressed' (easily confused in s.h. with *habilado* 'expert/skilled')

hablar = (S) 'speak'

hazer = (S) 'do/make', 'ejaculate/orgasm', thus *hazer me hazer*, 'make myself do' (and variants)

hermana/o = (S) 'sister/brother'

hija = (S) 'daughter'

ibi = (L) 'there'

jolie = (F) 'pretty'

jupes = (F) 'skirts'

laisser = (F) 'leave/let go/abandon/relinquish'

lecto = (L) 'bed'

lequel = (F) 'which'

lever = (F) 'rouse/get up'

lugar = (S) 'place'

main = (F) 'hand'

mamelles = (F) 'breasts'

mano = (S) 'hand'

manum = (L) 'hand' (accusative singular)

mari = (F) 'husband'

marido = (S) 'husband'

mas = (S) 'more'

mauvais = (F) 'bad/depraved/lewd'

meses = (S) 'months'

mi mismo = (S) 'myself', sometimes just *mi* or *me* (for 'my' or 'me')

minusier = (F) 'carpenter' (William Bagwell), Pepys's spelling of *menuisier*

mirando = (S) 'looking'

mit = (Ge) 'with'

móça = (S) 'servant girl/young maid/wench', written phonetically in s.h. *mosa*

moher = (S) archaic form of 'woman/wife', *mujer*/*mugger* (*moher* is not in Percivale, 1623)

monter = (F) 'go up/advance', but also 'to leap on' as in a man upon a woman (Cotgrave, 1611)

nada/*natha* = (S) 'nothing'. P sometimes blurred English and Spanish

negat = (L) 'says no', quoted from Martial

nudo in lecto = (L) 'naked in bed'

nulla = (L) 'no', quoted from Martial

nuper = (L) 'lately'

ómbre = (S) 'man' (contemporary variant spelling of *hómbre*)

ojos = (S) 'eyes'

ôter = (F) 'take off/remove' (e.g. gloves).

otra = (S) 'other', e.g. *otra cosa*, 'other thing'

ou = (F) 'where'

ouvert = (F) 'uncovered/open' or even 'large'

pas = (F) 'not'

pater = (L) 'father'

pernis = (L) 'legs/hams', as in ham-like thighs (Betty Martin's)

plaisir = (F) 'pleasure', also *plazer*

plein = (F) 'full'

poil/poyle = (F) 'hair', i.e. pubic hair

ponendo = (I) 'putting', e.g. 'putting her hand upon my thing', also *poner*

pragma = (Gk) 'thing', Pepys's s.h. transliteration of πρᾶγμα, used twice instead of *cosa* (q.v.)

primera = (S) 'first' (female)

puder/podra = (S) 'be able/could'

puella = (L) 'girl', quoted from Martial, *nulla puella negat*, 'no girl refuses'

quand = (L) 'when'

quicquid = (L) 'whatever'

rencontrar = (F) 'to meet'

sans fin = (F) 'endlessly'

sed = (L) 'but'

sedento = (S) 'sitting'

sequi = (L) 'follow'

sobra = (S) 'above/over'

sola = (S) 'alone'

taillée= (F) 'indented/proportioned', i.e. 'figure'

tocar = (S) 'touch', also *tocando*, 'touching'

tomar = (S) 'take', sometimes *tomando*, 'taking'

toucher = (F) 'touch'

traher = (L) 'drag/pull'

trouver = (F) 'find'

vaincue = (F) 'overcome'

vellem = (L) 'I would like'

venga = (S and I) 'come'

venida = (S) 'coming' (noun)

venir = (F) 'to come'

venter = (L) 'belly'

ver = (S) 'see'

vesper = (C) 'evening', s.h. *vespre* (9 April 1667) is certain, not the Latin *vesper veuve* = (F) 'widow' (applied to Elizabeth Burrows)

vezes = (P and S) 'times', today spelled *veces*

vida = (S) 'life'

visto = (S) 'seen', with *ensemble* (q.v.)

volebam = (L) 'I wanted'

volonté = (F) 'will', i.e. 'I had my will of her'

voluptas = (L) 'pleasure'

voudrais = (F) 'I would like/wanted', but used by P as a synonym for 'would'

χείρω̣<σις> = (Gk) Pepys's l.h. version in Greek characters of 'laying on of hands'

GLOSSARY OF PEOPLE AND PLACES

This list is not comprehensive but provides basic information about some of the people Pepys knew and some of the places he frequented that are mentioned in this book. Those interested in pursuing more detail should turn to the Latham and Matthews *Companion*, which is an unmatched compendium of information. Modern genealogical records have made some new details available, but the data is far from complete and lack of hard facts about personal origins can make isolating the correct individual difficult or impossible. Women are only listed here under their married names if they married during the diary period.

AXE YARD. Narrow lane in Whitehall that ran off King Street west towards St James's Park. The location of Pepys's and Elizabeth's rented home 1658–60 before moving to Seething Lane (q.v.).

BAGWELL, MRS ELIZABETH (c. 1640/2–1702). Wife of William (q.v.), Pepys's mistress in Deptford. Her first name survives in her sons' christening records in 1671 and 1673, her husband's will of 1697, and hers of 1702.[1] The first beneficiaries included her kinsman John Milbu<r>n, shipwright at Rotherhithe (see Redriffe), and her widowed kinswomen Elizabeth Couley and Sarah Bowles, both also of Rotherhithe, suggesting that

Elizabeth Bagwell was connected to a Rotherhithe family closely involved with dockyards. Her birth and marriage have not been traced.[2] In 1687 Mrs Bagwell was still appealing to Pepys to help her husband (see Epilogue). All her children were apparently dead by 1697. Buried at St Nicholas, Deptford 14 August 1702.

Bagwell, Owen (d. 1688). Yard foreman and shipwright at Deptford dockyard. He and his wife Alice were in Deptford by 1637.[3] Both were proactively engaged in facilitating Pepys's sexual relations with their daughter-in-law Elizabeth for the sake of their son William's (q.v.) career. They had several other children, none of whom Pepys mentioned. They included a brother John (b. 1646).[4] The will of Elizabeth Bagwell (q.v.) referred to William and John's sister Margaret, as well as several other kin, among them their Sutherland cousins (see Epilogue).[5] In March 1671 he was attacked by aggrieved unpaid shipwrights and caulkers at Deptford.[6] 'Owen Baggwell shipwright' was buried at Deptford 26 September 1688. Alice's burial may be that of 24 April 1681 at Bermondsey.

Bagwell, William (1637–97). Christened at Deptford 2 April 1637, son of Owen and Alice Bagwell (q.v.), the earliest evidence for Bagwells at Deptford. Ship's carpenter and later master shipwright willing, with the assistance of his parents, to allow his wife Elizabeth (q.v.) to have sexual relations with Pepys in return for his advancement. Died while a master shipwright at Portsmouth in 1697. The date of William's and Elizabeth's marriage is unknown but presumably c. 1659–62.[7] He had several siblings, see Owen Bagwell (q.v.).

Batelier, Joseph (d. 1667), his son William, and his daughters Mary and Susan, one of whom Pepys admired for her looks. A wine merchant family who lived close to Pepys. Not to be confused with the Botelers (see Butler below).

Batten, Sir William (c. 1601–67). As Surveyor of the Navy, he was a close business associate of Pepys's, who thought him incompetent, and with his second wife Elizabeth a familiar social contact.

Birch, Jane, *see* Edwards, Jane.

Birch, Wayneman. Pepys's servant boy for several years and the younger brother of Jane Birch. Pepys punished him with severe beatings.

Boteler, *see* Butler.

Brampton. Village near Huntingdon and Hinchingbrooke (q.v.) in Cambridgeshire where Pepys's uncle Robert lived until his death in 1661, the property then passing to Pepys's father John (q.v.). Frequently visited by Pepys and Elizabeth, she sometimes without him. The house is extant (see colour plate section).

Brouncker, William, 2nd Viscount (1620–84). Naval official and mathematician. As Navy Commissioner 1664–79 a constant professional colleague of Pepys's (who admired him), and the first President of the Royal Society in 1662.

Burrows ('Burroughs'), Mrs Elizabeth (née Crofts) (c. 1637–*p.* 1669). Birth records suggest she was born in 1633 or 1637, the latter being slightly more likely because of the location.[8] The widow of the naval lieutenant Anthony Burrows who was killed in 1665. Their marriage on 28 April 1653 (in online sources 'Anthony Barwis') is recorded at St Mary Somerset,

London. Elizabeth was of a similar age to her friend Betty Martin (q.v.). Her mother also ran a stall at Westminster Hall. Elizabeth Burrows came to Pepys in 1665 desperate to have her deceased husband's money paid, by when she had had several children. Pepys never referred to the children or what happened to them during his assignations with their mother. None has been successfully identified.[9]

Butler ('Boteler'), Frances. Her parents and siblings moved to Ireland in 1660. She remained in London, though in what capacity is unknown. Pepys was an enthusiastic admirer of her beauty and frequently socialized with her.

Carteret, Sir George (c. 1610–80). Navy Treasurer between 1660 and 1667. His competence was called into question.

Carteret, Jemima (Mrs/Lady Jem/Jemima) (1646–71). Eldest daughter of Edward Mountagu (q.v.). Pepys was charged with keeping an eye on her while she and her sister were living in London with their staff, but without their parents. She married Philip, son of Sir George Carteret (q.v.), in July 1665 and died in childbirth in 1671. Not to be confused with her mother Jemima Mountagu, Countess of Sandwich (q.v.).

Castlemaine/Castlemayne, *see* Palmer, Barbara.

Clerk of the Acts. Civilian royal naval officer who served on the Navy Board, managing the Navy Office for the Navy Board, and dealt with contracts and everyday administration. Pepys held the post from 13 July 1660 until 19 June 1673.

Cocke, Captain George (1617–76). Merchant, Navy contractor, and Treasurer of the Commission for Sick and Wounded Seamen. A drinking companion of Pepys's.

COVENT GARDEN. A piazza with church designed by Inigo Jones and burgeoning commercial market development to the north of the Strand and west of Drury Lane.

COVENTRY, SIR WILLIAM (1627–86). Secretary to the Lord High Admiralty (1660–67), Navy Commissioner (1662–7). Pepys thought highly of him.

CREED, JOHN (c. 1636–1701). Secretarial and administrative employee of Mountagu's (q.v.) and a rival of Pepys's for patronage, as well as marrying Mountagu's niece. He had Puritan sympathies and interests. Fellow of the Royal Society.

CRIPPLEGATE. One of the City of London's gates. Pepys knew the Cross Keys tavern near there.

CRISP (OR CRIPPS), DIANA/DINAH. Daughter of neighbours of Pepys's in Axe Yard, and an early sexual contact in the diary. Untraced.

DANIELS ('DANIEL'), MRS REBECCA. Daughter of Pepys's Greenwich landlady Mrs Clerke. Perhaps the Rebecca Clerke christened in Bermondsey on 5 August 1645. Marriage not traced.

DEPTFORD. Approximately 4 miles (6.5 km) south-east of London Bridge and by the royal dockyard, equipped with dry and wet docks and stores, and a vital installation for the Carolean Navy. Pepys frequently went there on naval business and also to meet Mrs Bagwell (q.v.). Deptford dockyard was operated closely with its counterpart at Woolwich, a little further downriver. Although supervised by the Navy Board officials, they functioned largely as depots for the private victualling contractors to the Navy.

DOWNING, SIR GEORGE (c. 1623–84). Pepys worked for him at the Exchequer 1656–60. A highly accomplished and ruthless politician with expertise in trade and finance, who served both the Commonwealth and Charles II, and as a diplomat.

DRURY LANE. Road connected at one end to the Strand and the other to what is now High Holborn. Home to the King's Playhouse theatre but also known for prostitutes and brothels around about which Pepys sometimes went to look at with professed disgust.

DUTCH WARS. The Second Anglo-Dutch War of 1665–7 was one of the defining historical events of the 1660s and with which Pepys was professionally involved at an important level. Although there were various causes, at the heart was intense commercial rivalry and therefore control of the waters lying between England and the Dutch United Provinces. The success of the English victory in the Battle of Lowestoft in June 1665 was to be followed by the Four Days Battle of June 1666 which was a hard-won Dutch victory. In June 1667 came the humiliation of the Dutch seizure in the Medway of several capital ships and destruction of others. The Peace at Breda that year ended the war, but another broke out in 1673–4.

EDWARDS, JANE (née Birch) (c. 1643/4–1715). The Pepyses' maid from 1658, with two breaks, throughout the diary period. By August 1662 Pepys was contemplating assaulting her. On 26 March 1669 she married Thomas Edwards, Pepys's clerk, in Islington. She was still living at Pepys's death in 1703. After Edwards's death she remarried, becoming Mrs Penny, and died in 1715.

EVELYN, JOHN (1620–1706). Scion of a family of landed gentry with a seat at Wotton in Surrey. Evelyn lived at Sayes Court,

Deptford. Evelyn was a founding Fellow of the Royal Society, a virtuoso esteemed by Pepys and others for his honourable manner, learning, and writing. As a Commissioner of Sick and Wounded Seamen and Prisoners of War, he and Pepys came to know each other well in a friendship that lasted until Pepys's death. There is no evidence that Evelyn ever had the slightest idea about Pepys's complicated private life. In 1685 Evelyn even tried to secure Pepys's official assistance after his daughter eloped with the nephew of a naval official at Deptford dockyard.

EXCHANGE. Used by Pepys to refer to the New Exchange in the Strand, a mercantile and shopping precinct, and the Royal Exchange, a similar development, between Threadneedle Street and Cornhill. The Royal Exchange was destroyed in the Great Fire and rebuilt. Both were used for casual socializing and as a source of news and gossip.

FENNER, THOMAS (d. 1664) ('Uncle Fenner'). Pepys's mother's brother-in-law.

FLAGEOLET ('flagelet'/'flagelettes' and other spellings). A woodwind instrument resembling a recorder.

FLEET STREET. The main thoroughfare that headed west out of the City, leading on to the Strand which itself led on to Whitehall. Pepys used Fleet Street constantly.

FOXHALL (now Vauxhall). Location of pleasure gardens on the south bank of the Thames a mile or so upriver from Westminster.

GENTLEMAN, JANE. Chambermaid in the Pepys household September 1663 to March 1664. Probably the girl christened at St

Margaret's, Westminster, on 5 April 1642. A woman of the same name married William Dolbey there on 13 April 1669.

GRAY'S INN. One of the inns of court and noted for its gardens ('walks') which were laid out in 1606 by Sir Francis Bacon (whose works Pepys enjoyed reading), often visited by Pepys.

GRIFFITH, WILLIAM ('GRIFFEN'). Navy Office doorman/janitor. Pepys lusted after his unnamed maid and was also godfather to a child of his.

GWYN, NELL (c. 1650–87). Actress and later mistress of Charles II, and mother of two of his children. When Pepys first saw her, she was still only in her mid-teens.

HALFWAY HOUSE. A tavern roughly equidistant between London Bridge and Greenwich at what is now 198 Lower Road, Rotherhithe ('Redriffe'), frequented by Pepys and his household, for example 26 April 1663. The site, marked on old maps such as John Cary's of 1786, is still occupied by a former pub.

HARMOND, SARAH, *see* Udall, Sarah.

HAWLEY ('HAWLY'), JOHN. Clerk to George Downing, former neighbour of Pepys, and unsuccessful suitor of Betty Lane to P's frustration (Martin, q.v.).

HAYLS, JOHN (d. 1679). Portrait painter commissioned by Pepys in 1665 to produce paintings of him and Elizabeth.

HEWER, WILL (1642–1715). Pepys's clerk and servant from 1663 and a frequent presence throughout the diary years. Beaten by Pepys on occasion for being idle but became a trusted confidant and friend for the rest of Pepys's life. He rose to be a high official in the Navy and a wealthy merchant. Pepys lived at Hewer's house in Clapham in the latter part of his life.

HINCHINGBROOKE, HUNTINGDONSHIRE. The mansion was the seat of Edward Mountagu, 1st Earl of Sandwich, close to the Pepys house at Brampton (q.v.).

HOLLIER ('HOLLYARD'), THOMAS (1609–90). The surgeon who operated on Pepys in March 1658 for his bladder stone, and who was consulted thereafter by Pepys on medical matters.

HOLMES, CAPTAIN SIR ROBERT (c. 1622–92). Naval commander and admirer of Elizabeth Pepys, to her husband's disquiet.

HOWLETT, BETTY, *see* Mitchell, Betty.

HUNT, MRS ELIZABETH, wife of John. Former neighbours of Pepys's in Axe Yard.

HYDE, ANNE (1637–71), Duchess of York, daughter of Edward Hyde, Earl of Clarendon, and mother of Mary II (1689–94) and Anne (1702–14)

JACKSON, MRS PAULINA ('Pall') (1640–89). Pepys's sister. She married John Jackson in 1668, and was the mother of Pepys's nephew and heir John Jackson jnr. From January 1661 she worked for Pepys as a servant and was routinely treated as being of lower status.

JAMES, DUKE OF YORK (1633–1701), and James II of England (1685–88). Soldier and naval commander. Pepys thought highly of him and remained a supporter throughout his professional career. Married first to Anne Hyde (q.v.), by whom he had the future Mary II (1689–94) and Anne (1702–14). Ousted in 1688 for his Catholicism.

Jervas, Richard ('Garvis') (d. c. 1669?). Pepys's barber who worked in New Palace Yard. Pepys pursued his assistant Jane Welsh (q.v.) from 1664 to 1666.

Jowles, Rebecca (b. c. 1640?). Married daughter of Captain John Allen, Clerk of the Ropeyard at Chatham dockyard. Married the naval Lt Henry Jowles on 12 August 1662 at St Bride's Fleet St. Pepys was captivated by her in 1661 but had to wait until 24 March 1669 to make progress.

King Street, Westminster. The main thoroughfare through Whitehall from Charing Cross to Westminster. Axe Yard (q.v.) was a side street.

Knepp ('Knepp'/'Knipp'/'Knip'), Elizabeth (née Carpenter). Actress and singer, and friend of Pepys's. Possibly the Elizabeth Carpenter christened in London on 31 January 1641.

Lane, Betty, *see* Martin, Betty.

Lane, Doll (Dorothy/Dorothie) (1646–*a.* 1673?). Younger sister of Betty Martin (q.v. also for their parents) and likewise a mistress of Pepys's. Christened 1 September 1646 in East Retford, Nottinghamshire.[10] She first appeared in Pepys's diary on 1 August 1666. Ran a drapery stall in Westminster Hall with her sister. Claimed to be the widow of a sailor called Rowland Powell (untraced). See the note for 11 April 1669 for the possible burial of her child born in 1669. Unmentioned in her brother-in-law Samel Martin's will of January 1673, unlike her siblings, and was probably deceased. No will located.

Lincoln's Inn and Fields. An inn of court with associated gardens to the west of Chancery Lane which runs from close to the site of Temple Bar up to Holborn.

Lowther, Mrs Margaret ('Peg') (b. c. 1646). Daughter of Sir William Penn (q.v.), she married Anthony Lowther in early February 1667. Pepys suggested she voluntarily offered him her favours.

Ludgate Hill. Road leading westwards downhill from St Paul's Cathedral to the site of Ludgate from which Fleet Street ran on to the Strand.

Magdalene College, University of Cambridge. Pepys's alma mater where he studied from 1651 to 1654. Today the Pepysian Library there houses Pepys's books in their original presses, including the diary volumes.

Martin, Mrs Betty (née Lane) (1636–86). Christened on 2 May 1636 in East Retford, daughter of John (probably d. 1677) and Ann/Anne Lane (buried 30 October 1662).[11] Pepys's long-term mistress, as was her sister Doll Lane (q.v.). Ran a drapery stall in Westminster Hall and was independent enough to be paying tax in her own right (as did Doll). Married Samuel Martin (d. 1678), a naval purser, on 14 July 1664 at St Benet Paul's Wharf in London, and had several children. Their infant daughter Katherine (b. 24 November 1666), Pepys's goddaughter, died on 5 May 1668. Samuel Martin's will of 1673 (proved 1679) specified his father-in-law as 'John Lane of East Retford' in Nottinghamshire. There were at least two other Lane siblings, James (christened 30 January 1637) and Mary (birth not traced), attested in Samuel Martin's and Betty's wills. Betty was outlived by another daughter, also Elizabeth (b. 1669 at Chatham), cited in her will.[12]

'MATT'. Maid employed briefly by Pepys and Elizabeth in early 1669. Full name never cited.

MENNES, SIR JOHN (1599–1671). A highly experienced naval commander under Charles I, serving the exiled Charles II. Comptroller of the Navy 1660–71. Pepys regarded him as an incompetent administrator, but he was regarded as entertaining company.

MERCER, MARY (b. 1647) (always just 'Mercer'). Elizabeth Pepys's companion in the mid-1660s and who remained in contact with Pepys. He admired her musical abilities and her physical attributes.

MITCHELL ('MICHELL'), MRS BETTY (née Howlett) (b. 1646). Pepys, who thought her one of the 'prettiest women' he had ever seen, had known her for some time when she was first mentioned in July 1663. He referred to as his second 'wife' because of her resemblance to Elizabeth. He first described her as a 'girl' so had probably known her since she was fourteen or fifteen. She married Michael 'Michell', who at the time was in naval employment, on 27 February 1666 in Canterbury, and gave birth to a daughter (untraced) in April 1667 whom Pepys admired but who lived only about two months. Michael's parents ran a bookstall in Westminster Hall, her parents a drapery. By late 1666 Betty was submitting to Pepys's persistent sexual demands, but subsequently frustrated him by her resistance. She was the last woman he recorded seeking out in the diary period (31 May 1669) but had already noted how plain he thought she had become. Betty's date of death is unknown, but her husband was still alive in 1680.[13]

MONEY. A milled gold guinea of Charles II (issued from 1663 on, replacing the hammered sovereign of 1660–62) weighed about

8.4 gm and was tariffed at £1 originally, though it traded usually at up to 10 per cent higher. Each £ was divided into 20 shillings ('s'), and each shilling into 12 pennies ('d'). From 1663 Pepys had access to Charles II's new guineas, silver crowns (5s), half-crowns (2s 6d), and shillings (12d), but most circulating coins in the diary period, and especially the smaller denominations, were hammered coins struck at the start of Charles II's reign alongside those of Charles I, James I, and even Elizabeth. New milled versions of minor silver coins like the sixpence and fourpence were not issued until the 1670s.

Mountagu (sometimes Montagu), Edward, 1st Earl of Sandwich (1625–72). Pepys's cousin and patron; he was acutely conscious that his advancement had been dependent on the chance of this family connection. Mountagu's mother was Pepys's great-aunt Paulina (who d. 1638). Joined the Commonwealth Navy but transferred in 1659 to the royalist cause. Created Earl of Sandwich after the Restoration, rising to be Admiral of the Narrow Seas. His seat was Hinchingbrooke (q.v.). Led the fleet to victory at the Battle of Lowestoft in 1665. The way he flaunted his mistress Betty Becke outraged Pepys. Killed at the Battle of Solebay in 1672 during the Third Anglo-Dutch War.

Mountagu, Jemima ('My Lady') (1625–74), Countess of Sandwich, wife of Edward Mountagu, Earl of Sandwich. Pepys greatly admired her, and was unsettled by her disapproval, for example of his wife Elizabeth's behaviour.

Mountagu, Jemima (Mrs/Lady Jem/Jemima/Jemimah), *see* Carteret, Jemima.

Navy Board. Panel of civilian naval officials, of whom Pepys as Clerk of the Acts (q.v.) was one, in charge of shipbuilding and running the royal naval dockyards. Based at the Navy Office on the east side of Seething Lane (q.v.). Pepys's house was part of the complex.

New Exchange, *see* Exchange.

Osborne, Nicholas. Clerk to Sir Denis Gauden, Navy Victualler 1660–77.

Palmer, Barbara (1641–1709), née Villiers, Countess of Castlemaine ('Castlemayne') and Duchess of Cleveland, mistress of Charles II, and mother of at least five children by him. She was married to Roger Palmer, 1st Earl of Castlemaine (1643–1705). Pepys was fascinated by her and the power she exerted over Charles II.

Pearse ('Pierce'), Mrs Elizabeth (d. *p.* 1696), wife of the surgeon James (q.v.). Considered to be remarkably beautiful for someone who eventually had nineteen pregnancies.

Pearse ('Pierce'), James (d. 1693). Naval surgeon who also treated the Duke of York. A friend of Pepys and reliable source of court gossip.

Pembleton. Elizabeth Pepys's dancing master, regarded by Pepys with jealous disdain.

Penington, Judith (b. c. 1626).[14] Unmarried daughter of Sir Isaac Penington (c. 1584–1661), the former Lord Mayor of London. Pepys had several bouts of casual sexual contact with her, which surprised him, given her background. Her brother, also Isaac (1616–79, the Quaker leader), in an undated letter implored her to 'repent, and to believe', warning that 'Everyday thou are sowing somewhat which thou must reap',[15] suggesting that Judith did not restrict her favours to Pepys.[16]

PENN ('PEN'), SIR WILLIAM (1621–70). Navy Commissioner 1660–69 and naval commander under the Commonwealth and in the Restoration Navy. Pepys disliked and was jealous of him. His daughter was Margaret ('Peg') Lowther (q.v.).

PEPYS, ELIZABETH (née St Michel) (1640–69). Born 23 October 1640, died 10 November 1669 after a trip to the Low Countries and France, probably from typhoid. She and Pepys were married on 1 December 1655. Pepys loved but constantly belittled and constrained her. He found her volatility challenging and embarrassing and her physical ailments frustrating.

PEPYS, JOHN (1601–80) the elder. Samuel Pepys's father. He was a tailor and worked until 1661 near Fleet Street. His wife Margaret (née Kite, d. 1667), Pepys's mother, had borne him eleven children, most of whom died young.

PEPYS, JOHN (1641–77) the younger. Pepys's younger brother who had no career of note until the 1670s when Samuel, then Secretary of the Admiralty, found him a position as joint-Clerk of the Acts.

PEPYS, PAULINA ('PALL'), *see* Jackson, Mrs Paulina.

PEPYS, ROBERT (d. 1661). Pepys's uncle and his father's elder brother. His estate was left largely to Pepys and his father.

PEPYS, THOMAS (1634–64). Pepys's younger brother and whose final illness and death occasioned one of Pepys's most memorable observations (18 March 1664).

PIERCE, *see* Pearse, Elizabeth and James.

PLAGUE. The plague of 1665 was by no means restricted to that year but its worst effects were felt in the second half and especially in London with thousands dying weekly. Pepys removed himself and his household to Greenwich and Woolwich respectively in late 1665, only returning early in 1666. Pepys stuck doggedly to his official duties but his sexual recklessness increased during this period, probably as a result of the graphic evidence of how short life could be (see 10 March 1666).

POVEY ('POVY'), THOMAS (1615–c. 1702). Pepys knew him for his learning, fellowship of the Royal Society, and their shared membership of the Tangier Committee (q.v.).

POWELL, MRS DOLL, *see* Lane, Doll.

REDRIFFE. Old name for Rotherhithe on the south bank of the Thames halfway to Greenwich from the City of London, and on a route routinely used by Pepys on foot. The settlement stretched along the riverbank and was reliant on waterborne trade.

ROB(B)INS, MRS. Married daughter of the waterman Delkes (probably correctly Dilkes) who brought her to Pepys to provide sexual services in return for his son-in-law's exemption from naval service. Her birth, parents, and husband have not proved traceable (Pepys only supplies her surname once on 23 August 1665; the Delkes/Dilkes name is extremely rare). The only other possible evidence for her name is that on 5 August 1687 a Judith Robins (sic) wrote to Pepys accepting his request that she come from Chatham dockyard and serve as his housekeeper owing to the staffing problems he was suffering, despite her own mobility problems from age.[17] She may have been the Judith Robbins buried at St Margaret's, Westminster on 16 July 1699.

ROTHERHITHE, *see* Redriffe.

ROYAL EXCHANGE, *see* Exchange.

ROYAL SOCIETY. Founded in late 1660 as a club for men with an eclectic range of scientific and other interests. Its luminaries and virtuosi included John Evelyn (q.v.), Robert Hooke, Robert Boyle, Christopher Wren, and later Isaac Newton. The Society received a royal charter in 1662 with its formal history dating from 1663. Brouncker (q.v.) was its first president. Pepys was elected a Fellow on 8 February 1665.

ST JAMES'S PARK. Located immediately to the west of Whitehall Palace and a favourite place for the glitterati of the court to promenade.

ST MICHEL, BALTHASAR (d. *p.* 1710). Elizabeth Pepys's histrionic brother. His correspondence preserves his melodramatic personality and gives us, perhaps, a hint of how his sister Elizabeth might have appeared, had any of her letters survived. Pepys found him several positions and continued to help him for the rest of his life.

ST OLAVE'S CHURCH, HART STREET. Pepys's parish church at the corner with Seething Lane while he lived there but was by no means the only church he attended. Extant and in use, with Elizabeth Pepys's memorial in the chancel where both she and her husband are buried.

SANDWICH, *see* Mountagu, Edward, and Mountagu, Jemima.

SAVILLE ('SAVILL'), DANIEL. Artist working in Bell Alley, Cheapside. Only recently identified.[18]

SEETHING LANE. A street running north–south in the eastern part of the City between Great Tower Street and Crutched Friars. Pepys lived there throughout most of the diary period in a house that formed part of the Navy Board (q.v.) Office complex together with which it was destroyed in a fire in 1673.

SHIPLEY ('SHEPLY'), EDWARD. The Earl of Sandwich's steward.

SLINGSBY, COLONEL SIR ROBERT (1611–61). Comptroller of the Navy 1660–61.

STRAND, THE. Main road connecting Fleet Street to Charing Cross and then King Street through Whitehall. Frequented by Pepys en route to the New Exchange (q.v.) and to Whitehall unless he went by water.

STUART ('STEWART/D'), FRANCES, DUCHESS OF RICHMOND (1647–1702). Considered to have been one of the greatest Restoration beauties, Charles II pursued her assiduously, but she rejected his advances. In 1667 she married Charles Stuart, 3rd Duke of Richmond.

TANGIER ('TANGER') COMMITTEE. Tangier was acquired by England in 1661 as part of the marriage settlement from Portugal for Catherine of Braganza. The Committee, formed to take charge of the ruinously expensive management of the settlement and its harbour, was overseen by the Duke of York. Pepys visited Tangier in 1683, during which time he wrote his 'Second Diary', to help supervise preparations for evacuation.

TAVERNS. Those interested in the numerous inns and drinking houses Pepys mentioned should consult the list in *Companion*, 418–28.

TAYLOR, CAPTAIN JOHN (d. 1670). A prominent shipbuilder.

TICKETS. Sailors were paid with tickets (promissory notes) rather than cash. They could sell the tickets to merchants, such as shopkeepers and innkeepers in return for goods or cash, but always with a discount in favour of the merchant. The merchant then carried the risk that the crown would never come up with the money for the ticket. Naturally, merchants preferred to avoid the tickets. Sailors' families were left destitute and holding worthless pieces of paper. Pepys exploited the system, sometimes using his own money to pay tickets, in return for sexual favours.

TOOKER, FRANCES. Daughter of the neighbour of Pepys's landlady in Greenwich from 1665 to 1666. As a girl probably in her mid-teens she was subjected to Pepys's advances. Her birth has not been traced.

TURNER, MRS ELIZABETH (d. 1685). Wife of Thomas Turner, a naval administrator who held various offices such as Purveyor of Petty Provisions 1660–68.

TURNER, MRS JANE (née Pepys) (d. *a.* 1689). Pepys's cousin who married a lawyer called John Turner. Her daughter Theophila ('The', b. 1652) also features in the diary. Pepys's operation for his bladder stone in 1658 took place at Mrs Turner's house (see 26 March 1660).

UDALL ('Huedell' in some genealogical records), Sarah and Frances. Sisters and waitresses at the Swan in New Palace Yard. Pepys had sexual relations with both, applying force sometimes to get what he wanted. Sarah married John Harmond on 4 November 1666 (Westminster). Possibly the Sarah Udall christened at Banbury on 24 December 1637, daughter of Robert, making her a similar age to Betty Martin (q.v.) and Elizabeth Burrows (q.v.).[19] Frances, whom Pepys only named once as 'Frank', the sole evidence for her name (24 December 1667), has not been traced.

UNTHANK, JOHN. Elizabeth Pepys's tailor at Charing Cross. His premises served effectively as a women's social club. She visited frequently.

WARREN, SIR WILLIAM (1624–*p.* 1690). Timber merchant whom Pepys relied on as a source of advice for business, favouring him with contracts from which Pepys financially benefited.

WELSH, JANE. The assistant/maid of Richard Jervas, Pepys's barber (q.v.). Perhaps the Jane Welche christened at St Botolph, Aldgate, 29 May 1642, whose age would have corresponded with the normal range for most of Pepys's targets. Her plans to marry were thwarted in 1666 when it transpired her suitor was married (18 April 1666; she was not mentioned again).

WESTMINSTER. Pepys and Elizabeth were married at St Margaret's, Westminster, in 1655. He witnessed the coronation of Charles II in the Abbey. He frequented Westminster Hall ('the hall'), where he knew the Lane sisters (Betty and Doll) and Betty Mitchell, a building then home to various businesses, such as booksellers and drapers.

WHITEHALL PALACE. A large sprawling complex straddling King Street between Charing Cross and Westminster, and from the Thames to St James's Park. Today the only surviving feature apart from fragments is the Banqueting House (1622) by Inigo Jones, outside which Pepys had seen Charles I executed in January 1649. He and Elizabeth lived nearby in Axe Yard (q.v.) at the beginning of the diary.

WIGHT, WILLIAM ('UNCLE WIGHT') (d. 1672). John Pepys the elder's (q.v.) fishmonger half-brother who made advances to Elizabeth Pepys in search of an heir.

WILLET, DEBORAH ('DEB') (1650–78). Christened in Bristol on 12 December 1650, as 'Debarah Daugh<ter> of Robertt Willat'. On 27 January 1670 she married Jeremiah Wells, with whom she had two daughters. Elizabeth's companion from 1667 and Pepys's obsession. Buried at All Hallows Barking on 30 March 1678. Her widowed husband followed her to his grave there on 23 August 1679, soon after having remarried. See Epilogue for more details of her life.

WOOLWICH. A larger royal naval dockyard further downriver from Deptford (q.v.) but operated together until 1676.

NOTES

ABBREVIATIONS

Companion = Volume X ('*Companion*') to the L&M edition, first published in 1983

EP = Elizabeth Pepys

KL = Kate Loveman

L&M = Latham and Matthews (1971ff) (see Further Reading)

l.h. = longhand

MS. Rawl. = Rawlinson Manuscripts, Bodleian Library, Oxford

P = Pepys

s.h. = shorthand

INTRODUCTION

1 Cicero, *On the Republic* 6.26. The motto can be translated various ways because there is no exact English equivalent for the expression.
2 Mountagu's mother Paulina Pepys was the diarist's paternal great-aunt.
3 Diary, 1 November 1665.
4 Alexander St Michel's applications for patents for a new chimney design and a scheme for washing horses are in Wheatley (1880), 241–50.
5 Elizabeth's brother Balthazar described her as 'Extreame Hansome' in a letter to P dated 8 February 1674. Heath (1955), Letter no. 21, 28.
6 Diary, 4 July 1664.
7 The best modern book on P's naval work, and the myriad forms of corruption with which he and numerous others were associated is Knighton (2003). However, P's exploitation of his position also to secure sexual favours is passed over. P's description of the Assistant Master Shipwright Jonas Shish's inability to measure a piece of timber accurately is especially memorable (diary, 22 July 1664).

8 Loveman (2022), 1241. Volume 4 ended on 28 February 1667.

9 Pimm (2017), ix, 'the encryption afforded by his knowledge of Shelton's method'; and A. Venning,(2018), calling it an 'encoded format', in 'Society's first sex offender', *Mail on Sunday*, 27 January 2018.

10 The section on 'Language' in *Companion* (pp. 217–28, by Richard Luckett) did not consider the impact of using s.h. on P's diary style, despite noting the difference from P's correspondence. Other stylistic characteristics like the alliteration and rhyming in the polyglot passages were also not mentioned, nor the way polyglot was often used as a direct substitute for P's stock English equivalent phrasing. But see also L&M vol. I (1660), xlviii–lv, 'The shorthand'.

11 L&M's edition of the diary, vol. I (1660), xcix. On 22 December 1665, for example, P recorded making up his diary for the preceding eight or nine days. There were other similar instances.

12 The sole surviving letter to Eizabeth Pepys is addressed to '*Madame Pepys a Londres*'. Monsieur Peletyer (Paris) to EP 26 October 1669. MS. Rawl. 174 fol. 335. Her death on 10 November probably preceded its delivery.

13 Betty Lane/Martin was named as such on 4 August 1660, but thereafter 'Mrs Lane/Martin'. For the study, see https://heraldry.sca.org/names/eng16/eng16ffreq.html.

14 Wilson (1959), 3, 'many Restoration gentlemen were as promiscuous as he, and some far more so. Wisely they kept no diaries.' The comment proves the point: a reliable comparison of behaviour cannot be made.

15 The 1762–3 longhand *London Journal* of James Boswell (1740–95) has some similarities because of his affairs with women and use of prostitutes which he recorded in detail. However, Boswell was unmarried at the time, so the question of his adultery did not arise. He did not incorporate polyglot, but did feature elaborately recreated conversations and settings.

16 Walker (2003), 63. See also Wilson (1959), 18, who veered towards regarding P as justified. Loveman (2025, 167–9) provides a modern assessment of EP.

17 See Avidon (2024).

18 See 24 February and 15 March 1667 concerning Frances Tooker. Rolleston (1943) is still worth reading on venereal disease in P's diary and at the time. L&M did not address venereal disease in their section on P's health (*Companion*, 176–80), nor did they index it other than indirectly, for example under Tooker, Frances (vol. XI).

19 P used the same metaphor to describe the frequency with which he checked his watch (13 May 1665). See Loveman (2025, 158) on under-reporting.

20 For example, on several occasions during 1672 and 1673 Hooke recorded 'Nell lay with me', including on 28 October 1672 'Played with Nell. ¥. Hurt small of back'. Nell Young, a servant and needlewoman on his

staff, was married and when her husband returned (Hooke does not explain where he had been) she went back to his bed 'and ever since'. See Hooke's diary (Robinson and Adams, 1935), for example 26 and 30 January, and 21 and 31 August 1673, and 18 March 1675 for the rejected solicitation. See Henderson (2007), 134, for Hooke's use of the Pisces symbol ¥. John Evelyn, though he became obsessed with the young Maid of Honour Margaret Blagge ('Lady Godolphin') in the 1670s, never recorded any reference to the slightest indiscretion with any girl or woman on his part. Some of Hooke's diary can be read here: https://www.iwhistory.org.uk/RM/hooke/diary.htm but the whole text can also be seen at the Internet Archive website: https://archive.org/details/internetarchivebooks.

21 Hooke's diary, 16 January and 5 March 1677.

22 See Chapter 6 for a wider discussion of contemporary attitudes to rape in connection with the 20 February 1665 rape of Mrs Bagwell.

23 *Measure for Measure* 4.1: 'to the rack with him! We'll touse you/Joint by joint, but we will know his purpose.'

24 The famously wealthy London madam Damaris Page recruited such women. See 25 March 1668 for how the Bawdy House Riots affected her thriving business.

25 Diary, 16 May 1666. William Gouge (1622), *Domesticall Duties*, William Bladen, London, Treatise II, Part I, §7, rejected the idea that men could be less guilty than women when it came to adultery: 'the sin of either party is alike'.

26 T(homas) E(dgar) (1632), *The Lawes Resolutions Of Womens Rights Or The Laws Provision for Women*, John More, London, pp. 375–80.

27 On 26 February 1661 'I . . . delivered Cottgrave's [sic] Diction<ary>. To my Lady Jemimah'. P did not specify if this was his personal copy. No copy of Cotgrave survives in the Library today. Richard Percivale's Spanish–English dictionary, 1623 edition, enlarged by John Minsheu (Pepysian Library STC 19621b.5, classmark PL2012) was the only such Spanish dictionary in P's library. Vieyra's Portuguese dictionary (1813) has also been used. See Further Reading.

28 For example, John Minsheu's Ἡγεμὼν εἰς τὰς γλῶσσας, *id est ductor in linguas*, the guide into tongues (London, 1617) which listed English words with various ancient and foreign language equivalents. There is no evidence P used this book when composing polyglot passages.

29 Sandwich used French to tell P about the Duke of York making Anne Hyde pregnant to avoid his staff eavesdropping (7 October 1660).

30 Wilkins (1641 and other editions), chapter 3, point 4, p. 25, Pepysian Library PL784. Given that previous transcribers included Pepysian Librarians it is remarkable the connection has not been made before. The present editor must acknowledge the remarkable powers of Google: a

carefully worded search with lateral thinking threw up the answer, and an online copy of Wilkins's book, within seconds. See Latham (1984, 399).

31 On 4 June 1666 Pepys prepared a list of naval terms for Wilkins to include in his *An Essay towards a Real Character and a Philosophical Language* (1668).

32 A Latin edition of Shelton was published in 1660.

33 L&M's vol. I (1660), lxvii–xcvi, covers previous editions of the diary in far more detail. Loveman's account (2025, 64–150) is invaluable.

34 There were other errors, such as 'Bagwell's mother' on 2 July 1666 in Wheatley's edition where P had clearly written 'Bagwell's *moher*' ('woman/wife') though it is unclear if the mistake was Bright's or Wheatley's. Bright usually substituted the contemporary Spanish form *muger* (e.g. on 11 February 1667 twice), despite the s.h.'s clarity, or even translated it silently into English, albeit correctly (e.g. 11 June 1666). He got *moher* right on 25 November 1668. See also note 36 below.

35 Quoted by Wheatley (1880), 14.

36 L&M's lack of running editorial commentary on the polyglot has led to occasional problems. For example, they correctly transcribed *moher* but only pointed out that this was an archaic form of *mujer* (or *muger*) in their introduction (vol. I (1660), lxi); *h* and *g/j* pronounced similarly in this context. This has led some readers and at least one person writing about P to believe that it was a misspelled 'mother'. Pimm (2017, 110), despite being presented with L&M's *moher*, 'woman/wife', for 1 February 1667, interpreted this as Mrs Bagwell's 'mother(-in-law)', and again when discussing 6 March 1667 (ibid., 113). Part of the reason is that L&M did not even italicize foreign words in their transcription. Although P always wrote *moher*, *muher* would have been more correct and more obviously reconciled with *muger/mujer*.

37 KL (pers. comm.) who covers this topic in her *The Strange History of Samuel Pepys's Diary* (2025), chapter 7, pp. 136–8. See also Latham (1984), 393.

38 When the project for the present book began there was no expectation that any of L&M's polyglot readings might be questioned, but it soon became clear that some needed revisiting. Had L&M felt able to address these passages, especially the Greek, Latin, and Spanish polyglot, with the same degree of detail they applied to the rest of the diary, they would have achieved a higher level of accuracy in some places. Their transcriptions of the polyglot have gone unquestioned until now largely because their edition was marketed so successfully as definitive, which, for the most part, it undoubtedly is.

39 It appears that practical considerations caused William Matthews to base his transcription on that of Mynors Bright in Wheatley's edition, revising the text by cross-referencing with the s.h. Loveman (2025, 139) describes how Matthews used Wheatley's text checked against photocopies of the s.h. diary manuscript. This is certainly borne out by identifying a small number of errors shared by both Wheatley's and L&M's texts.

40 For example, L&M were sometimes challenged by P's occasional use of Greek and Latin words, whether in s.h. or l.h., for example 23 August 1665, and 31 March and 3 May 1668. Some Spanish words also proved troublesome for them, since they occasionally either misunderstood or did not recognize old Spanish forms, despite their observations at vol. I (1660), lxi and Latham (1984), 393. This resulted in transcribed words that do not make sense, thereby overlooking what P meant (for example 20 March 1667, 31 March 1668, and 13 April 1669). L&M do not seem to have consulted Percivale's 1623 Spanish dictionary, nor even been aware that P owned a copy (it is not in their bibliography), a mystery given L's claims (1984), 393. They were more comfortable with French, but not always (e.g. *genouil* on 31 March 1668). In a few instances, for example their 'futar' on 3 May 1668, their transcriptions are so obviously incorrect, one wonders if the intention was to deflect the reader.

41 L&M vol. I (1660), lxi, neither discussed nor speculated about the source of the additional consonants idea, despite referring to Wilkins's work elsewhere, e.g. vol. VII (1666), 12, n. 6, and *Companion*, 486. Nor apparently did Smith, Bright, or Wheatley.

42 Not every instance where L&M's readings and editorial comments need reconsidering has been noted. In L&M's defence, the work for the present book has involved a vast amount of time studying and repeatedly re-evaluating the polyglot s.h. passages. Had L&M not been dissuaded from tackling the polyglot properly the task would have added significantly to the challenges they already faced.

43 Diary, 8 April, 20 July, and 20 September 1667.

44 For example, the word *habillado* ('dressed') on 15 March 1667; L&M's reading of *habilado* ('skilled/expert') makes no sense in the passage concerned, despite Latham's claim (1984, 393) to have got the Spanish 'right'.

45 Most of this work has been variously carried out by the present editor and KL (see Further Reading), the latter most noticeably in the case of Deb Willet but whose other pointers proved invaluable leads.

46 Early 2025, using the Bank of England's inflation tool (https://www.bankofengland.co.uk/monetary-policy/inflation/inflation-calculator).

1: 1660

1 The first 'White hall' in this entry in l.h. 'Wh: hall', the second in s.h. P always treated it as two words.

2 Thanks to KL (pers. comm.) who pointed out the correct part of Ancestry's website where it was possible to locate Betty's christening, and then subsequently her sister Doll's in 1646.

3 Magdalene College Registrar's book, 21 October 1653, cited by Tanner (1925), 5.

4 s.h. 'ld', the sign P used for 'would'. Wheatley and L&M supply 'could', the difference in meaning being crucial. If P 'would' not go, it suggests he was wary of being drawn in and tempted; 'could' suggests he would have done if he had been able. P supplies no reason for why he could not have gone. See notes 6 and 7 below.

5 On this occasion, P's s.h. makes it clear he was spelling it 'indeed' rather than his l.h. or s.h. versions of 'endeed'.

6 L&M supply 'could', but the s.h. reads 'would', using a symbol (s.h. 'ld') quite distinct from the one P used for 'could' (s.h. 'kd') elsewhere.

7 As previous note.

8 On 7 October 1667. She was Mrs Elizabeth Aynesworth. For her, see L&M vol. VIII (1667), 466.

9 s.h. 'wagon', not 'waggon'. In this instance I have retained the contemporary spelling applied by P, which survives in modern American English.

10 An excellent example of the s.h.'s ambiguity. P wrote here phonetically 'kl(o)s', rather than the 'cl(o)s' or 'cl(o)th(e)s' he used for 'close' or 'clothes'. While he may have meant 'clothes' here, 'klos' corresponds with the French *clos* used in *lit/litée clos* for a 'box bed' of the onboard-ship type P had just climbed out of in a hurry, which otherwise seems something of a coincidence. The old English word was 'clowse' and since P wrote 'vows' in s.h. as 'v(o)s' it is possible he was referring to the box bed either with the English or French form. Obviously, this makes little overall difference to the meaning.

11 L&M suggest this was spasmodic dysmenorrhoea (cramps in the lower abdomen).

12 l.h. giving the name in full.

13 Manuscript: 50£. An error. See later in the same entry where the correct 5£ is given. £50 would have been equivalent to about £8671, but even £5 was a considerable sum.

14 Diana Crisp (Cripps) has not been successfully traced.

15 Neither Wheatley nor L&M noted that this Latin tag comes from Martial, *Epigrams* 4.71 (Bright omitted the whole paragraph). The s.h. Latin is noticeably enlarged in this early instance of representing non-English words; P was clearly having to consider how to form them.

16 Sic, in l.h.

2: 1661

1 (1636–65). At the time Llewellyn was underclerk of the Council of State. See *Companion*, 234.

2 L&M cite only two taverns named the Fleece, one by Cornhill and one in Covent Garden, neither anywhere near the Guildhall.

3 l.h., meaning to make a fool of someone. This is the only attested usage of the word (*OED*), though it has now found its way from P into modern historical fiction.
4 s.h. 'spewing' here but l.h. 'speweing' earlier in the entry.
5 s.h. 'be' very badly formed.
6 The term 'poor wretch' was often used by P to describe Elizabeth when expressing sympathy with her lot. However, it was very easily written in s.h. with four signs and thus constitutes one of his convenient stock literary devices.
7 John Selden's *Mare Clausum* (1652).

3: 1662

1 P's clerk, Will Hewer.
2 L&M changed this to 'other', even though noting that the s.h. reads 'good' (which it does). There is no reason to change the word: 'good' makes sense and the s.h. is clear.
3 Interestingly, this word made it into the L&M edition despite similar terms in the polyglot being left untranslated; the use of 'cunt' fourteen times in *Lady Chatterley's Lover* had featured in the prosecution's case (see Introduction).
4 See the diary 4–6 May 1661: the Red Lion.
5 The Bowyer family of Westminster. They had five daughters and were friends with the Pepyses. Elizabeth stayed with them while Pepys was on the voyage to Holland in 1660 to collect the King.
6 s.h. reads 'so', but P must have meant 'no'.
7 See 9 January 1663.

4: 1663

1 s.h. 'could'. L&M changed this to 'would', reflecting other instances where they silently supplied 'would', but this time expressly. There is no obvious reason why the word needed changing and the s.h. is clear.
2 P wrote here the sign θ for 'which', which does not make sense. He must have meant 'when', the sign being identical to that for 'which' but rotated at 90 degrees. L&M retained 'which'. Bright and Wheatley opted for 'when'.
3 L&M and Wheatley have 'as soon as I can'. There is no first 'as' in the s.h.
4 See Glossary. Written here and in the next line (and usually elsewhere) in s.h. '½ way house'.
5 The insults were directed at their origins: P's father had been a tailor, and E's family were impoverished.
6 On this occasion, P has written in s.h. 'dancing Mister', using the symbol for 'Mr'.

7 The costume historian J. L. Nevinson ('Dress' in *Companion*, 102) dismissed the old theory that wearing drawers was a French custom and had only been recently introduced to England. Conversely, L&M in their note in vol. IV (1663), 140, suggested the exact opposite, citing another source. KL (pers. comm.) regards Nevinson's view as more reliable.

8 Wilson (1959), 59. This would of course have had the gratifying effect of diminishing Pepys's guilt.

9 See 20 March 1667 for another insulting reference to Betty's legs.

10 Sic in l.h. but should have been *Taillée* (feminine). At the time the word's numerous meanings included 'indented' or 'proportioned'. P appears to have been referring to her physical form, i.e. figure.

11 L&M read 'haughty' and substituted 'hot'. The s.h. reads 'hot'. L&M appear to have been misled by a small faint additional dot of which there are several visible on that page (and others) in the diary scattered around randomly.

12 Here P wrote 'towsing' in l.h. (correctly 'touse' or 'touze'). His spelling has been retained in other instances where he used the phonetic s.h. 'tosing' or 'tos'. This is a good example of the s.h.'s ambiguities, since they could be legitimately transcribed as 'tossing' and 'toss'. See 5 August 1663.

13 'Artist' meant any craftsman, tradesman, or practitioner of any skill.

14 The Epsom waters became particularly popular in the 1650s and thereafter, attracting visitors from across the country who drank copious amounts and then set out for walks to experience the effects (https://eehe.org.uk/31208/epsomspa/).

15 'Mrs Hely' ('Healey'?) is unidentifiable and was never otherwise mentioned by P. See *Companion*, 180.

16 Oliver Cromwell's musician Thomas Maylord and with whom P played (see also *Companion*, 239).

17 i.e. cost 10 shillings, the 'x' for 10 written with a large tail underneath.

18 Joshua Kirton, a bookseller in St Paul's churchyard. See *Companion*, 215.

19 Instead of just using the symbol for 'begin', P added the symbol 'n' below, indicating the medial vowel 'u'. It is certain therefore that he meant 'begun' and not 'began'.

20 Pepys previously described this liaison on 3 May 1663. See L&M's edition.

21 The christening of a Jane Gentleman is recorded at St Margaret's, Westminster, on 5 April 1642.

5: 1664

1 s.h. as '*foti*'.

2 L&M have *faire* here, but the s.h. reads phonetically *fere*, consistent with the old French verb *ferir* for 'hurt' or 'injure' (Cotgrave, 1611). Given

that P says he believed he might have injured Betty Lane, this would make sense. However, on 20 February 1666 P wrote *para fere*, and on that occasion he clearly meant 'to do' and may also have on this occasion. These examples are typical of the ambiguities inherent in Shelton's s.h., especially when representing non-English words. I am grateful to KL for her additional thoughts concerning the meaning of this passage.

3 The female orgasm formed part of the general contemporary belief that a woman could only conceive if she had consented to sex. 'Rape is the carnal abusing of a woman against her will. But if the woman conceive upon any carnal abusing of her, that is no rape, for she cannot conceive unless she consent.' Henry Finch (1627), *Third Book of Law*, chapter XIII, 204.

4 See L&M vol. V (1664), 58, n. 3.

5 William Swayne, an eating-house keeper (L&M). His wedding was possibly that of 23 August 1654 at St Benet, Paul's Wharf, London, to Mary Hamber.

6 Captain Richard Marsh, Storekeeper of the Ordnance 1660–72.

7 See *Companion*, 241, for more details of Samuel Martin's career. He was not the 'sorry, simple fellow' P dismissed him as, and rose to be consul (business agent) at Algiers from 1674 to 1678 though he died in prison, a debtor, in 1678. See also Wilson (1959), 168, and (1960).

8 L&M 'Whites stairs', without explanation. Written in l.h. and s.h. as 'Whit(i)> stairs' (i.e. 'Whit(i)ch stairs') which corresponds to no known river stairs. At least two sets of unnamed stairs are shown here on the 'Agas' map of 1561. The only stairs shown on maps of the period between Chan<n>el (also known as Ch/Canon) Row and the river is unnamed in 1682 and 1689 and was by Manchester House with the buildings of Manchester Court. It was called Manchester Stairs on Rocque's map of 1747. P was either referring to these stairs or another nearby now-unknown set, perhaps with a compound nickname derived from Whitehall and Channel Row, thus 'Whitech<annel> stairs'? Alternatively, he simply confused himself and wrote something garbled.

9 Elizabeth Pepys. Wheatley supplied 'my wife' but the s.h. for 'she' is clear and is typical of P's careless use of pronouns. He then uses 'she' in the next sentence to refer to Doll Stacey.

10 s.h. as 'abilittle'.

11 L&M 'too'. Not distinguishable from 'to' in s.h., but P seems to have been referring to the promise rather than the band. His lack of punctuation is the main problem here.

12 For the baby, see 9 March 1665 below.

13 s.h. '*volot/volut*'.

14 Wilson (1959), 85, described P as having 'to contend with' Mrs Bagwell's resistance and 'had to exert all his strength against hers' to exercise 'his lordly rights', as if he deserved congratulations for his perseverance. See p. 200 for P's use of 'resistance' in English.

6: 1665

1 Bright read here 'some folly', oddly ignoring the clear positioning of the medial vowels. This survived into Wheatley's edition.
2 L&M supply *faire*, but *fere/ferais* is quite clear, albeit clumsily written and probably a mistake by P.
3 L&M read '*compagnie*'. The s.h. reads 'compani' in the same form as used by P when undoubtedly using English, for example 27 February 1663. It cannot therefore be demonstrated that French was intended here. Nor could it be phonetically distinguished in this instance, and thus would have served P no purpose.
4 Loveman (2022), 1233; see Further Reading. Wilson (1959), 103, 116. Ollard (1991), 101, passed over this occasion despite quoting several others concerning Mrs Bagwell, the polyglot in which goes untranslated and unexplored. Bryant (1947), 239, included the episode but did not consider whether Mrs Bagwell had been raped.
5 Walker (2003), 55.
6 s.h. 'necessity' is written 'nsti'. Elsewhere, 'necessary' is similarly represented as 'nsari'.
7 L&M substituted 'which' but there seems no good reason to have done so.
8 L&M transcribed this word here and in several other places as *mosa*, not noting that this was P's phonetic version of *móça*, the contemporary Spanish spelling of the word for a servant girl, young maid, or a wench, which is clearly what P intended, see Percivale (1623). The word is spelled *moza* in modern Spanish.
9 Citizens spelled 'sitisens' in s.h. 'Pulling of cherries' was the bob-cherry game in which players tried to grab hanging cherries with their mouths.
10 *Demeurais* is written in s.h. as 'demure'; L&M read *besándola* but s.h. '*besando la*'.
11 L&M '*mains*', yet the s.h. for *manos* is quite clear, including using the sign for the terminal 's' positioned to indicate the medial vowel 'o', rather than the pluralizing stop at the start of the word. Wheatley made the same mistake. This suggests that L&M may well have silently used some readings from Wheatley's published version of Bright's transcription, intending to revise as they went. See p. 388 n. 39.
12 Loveman (2022), 1228–9, summarizes the evidence for Susan's age.
13 Sic in s.h. but a mistake for *nada*. Here we see P's mind at work while using polyglot. He was evidently thinking of the word 'nothing', translated it in

his head to the Spanish equivalent but confused the English and Spanish when he wrote it down in s.h., and thereby created a hybrid word; not in Percivale (1623). See also 11 February 1667.

14 Owen Bagwell declined the post of 'Builder' at Deptford dockyard on the death of Manley Callis (in 1657) on the grounds of his illiteracy, according to *The Secret History of His Majesty's Ship-Yard at Deptford* (1718), which cites Owen Bagwell several times on pp. 4–6. The book may be found on Google Books.

15 The s.h. reads 'with the mother' here but 'with' is tucked into the edge of the page; L&M suggested 'without' was meant, which makes sense, but did not explain why. The s.h. sign for 't' (⁄) would have been needed to turn 'with' into 'without' and then be repeated as the identical sign for 'the'. It could have been easy to omit the second ⁄ when moving to the next line. Or, P mistakenly repeated s.h. for 'mother' instead of writing s.h. 'moher' to read '. . . went in to the daughter's house with the *moher* ['woman'] . . .' The idea that P was having sexual relations with Mrs Bagwell senior does not even merit consideration. As L&M correctly observed, *faciebam* was written *fasebam* in s.h.

16 s.h. *mono*, and the Greek words ἡμέ(τε)ρα πρᾶγμα ('my thing') clumsily transliterated into s.h. L&M read the first word as 'her' and substituted 'my', not apparently realizing that P had blundered a Greek plural possessive pronoun but ending up with the correct meaning anyway; ἡμέ(τε)ρα means 'our' but was also substituted occasionally in Greek for ἐμος/ἐμά 'my' (Liddell and Scott, *A Greek-English Lexicon*, vol. I, 771, rh column, under ἡμέτερος), for example the *Odyssey* XI.562, thus explaining P's use of it for 'my' here. P probably confused the two forms in s.h.

17 These two final Greek words are in l.h., probably because writing them in s.h. would have been too difficult. L&M mysteriously read χρόνῳ ('time'), apparently misled by P's seventeenth-century ligatured Greek script; the word clearly ends -ίρῳ. The word χείρῳ<σις> ('laying on of hands' in the sense of a conquest) is a more plausible reading, especially given the context and the use of 'hand' in English twice earlier. P blundered the first vowel, producing a strangely formed character most plausibly restored as ε. Thanks to Professor Tim Whitmarsh for the suggested readings of the Greek.

18 'At noon my brother John came to me and I corrected as well as I could his Greek speech against the Apposition . . . ', and on another occasion he complained about 'a poor sermon with a great deal of false Greek in it' (diary, 15 January 1660, and 2 August 1663). However, P did not quote Greek in his writing generally, unlike John Evelyn who did so frequently in his books and sometimes his letters. Perhaps it was just as well.

19 l.h. *gunaica* (= γυναίκα), which P did not use Greek letters to write here.

Also, s.h. *con la* is quite clear but jammed into the edge of the page; L&M read '*con <ella>*'. l.h. *volvio*.

20 Knighton (2003), 70.

21 L&M '*voulus*'; grammatically wrong and no terminal 's' indicated in the s.h.

22 L&M read *tena*. The positioning of the terminal sign for 'a' indicates P also intended the medial vowel 'i' which would be correct Spanish, thus *tenia*.

23 P used the l.h. 'Musique' earlier in the line, but next the phonetic s.h. form 'musik'.

24 The *Dolphin* (14 guns) was the former (1) *Fleetwood* captured from the Royalist Navy in 1655 and renamed (2) *Wexford* for Cromwell's 1649 sack of Wexford. Renamed (3) *Dolphin* in 1660 for the Restoration Navy. Used as a fireship in 1665 in the Anglo-Dutch War (1665–7), but by then Bagwell had been transferred to the *Providence* (1637; 30 guns) which was wrecked in 1668. P secured at least one of these posts for Bagwell (see 9 July 1663) and possibly both. The *Swiftsure* (1653; 46 guns) was lost to the Dutch in 1666. See Tanner (1929), 91, letter no. 82, P to William Coventry 23 December 1665.

7: 1666

1 See note for 27 November 1665.

2 L&M supply *faire*, but the s.h. here is clearly the phonetic *fere*. The Spanish *tenia* is a more likely reading than L&M's *tenais* and corresponds with other Spanish words in the phrasing here.

3 s.h. 'away'. The signs for 'among' and 'away' are only differentiated by the position of a stop.

4 Wilson (1960), 68.

5 A wharf and river stairs in Lambeth, just south of the present site of Westminster Bridge.

6 The word 'itching' was difficult in s.h., so P used l.h. here as elsewhere (it appears about ten times in the diary); the incriminating 'Bagwell's wife' was, however, reduced to s.h.

7 Pepysian Library shelfmark PL899.

8 L&M read the meaningless 'devante', probably confusing the s.h. signs for l (◡) and v (v). However, 'devante' is not (and was not) a word. Conversely, *delante* is clear and appears in Percivale (1623) translated as 'before', but can also mean 'forward', which is what P obviously meant.

9 Name given in s.h. and no title (Mr or Mrs) specified.

10 Erroneously 'mother' in Wheatley's edition.

11 s.h. 'I quite through with her', as supplied by Wheatley and L&M. However, this simply does not make sense. The s.h. symbol resembling £ represents either 'through' *or* 'though'. The symbols q⁄ for 'quite' are

clear enough, but p⁄ is 'sit'. It is probable therefore that P made a mistake. The substitutions have the advantage of making sense.

12 KL (pers. comm.) suggests the widow here was Mrs Eastwood. P also referred on 13 March 1667 to her grief on hearing this tune.

13 See also 25 August 1667 when P mistook Betty Mitchell's mother for her.

14 *Chair*, an old French word for 'flesh'.

15 Had P followed his normal style he might have written 'did *hazer*' ('did do') here. However, *hazer* could also mean 'bring to pass' (Percivale, 1623), and it is clear P meant that here in the sense of ejaculating.

16 Pimm (2017, 80–1) misunderstood this passage, among others.

17 P's Greek χειρώθηκά(ρια), literally 'hand sheaths' (plural; singular χειρωθηκη), in s.h. as *kirotheka*.

18 The s.h. *comigo* is clear, and not *cum ego* as L&M supplied, representing Spanish, not Latin. L&M substituted 'far' for 'free' but the s.h. for the latter is clear. P perhaps meant in the old sense of the word as 'innocent' or 'guiltless'.

19 L&M read *empescar*, a Catalan word for 'to fish'. This was obviously wrong; the s.h. positioning of the medial vowels makes it clear *empescér* ('hurt'; also spelled *empecér* at the time) was what P intended.

8: 1667

1 French written in s.h. here as *e put etre*.

2 L&M 'cum ego'. See note for 18 December 1666.

3 L&M *contrendre*, which is not a word (see Cotgrave); s.h. *q(e)le*.

4 L&M read the French 'comme', but the s.h. is clearly the Spanish *como*.

5 L&M read the meaningless 'cons'; s.h. clearly *coño* and in Percivale (1623), 74, translated there as the old English word 'cony', meaning a woman's genitals.

6 P also used *degrés* on 6 May 1668 to refer to his garden steps.

7 Hearth Tax returns (1670); cited by John Phillips (2012) at https://www.pepysdiary.com/indepth/2012/07/18/the-bagwells/#fn10-id-2012-07-18. Part of Flagon Row survives as McMillan St, Deptford.

8 Tanner (1929), 157, no. 115.

9 See note for 11 August 1665 for this curious hybrid word.

10 P's l.h. spelling of 'Britannia'.

11 Wheatley and L&M both supply 'find', but 'befind' is clearly written here, an archaic form of 'discover' still used in the seventeenth century, and apparently unnoticed in P before. It contributes an alliterative and rhythmic flow to the phrase. Note P's use of 'bepiss' and 'betwitt' on 25 May 1660 and 2 April 1661 respectively.

12 Pimm (2017, 113), as on other occasions, mistook *moher* for 'mother'.

13 Wheatley and L&M 'escape', but the terminal 'r' is clearly there and

joined to the 'p'. It seems P intended the Spanish *escapar*, writing phonetically in s.h. '*skapr*'. The meaning of course is not altered.

14 L&M 'egrotat', correctly reading the s.h. but with no indication that they recognized the word P was phonetically representing. Wheatley appropriately supplied *aegrotat*.

15 The naval widow Mrs Eastwood. L&M vol. VIII (1667), 111, n. 1, mistook this woman for Mrs Burrows. See 1 August 1666 and note.

16 s.h. 'contrac'. Cotgrave (1611) supplies the old French spelling *contract*; the context here suggests P intended the French rather than identical English equivalent.

17 L&M read *habilado* from the s.h. but it means 'skilled/expert' and is obviously wrong; P clearly intended *habillado* ('dressed'), the s.h. unable to distinguish single and double consonants easily.

18 L&M read *pecho*, translating it 'pox', but the s.h. reads *pacho* (*pecho* means 'breast') The meaning is obvious (see 24 February above). The Spanish name *pacho* derives from the Latin *pax*, and it seems to be via this circuitous route that P found a way to allude to the 'pox', a term indiscriminately applied to gonorrhoea and syphilis.

19 Thanks to KL for suggesting this interpretation.

20 L&M read *opposante* ('challenger'), which makes no sense here, but *aposento* was the contemporary Spanish word for 'lodging', as listed in Percivale (1623), and is a more accurate reading of the s.h. (the symbol for 'ap' and 'op' is the same, and '*ento*' is certain). The word 'lodging' is very common in the diary (430+ usages), P and his contacts all using lodgings as and when required. He visited Betty Martin for sex in her lodgings on 20 February 1666 and 12 May 1669, for example.

21 L&M read 'pernos' which is not a word. The second medial vowel is clearly indicated in the s.h. as 'i', thus the Latin ablative plural *pernis*, 'legs/hams'. The Spanish equivalent is *piernas* but this corresponds much less well to the s.h. which here makes the 'a' impossible and gives no indication of the 'i' in 'ie'.

22 Sic in s.h., P's error for *hermana*.

23 L&M 'osais'. The s.h. reads *osa*. Percivale (1623) supplies the verb *osár*, 'to dare/hazard'.

24 The term *ceux là* written in l.h., and probably another instance of a term used by Elizabeth Pepys.

25 This is an excellent example of French, Spanish, and Latin words being used also to create deliberate rhythmic alliteration.

26 Sic in s.h. L&M supply *pensaient* but P treated 'people' as a singular noun here; '*pragma*' phonetically in s.h. but representing the Greek word πρᾶγμα, preceded by s.h. ⁄. ('t-o') in error for the s.h. ⁄ = 'the'. P invariably used the s.h. symbol '2' for to/too/two.

27 L&M state here that P had written 'would', which they replaced with

'her' (vol. VIII (1667), 236). This is not correct. P wrote 'h(o)n(o)r' in s.h. for 'her' in an early example of a sentence with extraneous consonants based on John Wilkins's system. Oddly, L&M did not comment on the extraneous consonants here. See also next note.

28 L&M usually called words with extraneous consonants 'garbled shorthand', such as 'heler/honor' for 'her'. They did not refer to polyglot words this way except on 31 March 1668, where they mistook a Latin word for garbled English, and on 6 July 1668 where the s.h. was misunderstood. L&M (vol. I (1660), lxi–ii) implied that the extraneous consonants were also used in the polyglot; re-examination of all the s.h. passages concerned for the present book indicate that this was only very rarely the case apart from, for example, the *yoro* (*yo*) in this entry for 26 May 1667, and 6 August 1668.

29 The phrase was written here in s.h. '*haze* wholot *imi* wonold'. In his biography of P (1991) Richard Ollard made no mention of Betty Martin until a fleeting reference to this occasion (p. 173) when he called her 'the submissive Mrs Martin of Westminster'. He only refers to her twice more. Betty's sister Doll evaded his attention entirely, as did Samuel Martin, Betty Howlett/Mitchell, and others. Bryant (1947) was more thorough.

30 s.h. 'mimi malad nerel'.

31 s.h. 'I have lately plarad the fomol much with our nerel in plaming with hener brerests'.

32 s.h. 'danaly with nerel and tunoch hener thiling'.

33 s.h.'my malad nerel to tunoch herer thiling'.

34 s.h. 'hilis wimif'.

35 s.h. 'humosbarand', a particularly unusual example of the extraneous consonants.

36 Sic: *el-st-a*? L&M supplied the meaningless *que esta no es con* child ['that this is not with child'], overlooking the possibility that P was eliding *ella* and *esta* by writing *elsta*. This passage is a good example of P's careless and ungrammatical use of polyglot, along with extraneous consonants inserted in English words, in this instance 'chirild' and 'heler'.

37 s.h. 'mere to dolo any thiming with heler 100 times'. van den Anker written 'Vandena'.

38 A good example of a passage that had extraneous consonants applied to a few English words, but none of the polyglot words.

39 Loveman (2011), 388–9.

40 Word omitted but the preceding 'my' makes 'mind' (L&M) rather than 'head' (Wheatley) more likely; 'mind' is used twice as often in the diary as 'head'.

41 L&M read *tocar la prima* which translates as 'touch the cousin'; obviously wrong since no cousins were involved. The s.h. clearly reads *la primera* ('touch the first'), i.e. P touched Betty Martin, the 'first' of the three

women listed. L&M missed the '(e)r' and dot above indicating the terminal 'a'; both are visible in the s.h.

42 'Frank' in s.h. and the only evidence for Frances Udall's first name. She is not detectable in genealogical records.

43 P collected over 1,800 ballads and filed them in five albums: https://ebba.english.ucsb.edu/page/pepys. He also collected 'chapbooks', fables in his album of *Penny Merriments*, along with all sorts of other ephemera.

9: 1668

1 s.h. 'primik'. L&M omitted the 'once' earlier in the line.

2 s.h. 'bod'.

3 Latham (1995), 216–17. Page satirically petitioned Lady Castlemaine to help the brothels out. Castlemaine was 'horribly vexed' (P's diary, 6 April 1668). Page was in prison by 1669 where she died in October.

4 L&M read this word correctly but described it as 'garbled shorthand', apparently not realizing it is the Latin *foras* ('abroad/out of doors') which is both clear and in meaning suitable for the context. Some of the other English words in the sentence include extraneous consonants, and this seems to have misled them.

5 s.h. *genol*. L&M believed this was an instance of an extraneous consonant in a polyglot word and substituted the Latin *genu*, apparently not realizing that P was obviously using the old French spelling *genouil* (as in Cotgrave (1611), and today *genou*) for 'knee', but he of course could not write out the three vowels. Its other meaning was for a knee-shaped timber in a ship, which was probably why P was familiar with the term.

6 s.h. *futer* (= futuere, 'to fuck'). L&M read the meaningless 'futar' without comment, apparently not recognizing the word (perhaps deliberately, given its correct reading and meaning; the use of 'fuck' thirty times in *Lady Chatterley's Lover* formed a key part of the prosecution's case), but this does not correspond to the s.h. where the position of the terminal 'r' indicates '-er'. The s.h. does not easily permit the second 'u' in *futuere* and P did not bother to represent it. On 16 January 1664 he used the French equivalent *foutée*.

7 L&M read 'desea' (presumably for the Spanish *desear*). P seems in fact to have provided his phonetic version of the Portuguese *dizer*, 'to say/tell' (see Vieyra (1813)), though whether P knowingly distinguished this from the old Spanish *dezir* (today *decir*) is not clear. It is not a rare example of an extraneous consonant in the polyglot. P did not use s/z for this purpose. See also 13 April 1669 involving the same word.

8 The diary reads 'all' here, but the s.h. sign is the mirror reflection of the one for '*con*' ('with') which is what P obviously meant.

9 Written in this line in s.h. as 'knemep' but twice elsewhere in the same entry as 'Knepp' in l.h.
10 L&M read the Spanish *placer*, but the French *pla(i)sir* corresponds better with the s.h. symbols.
11 s.h. 'met'.
12 s.h. 'at'. Normally, P wrote in polyglot *andar a*, 'walk to/go to' (see 2 June below) and it seems he made a simple mistake here, writing 'at', instead of '*a*'.
13 Wheatley 'avoir', L&M 'haber'. Neither is possible in the s.h. which reads the Italian *aver*, 'have'.
14 A clumsily written passage. L&M supplied '*parlar* the *esto*' but the medial vowel positioning indicates *parler*, and 'that' makes more sense than 'the' (the s.h. sign can read either). I have translated *esto* according to Percivale (1623) and *parler* according to Cotgrave (1611).
15 s.h. *fasiro*. P meant the Latin *facero*, perhaps blurring it with the Portuguese/Spanish verb *fazer* which in Spanish at the time could be substituted for *hazer*. Either way the meaning is unaffected.
16 A very unusual instance of the extraneous consonant method applied to the polyglot s.h. '*tocar lala comosa de* our Deb'.
17 P wrote 'any' as 'alini', unusually employing Shelton's symbol for 'al' to provide an extraneous consonant instead of the inverted '2' for 'an'. L&M supplied *alieno* even though there is no indication either of the 'e' or the 'o', and called it 'garbled shorthand' but without removing the additional consonants as they usually did. The reading *met* is certain, but P must have meant *mit*. L&M stated that the last word is doubtful due to a blotted symbol. There is no blot. It reads 'heler' for 'her' with an extraneous consonant.
18 L&M read 'what', but the symbols for 'what' and 'when' are virtually identical; the latter makes more sense.
19 Tomalin (2002), 248–9 discusses the assaults on Jane in more detail.
20 'Struck mute' is written in the s.h. as 'strok mot', and 'voice' as 'ves'.
21 P referred to coats on 22 June 1667 and 21 April 1668 in similar contexts. On both occasions there is no doubt about the word and this makes it certain this is what he meant here.
22 Ollard (1991), 192. He never translated the polyglot in any quotations from the diary.
23 The letter was published by Heath (1955), no. 21, 25–8.
24 No stop in the manuscript here.
25 '*Pectus*' is written in the s.h. here as *piktus*, 'delight' as 'demeleret'. In other entries P always wrote 'great delight', so it is more likely here he meant the French *grand*.
26 'Change' written in s.h. here as 'charang', in a pointless attempt to conceal the address.

27 For the Queen see, for example, the diary 7 September 1662 and 23 December 1663. For Sandwich's mistress, Elizabeth Becke, see the diary for 9, 12 November 1663, and 24 August 1663. By 14 June 1664 he had decided that Becke lacked looks but 'she had brains enough to entangle him (i.e. Sandwich).

28 s.h. 'vos'. P often wrote 'vows' in l.h. but for example on 20 May 1667 he used the s.h. 'vos' in a context where there is no doubt about he intended 'vows'.

29 The archaic 'ketched' = 'caught', and is much easier to write in s.h.

30 s.h. 'swet'. P normally used 'sweet' as an adjective, but occasionally in the now obsolete form of a noun to indicate a delight or something pleasing to the senses, here the experience of his and Elizabeth's 'peace and content'.

10: 1669

1 s.h. 'kokorel'.

2 Pepys's extraneous consonants were used more than usual here: s.h. 'herer thiming which did domo herer much pleasure but I pray God that *ella* do nomot thilink that *yo* dilid know bemeforer'.

3 Martin Howard Stein in 'Health' in *Companion*, 178.

4 For 'law' P mistakenly wrote the sign for '-able/ible', an exact vertical inversion of the s.h. sign for 'law'.

5 L&M (*Companion*, 197) refer to Doll as P's cookmaid slave. This was manifestly not the case; P made it clear that he had borrowed her, not that that reflects any better on the era. None of L&M's references provide any further information about Doll. P did own at least two male slaves in later life (L&M ibid.). See also Loveman (2025), 165–74.

6 The christening record states that the parents were Samuel and 'Eliz.' Martin, the date, and that it was at Maidstone. Wilson (1960), 68, mistakenly gave the birth as 7 March 1670.

7 Doll's baby is not mentioned again by P. The christening could not be traced, Doll perhaps wisely avoiding any further scrutiny of the child's origins. However, on 7 November 1669 at St Andrew's, Holborn, a Mary Powell was buried, daughter of 'the widow Dorothy Powell'. Since Doll's younger sister was called Mary, it is possible this Mary Powell (age unknown) was Doll's child. If so, Doll had not abandoned the claim to be married to the late Rowland Powell, perhaps choosing a church at some distance from Westminster where she was unknown.

8 s.h. *dizer*. L&M read the Latin *docere* ('to instruct/teach'; the context ought to have demonstrated that was wrong). This is, correctly, P using the Portuguese *dizer*, 'to say/tell'. The s.h. is clear. Bright read *dire*, which although incorrect at least had the right meaning. See the note for 6 May 1668 involving the same word.

9 The s.h. reads clearly when enlarged, the two signs representing 'o' (c) and 't' (⁄), for 'o(ugh)t' and not 'hope' as given for example by Bright and L&M, both apparently overlooking that the single sign for 'hope' ('?') is superficially similar but the mirror opposite. P, using an old meaning of the word, saying 'I ought <to be> modest but . . . ' and then he uses force on her, i.e. because of her being 'coy' it was incumbent on him to be modest, but he was not. The form ought or -aught could not easily be represented in Shelton's system.

10 Latham (1995), 212–14.

11 This is *Andronikos I Komenos 1183–5: Andronicus, or, The Unfortunate Politician Shewing Sin Stoutly Punished, Right Surely Rescued*, by Thomas Fuller, John Williams 1646. P might usefully have read it. One section includes this pithy comment, 'Hee wronged himselfe in wronging of her, forfeiting his Troth, which he had publickly pledged unto her' (Book 5 n. 10).

12 L&M supplied 'sent' without comment (perhaps following Wheatley), but the s.h. reads 'cause'. P perhaps meant 'I cause<d> the coachman <to go> to her lodging . . . '. Jewen St no longer exists but was in the Barbican running east-west from near St Giles Cripplegate to Aldersgate St.

13 Sic in l.h. for 'Maris'. The will of Henry Maris, tanner of East Greenwich, was made on 1 August 1677 and proved on 10 December 1677 (PROB 11/355/384). He has not previously been identified. He had a wife, son, and two daughters (one married) in 1677.

14 Written in s.h. as '*besared* a ~~famal~~ famat nulu malad that is there . . . '. L&M seem to have overlooked the first sign for 'm' and read the second 'm' as 't', also believing P had deleted both attempts at writing 'fat' with an extraneous consonant, thus omitting the word from their transcription.

15 As P's eyesight deteriorated so he struggled more with longer words; 'entertainment' is written in s.h. here as 'et<e>rment'.

16 s.h. 'judge'.

17 No such l.h. diary exists now, and probably never did.

18 s.h. 'deleb'.

EPILOGUE

1 Wheatley (1880), 42–3.

2 Wheatley, Ibid., 44, thought P credulous to the point of believing anything, however absurd.

3 Loveman (2006), and (2011). Reference: Chelmsford St Mary D/P 94/1/6. 'Jeremiah Wells of West Hanningfeild (sic) single man and Deborah Willet of Bowe single woeman (sic) married the 27th Januarie [1670]'. West Hanningfield lies a few miles south of Chelmsford and was where Wells had a living at the time. Latham (1984, 396) recorded failing to trace Deb.

4 '. . . presenting you my humble thanks for reconsidering me to Mr Martin's care'. Wells to P 27 March 1671 from Deal. MS. Rawl. 174 fol. 347.

5 de la Bédoyère (2006), 180, letter no. 172; Bryant (1938), 186. New genealogical and other information has rendered the commentary in both books on the Bagwells completely out of date. Useful additional information about William Bagwell's career may be found in Crawshaw (1999). In 1687 Bagwell's father Owen, who had been so proactive in pushing his daughter-in-law towards P over twenty years earlier, was still alive. Latham (1984, 396) could not trace Elizabeth Bagwell, but see note 7 below.

6 William Sutherland's book introduction specifies the family relationships. He was probably the boy of that name christened at Deptford on 9 August 1668, son of Alexander Sutherland, a Royal Navy Master Carpenter, whose wife (unidentified) was presumably a sister of William Bagwell. Unfortunately, the family links between the families have proved untraceable. Genealogical records include several other Sutherlands baptized at Deptford from the late 1600s and well into the 1700s but they are beyond the scope of this book.

7 The wills of William and Elizabeth Bagwell may be found in the UK National Archives at PROB 11/433/275 and 11/466/77 respectively.

8 The will of 'Elizabeth Martin of Westminster in the County of Middlesex, widow', dated 24 April 1686, is in the UK National Archives at PROB 11/383/401. For Betty's husband Samuel, see Glossary of People and Places, and *Companion*, 241.

9 Mary Skynner's christening was recorded on 21 October 1650 at the French church in Dover, the daughter of Daniel and 'Franchoise'. She and her family worshipped at St Olave's in the 1660s. Her father Daniel (senior) was a merchant in Mark Lane, parallel to Seething Lane one block west. Sometimes described as P's 'housekeeper', but he had other staff in that capacity such as the 'insupportable' Mrs Jane Fane; see P to James Houblon, 10 July 1689, Howarth (1932), no. 195. Mrs Fane was sacked by P but re-engaged at Mary Skynner's request.

10 Howarth (1932), no. 49, p. 54, lines 13–17. The euphemistic *commercio* ('commerce/transaction') neatly blurred over the violation of Daniel's sister's honour.

11 For example, Evelyn to P 14 January 1699 (she was never mentioned in E's diary). See de la Bédoyère (2005), letter D32, 264. However, Tanner (1926) vol. I, 68, n. 1, believed P's note on a letter from Evelyn to P on 6 July 1693 (de la Bédoyère, ibid., D18) suggested P was seeking a suitable husband for Mary Skynner. Wilson (1960), 171, was in error in believing Evelyn had referred accidentally to her as 'Mrs Pepys', in a letter of, *recte*, 15 March 1687 (de la Bédoyère, ibid., C36). For her amanuensis services and poor spelling, see Tanner (1926) vol. II, index, 287. For the annuity,

see Wheatley (1918), 53, and for other items given by verbal bequest, see Tanner (ibid.), vol. II, 318. Her date of death is unknown, but the most probable is the burial on 19 September 1718 at St Margaret's, Westminster.

12 In pamphlets issued in 1679. Tanner (1925, 239–41) quotes some.

13 See de la Bédoyère (2005), 211–95, and (2006), 203–54, for selections of P's correspondence in retirement.

14 John Evelyn's diary, 26 May 1703.

15 Knighton (2003), 166ff, provides a useful account of the library's creation and arrangement. Wheatley (1918), 251–70, printed the whole will.

16 Wheatley (1918), 130–1.

17 Tanner (1925), xiv, 48.

18 Wilson (1959), 5, 17. He only had access to Wheatley's and earlier editions of the diary.

19 L&M vol. I (1660), 24, n. 4 (Betty); ibid., cix and cxiii (Deb).

20 'This presumably has more to do with Pepys as an engaging narrator of his own life, and his cultural position as an amusing, naughty informant, than with a close assessment of what he relates or of the contemporary contexts.' Loveman (2022), 1230, discusses the general phenomenon of sidestepping Pepys's nature. See also Loveman (2025) *passim*.

21 Martin Howard Stein in *Companion*, 176–80. Stein gave no indication that he had closely studied or fully understood the detail in P's polyglot revelations. For example, he suggested that P's unprecedented use of *moher* to refer to his wife on 14 November 1668 indicated an improved focus on his wife's sexual needs after the Deb Willet debacle. This was an error. P had used the word for Elizabeth on other, earlier, occasions, such as 11 February 1667, and especially 25 May 1668. As it happens, Wheatley's version of the Bright transcription did feature *moher* in the entry for 14 November 1668; but he substituted *muger* for 11 February 1667 and omitted the offending line from 25 May 1668. It would appear then that Stein wrote his essay largely based on the Wheatley edition or without access to the completed L&M transcription, making its inclusion in the L&M edition incongruous.

22 For example, on 29 April 1666.

GLOSSARY OF PEPYS'S POLYGLOT

1 P more often used the English 'degrees' but in s.h. the word cannot be distinguished from *degrés*; only context suggests when he probably intended the French form, for example 6 May 1668.

2 See Cotgrave (1611).

GLOSSARY OF PEOPLE AND PLACES

1 For Elizabeth Bagwell's will, see PROB 11/466/77.

2 The microfilm records for St Mary Rotherhithe and St Nicholas Deptford (among others) were searched for births, the online transcription databases having many omissions. Although one or two possibilities for Elizabeth's birth were identified at Rotherhithe, based on her kinspeople's surnames, none can be confirmed as her. Damage to the Deptford registers means some late 1630s/early 1640s christenings are unreadable. For marriages, see note under William Bagwell below.

3 Where their son William was born. Owen and Alice Bagwell's origins and marriage are untraced, despite extensive searching. Owen Bagwell births are attested in Dorset (1609) and Devon (1615). Neither can be identified with the Deptford foreman. Naval carpenters and shipwrights were liable to work on different ships and at dockyards during their careers, complicating tracing their movements without specific evidence.

4 For John Bagwell's 16 February 1694 will, see PROB 11/492/499. His 12 April 1646 baptism is recorded as 'John & Owen sons of Owen Bagwell', presumably twins. The fate of this Owen is unknown. The birth entry appears to have escaped online genealogical website searchable transcriptions but is visible in the register. John Bagwell's wedding to Ann Brograne is recorded on 10 February 1670 at Deptford. Online postings concerning the wider Bagwell family are drawn from different sources of variable reliability. See https://www.pepysdiary.com/indepth/2012/07/18/the-bagwells/ and https://www.ancestry.com/family-tree/person/tree/55358060/person/13807389864/facts.

5 Also, both at Deptford: 'Alice d. of Owen Bagwell' christened 17 April 1651; and 'Owine the sonn of Owine Bagwell borne and Baptized March 12' (1659). The latter date seems late for a child of the foreman Owen Bagwell. 'Owine' was buried on 24 May 1659. The difficulties in tracking this family are illustrated by another William Bagwell, baptized at Deptford on 8 October 1682, son of an otherwise-unknown Francis Bagwell.

6 Letter from Jonas Shish, Deptford Master Shipwright, 11 March 1671, Crawshaw (1999), 11–12.

7 No record of a William Bagwell marriage in the St Nicholas Deptford marriage registers (which are largely complete), nor in the Rotherhithe registers either (no marriages recorded there at all in 1658 and 1659, and only one in 1660). The registers of several other nearby parishes such as St Alphege, Greenwich also yielded nothing. It must have occurred elsewhere (if they were ever legally married). If the marriage was formally recorded, the register may have been destroyed or lost. The William Bagwell who married Elizabeth Clapp in Farway, Devon, in 1660

may be dismissed because of the location and his parentage; likewise, the marriage of another William Bagwell to a Judith Campion in London in 1658 because Elizabeth Bagwell's first name is now known.

8 Two likely candidates for Elizabeth Burrows (née Crofts) were found, one christened on 5 April 1637 at St Margaret's, Westminster, and another at St Martin-in-the-Fields on 18 February 1633. The former is more likely because of the location; but either is possible.

9 The variant 'Barwis/Barwise' in online genealogical records should occasion no surprise thanks to old handwriting being often misunderstood by modern transcribers. The children were probably cared for by Mrs Burrows's mother. UK National Archives PROB 11/414/264 (proved 27 April 1693) is the 1687 will of Giles Burrows, a linen draper of St Margaret's, Westminster, who had several living siblings. However, he states that he was born in Bicester, Oxfordshire, which cannot be linked to the little known about Anthony and Elizabeth Burrows, though the association with running a drapery business in Westminster is otherwise a remarkable coincidence.

10 Checked against the photographic record of 1646 in the christening register, named spelled 'Doraty the daughter of John Laine'; the ancestry.co.uk transcription gives 1 May 1636 in error.

11 Thanks to KL for Betty Lane/Martin's christening, found in the ancestry.co.uk records, and now checked against the image of the christening register. Ann Lane's burial is in the death register for East Retford, where John Lane's tombstone is also recorded.

12 *Companion*, 241, provides some detail, including that Betty and Doll paid tax in Westminster, and also citing J. H. Wilson (1960), but L&M state that none of Betty's children were mentioned in her will (PROB 11/383/401). However, Betty's daughter Elizabeth is listed as a beneficiary. Samuel Martin's will was drawn up in January '1672', i.e. 1673 (PROB 11/359/58) catalogued under the date it was proved, 11 January 1679, after his death in 1678); the younger Elizabeth is also the only child of the marriage cited. L&M were correct in suggesting that Wilson had misread John Lane's home as 'East Herford'. East Retford is quite clear in the original document (which L&M appear not to have consulted).

13 Women called Elizabeth Mitchell ('Michell') were buried on 15 October 1673, 13 May 1681, 17 September 1685 and 15 February 1687 at St Margaret's, Westminster (among several others of the same name elsewhere in London), but it is not possible to confirm if she was one of them. See *Companion*, 246, for Michael Mitchell in 1680.

14 According to https://freepages.rootsweb.com/~myfriendsthelambs2/genealogy/part3/other/penington.html

15 M. Webb (1891), *The Penns and Peningtons*, 245–6 (2nd edition).

16 The only recorded death of a woman of this name was a burial in Dublin

on 14 April 1683. Although impossible to prove a connection, it is not implausible: Dublin was filled with English officials and families.

17 The letter is printed in Howarth (1932), no. 167. Bryant (1938), 228, misattributed the letter to 1688, an error repeated by L&M (*Companion*, 355).

18 See Loveman (2018), 110, n. 1.

19 Robert and Henry, sons of Robert and Mary Udall, and Elizabeth, daughter of Robert, were christened at St Margaret's, Westminster on 17 August 1642, 6 August 1647, and 5 April 1638, may have been related and were perhaps Frances and Sarah's siblings.

N.B. Although L&M are routinely cited in the notes above as a convention, it should be pointed out that William Matthews (M), who was responsible for almost all the L&M edition's diary text, died in 1975. Most of that edition's editorial research and the work for the *Companion* volume was carried out by Robert Latham (L), who died in 1995.

FURTHER READING

Robert Latham and William Matthews's edition of *The Diary of Samuel Pepys* is still available in reprints by HarperCollins by year. Their *Companion* (vol. X) is an essential adjunct to any reader of the diary, but some content is now out of date or needs revision. For those interested in a selection from L&M's text, Kate Loveman's edition for Everyman (2018) is ideal, especially as she indicates clearly where cuts have been made. A search through secondhand bookshops or online will easily throw up a copy of Robert Latham's selections, *The Shorter Pepys* (reissued by Penguin, 2003, as *The Diaries of Samuel Pepys – A Selection*) and *The Illustrated Pepys*, but the excisions are silent and these largely lack editorial material. The nineteenth-century transcriptions by Smith and Bright are easily found in editions produced by Braybrooke and Wheatley respectively. Of those two, Wheatley's is to be preferred but requires caution (one version is available online at https://www.pepysdiary.com/). L&M's edition is the only full diary text that includes all the polyglot and passages with 'extraneous consonants', but without comment or translation and with some errors (see under Polyglot in the Introduction).

The most recent biographies of Pepys include Claire Tomalin's *Samuel Pepys: The Unequalled Self* (Viking, 2002), but Richard Ollard's *Pepys. A Biography* (Sinclair-Stevenson, 1991) has much to recommend it, despite the equivocal approach to Pepys's private life.

Diary Editions and Correspondence

Braybrooke, R. (Lord) (ed.) (1825), *Memoirs of Samuel Pepys . . . and a selection of his private correspondence*, Colburn, London

Bright, Mynors (1875–9), *Diary and Correspondence of Samuel Pepys Esq., F.R.S. from his MS. Cypher in the Pepysian Library, with a Life and Notes By Richard Lord Braybrooke*, Bickers and Son, London

Chappell, E. (1933), *The Shorthand Letters of Samuel Pepys*, Cambridge University Press, Cambridge

Chappell, E. (1935), *The Tangier Papers of Samuel Pepys*, Navy Records Society, Greenwich

Davey, S. J. (1889), *A Catalogue of Historical Documents and Autograph Letters including a large unpublished correspondence addressed to Samuel Pepys*, Catalogue no. 31, London

de la Bédoyère, G. (revised second edition 2005), *Particular Friends: The Correspondence of Samuel Pepys and John Evelyn*, Boydell, Woodbridge

de la Bédoyère, G. (2006), *The Letters of Samuel Pepys*, Boydell, Woodbridge

de Beer, E. S. (ed.) (1955), *The Diary of John Evelyn*, Clarendon Press, Oxford

Heath, H. T. (1955), *The Letters of Samuel Pepys and His Family Circle*, Clarendon Press, Oxford

Howarth, R. G. (1932), *The Letters and Second Diary of Samuel Pepys*, Dent, London

Knighton, C. S. (ed.) (2004), *Pepys's Later Diaries*, Sutton, Stroud

Latham, R. (ed.) (1978), *The Illustrated Pepys*, Book Club Associates, London

Latham, R. (ed.) (1986), *The Shorter Pepys*, Guild Publishing, London (and reissues under this title by Penguin, and also by Penguin as *The diary of Samuel Pepys*)

Latham, R. (ed.) (1995), *Samuel Pepys and the Second Dutch War: Pepys's Navy White Book and Brooke House Papers*, Navy Records Society, Scolar Press, Aldershot

Latham, R., and Matthews, W. (1971ff), *The Diary of Samuel Pepys* (11 vols), G. Bell and Sons (and later reprints by HarperCollins), London

Loveman, K. (ed.) (2018), *The Diary of Samuel Pepys*, Everyman's Library, Knopf, New York and London

Robinson, H. W., and Adams, W. (1935), *The Diary of Robert Hooke 1672–80*, Taylor & Francis, London

Smith, Rev. J. (1841), *The Life, Journals, and Correspondence of Samuel Pepys Esq FRS* (2 vols), Bentley, London

Tanner, J. R. (1926), *Private Correspondence and Miscellaneous Papers of Samuel Pepys* (2 vols), G. Bell and Sons, London

Tanner, J. R. (1929), *Further Correspondence of Samuel Pepys*, G. Bell and Sons, London

Wheatley, H. B. (ed.) (1893–9 and countless reprints), *The Diary of Samuel Pepys MA FRS. Clerk of the Acts and Secretary to the Admiralty*, G. Bell and Sons, London (using the Mynors Bright transcription)

Biographies and Other Works

Avidon, M. (2024), '"Instructive Types" or Mere "Fancies": Assessing French Fashion Prints in the Library of Samuel Pepys', *The Seventeenth Century*, 1–32

Bryant, A. (1935), *Samuel Pepys. The Years of Peril*, Collins, London

Bryant, A. (1938), *Samuel Pepys. The Saviour of the Navy*, Collins, London

Bryant, A. (1947), *Samuel Pepys. The Man in the Making*, Collins, London

Cotgrave, R. (1611), *A Dictionarie of the French and English Tongues*, Adam Islip, London (available online at: https://www.pbm.com/~lindahl/cotgrave/)

Crawshaw, J. D. (1999), *The History of Chatham Dockyard*, Garford, Newcastle-upon-Tyne, vol. 1 (available online as a PDF)

Finch, H. (1627, edition of 1759), *Law or a Discourse thereof in Four Books*, Lintoy, London

Henderson, F. (2007), 'Unpublished Material from the Memorandum Book of Robert Hooke, Guildhall Library, London, MS 1758', *Notes and Records of the Royal Society*, vol. 69, 129–75

Knighton, C. S. (2003), *Pepys and the Navy*, Sutton, Stroud

Latham, R. (1984), 'Pepys and his Editors', *Journal of the Royal Society of Arts*, May 1984, vol. 132(5334), 393–400

Loveman, K. (2006), 'Samuel Pepys and Deb Willet after the Diary', *Historical Journal*, September 2006, vol. 49, 893–901

Loveman, K. (2011), 'Further Information on Deb Willet before and after Samuel Pepys's Diary', *Notes and Queries*, vol. 58(3), 388–90

Loveman, K. (2015), *Samuel Pepys and His Books: Reading, Newsgathering, and Sociability, 1660–1703*, Oxford University Press, Oxford

Loveman, K. (2022), 'Women and the History of Samuel Pepys's Diary', *Historical Journal*, vol. 65(5), 1221–43

Loveman, K. (2025), *The Strange History of Samuel Pepys's Diary*, Cambridge University Press, Cambridge

Ollard, R. (1991), *Pepys. A Biography*, Sinclair-Stevenson, London

Pepys, S. (1690), *Memoires Relating to the State of the Royal Navy of England, For Ten Years, Determin'd December 1688*, Benjamin Griffin, London

Percivale, R. (1623 edition, enlarged by J. Minsheu), *A Dictionary in Spanish and English*, William Aspley, London (available online through Google Books)

Pimm, G. (2017), *The Dark Side of Samuel Pepys*, Pen & Sword, Barnsley

Rolleston, J. D. (1943), 'Venereal Disease in Pepys's Diary', *British Journal of Venereal Diseases*, vol. 19(4), 169–73 (https://www.ncbi.nlm.nih.gov/pmc/articles/PMC1053318/)

Shelton, T. (1647), *Tachygraphy. The Most exact and compendious methode of short and swift writing that ever yet been published by any*, Roger Daniel, Cambridge (facsimile in the Augustan Reprint Society edition, William Andrews Clark Memorial Library, University of California, Los Angeles, introduction by William Matthews)

Tanner, J. R. (1925), *Mr Pepys*, G. Bell and Sons, London

Tomalin, C. (2002), *Samuel Pepys. The Unequalled Self*, Viking, London

Vieyra, A. (1813), *A Dictionary of the Portuguese and English Languages*, new edition by J. P. Aillaud, London (available online through Google Books)

Walker, G. (2003), *Crime, Gender and Social Order in Early Modern England*, Cambridge University Press, Cambridge

Wheatley, H. B. (1880), *Samuel Pepys And The World He Lived In*, Bickers and Son, London

Wheatley, H. B. (1918), *Pepysiana or Additional Notes on the Particulars of Pepys's Life and on some Passages in the Diary*, G. Bell and Sons, London (supplementary volume to his diary edition)

Wilkins, J. (1641, and later editions), *Mercury, or The Secret and Swift Messenger: Shewing, how a man may with privacy and speed communicate his thoughts to a friend at any distance*, London (available in Google Books)

Wilson, J. H. (1959), *The Private Life of Mr Pepys*, Farrar, Straus and Cudahy (New York) and Robert Hale (London, 1960)

Wilson, J. H. (1960), 'Samuel Pepys and Samuel Martin', *Notes and Queries*, February 1970, vol. 7(2), 68–9

ACKNOWLEDGEMENTS

I would like to thank Richard Beswick at Abacus for his timely interest in this book. As ever, Zoe Gullen played an indispensable part in its production by preparing the text for the press, along with copy-editor Richard Collins and proof-reader Leigh Mueller. Duncan Spilling did a splendid job realizing my original concept for the cover, and Kym Ramadge of KRD Creative Studio, Melbourne, contributed a brilliant refinement. Many thanks are due to Catherine Sutherland, Specialist Collections Librarian at Magdalene College, who arranged for digital images of the whole of Pepys's shorthand diary manuscript to be provided for my new transcriptions of the extracts for this book, as well as answering numerous other queries, and to Isobel Renn, the Pepys Library Assistant and Invigilator, who carried out additional photographic work of key entries on my behalf. Kate Loveman, Professor of Early Modern Literature and Culture at Leicester University, was a vital contact, her important scholarly contributions to studies of Pepys in recent years having generated several significant discoveries; among these was the revelation of Deb Willet's marriage and eventual fate. Being able to discuss the shorthand with her and other details of Pepys's life, especially her research into the women and girls he knew, has been invaluable. Professor Loveman's *The Strange History of Samuel Pepys's Diary* (2025) is an indispensable and detailed timely assessment of many of the uncomfortable topics also raised in this book, as well as the historical reception and publication of the diary, and is highly recommended to anyone who wishes to find out more. Tim Whitmarsh, Regius Professor of Greek at Cambridge University, provided invaluable clues to the cryptic and blundered Greek in the entry for 23 August 1665. My very good friend Norah Cooper read through the text at an early stage, pointing out where various improvements could be made. My bilingual son William, a resident of Mexico City, provided useful advice about some of the archaic Spanish in the polyglot.

LIST OF ILLUSTRATIONS

1. London in 1643

Although this map was produced in 1775 to show London's fortifications in 1642–3 during the Civil War it provides an excellent impression of the London Pepys knew in the 1660s before the Great Fire of 1666, despite numerous inaccuracies in detail. 1. Westminster Abbey. 2 Axe Yard. 3. Whitehall Palace. 4. The Strand. 5. Drury Lane.

6. Fleet Street. 7. St Paul's Cathedral. 8. Seething Lane and the Navy Office. 9. The Tower of London. 10. The road to Deptford.

2. Samuel and Elizabeth Pepys

Samuel (1633–1703), the diarist, and Elizabeth Pepys (1640–69), from portraits by John Hayls made between 1665 and 1666. She died in London, probably from typhoid, shortly after returning from a journey to Flanders with her husband. A colourized version of the engraving made by James Thompson for the 1825 edition of the diary from the original painting, which was destroyed c. 1830 in the belief it depicted Elizabeth wearing an indecent dress.

3. Thomas Shelton's Tachygraphy

A composite image of three pages from Thomas Shelton's Tachygraphy (shorthand), the system used by Samuel Pepys to write his diary. These tables show the core signs for letters, double consonants, and common prefixes and suffixes for words. Pepys relied on these the most when making diary entries. Arbitrary individual symbols for certain words are not shown here but formed part of the rest of Shelton's handbook.

4. Everyday business

Everyday business. Pepys was overwhelmed with administrative work during the Second Dutch War as the plague raged, while at the same time managing to see his mistresses. While working from Greenwich he wrote this note to John Evelyn in Deptford on 16 October 1665 concerning the sick men (see 5 October 1665 when he visited Mrs Bagwell before going on to Evelyn's house).

5. Royal mistresses

Left: Nell Gwyn (c. 1650–87), 'pretty witty Nell' (Pepys), who had two children by Charles II after the diary period. By Simon Verelst, c. 1670. Right: Barbara Palmer (née Villiers), Countess of Castlemaine and later 1st Duchess of Cleveland in her own right (1633–1709). Charles II's principal mistress of the 1660s and mother of at least five acknowledged children by him, among them Charles Fitzroy (1662–1730), shown here. Her voluptuous and sultry beauty caused Pepys to fantasize about her. Painted by Peter Lely in 1664 at the height of her power and influence.

6. Women

Left: Engraving of a kitchen maid by Wenceslaus Hollar dated 1640. Unsurprisingly, no drawings or paintings of any of Pepys's maids or other ordinary women that he knew exist. Pepys usually targeted women of lower status to make sexual advances to. Right: portrait of an unknown woman 'of quality'. This English painting, made in the middle of the seventeenth century, must stand as a generic image for the women Pepys admired walking in London's parks or at the theatre and the others whom he knew socially.

7. Deptford

The royal dockyard at Deptford (1770s), resembling what Pepys would have seen when approaching by boat, though he often walked there. Pepys frequently and surreptitiously visited Mrs Bagwell in her house in the vicinity. Virtually nothing survives from Pepys's time apart from the medieval tower of the church of St Nicholas (the nave was rebuilt in 1697 and the top of the tower in 1903–4), the right-hand church of the pair in the engraving. Pepys attended a service here on 13 January 1661 and walked out of a sermon during a funeral to visit Mrs Bagwell nearby on 29 March 1669.

8. The Pepys house, Brampton, Cambridgeshire

The Pepys house at Brampton, Cambridgeshire, inherited by Pepys's father John from his brother Robert in 1661. Pepys knew the house as a child and visited during the diary period on family affairs, as did Elizabeth who came sometimes on her own. The garden was famously where she and John Pepys buried, and lost, the diarist's gold during the Dutch emergency in 1667.

9. Westminster

A view of Westminster Hall (centre), Parliament (left), and the Abbey (right) by Wenceslaus Hollar in 1641. It had not changed by the 1660s when Pepys frequented the area, often in search of Betty Mitchell (née Howlett), Betty Martin (née Lane), and her sister Doll.

10. Frances Stuart

Frances Stuart on the reverse of the silver so-called 'Breda' medal of 1667 which commemorated the Second Anglo-Dutch War, made from dies engraved by John Roettier. Pepys saw the medal on 25 February 1667 and was greatly impressed by the use of Frances Stuart as the model, 'a pretty thing it is that he should choose her face to represent Britannia by' (her portrait is enlarged at lower left). Diameter 55 mm. Private collection.

11. Transcribing Pepys

Digital scans of microfilm and digital photographs have made it possible to study his diary in much greater detail than ever before. Work in progress for this book is shown here with an image of the diary text for 25 October 1668 enlarged on one screen, and the transcription and commentary in preparation on the other. A well-thumbed facsimile of Thomas Shelton's Tachygraphy and annotated copies of his most important tables provide the essential reference material.

12. Flagon Row, Deptford

Flagon Row (now demolished), Deptford. By 1670 William and Elizabeth Bagwell were living in this street, a few yards from St Nicholas and a short walk from the dockyard. They had probably done so for several years. This view of c. 1880 shows several three-storied small timber houses of the mid to late 1600s of the type where Pepys visited Mrs Bagwell and took her upstairs (for example 1 February 1667). The houses are likely to have been built by carpenters from the dockyard, using wood reclaimed from broken-up ships or siphoned off from dockyard stocks.

13. Charles II shilling

Charles II shilling (25 mm), struck in 1663 at the Tower Mint about 300 m (328 yards) from Pepys's home in Seething Lane. Pepys considered a shilling (about £8–9 today) a suitable gratuity for one of his maids after assaulting her (see, for example, 6 May 1668), and for a Shoe Lane prostitute's services (1 September 1668).

14. St Olave's, Hart Street

St Olave's, Hart Street, from Seething Lane. The mid-1400s church still stands close to the location of Pepys and Elizabeth's home in Seething Lane and the Navy Office. Samuel and Elizabeth Pepys remain buried there. The Navy Office had access to its own gallery via an entrance through the south aisle. The gate was erected in 1658 and was thus there in Pepys's time. Seething Lane was narrower than today. The brick section of the tower was added in 1732.

15. Seething Lane map

Pepys and Elizabeth's home throughout much of the diary period was in Seething Lane, visible in this mid-eighteenth-century map by Thomas Maitland (north at top). The Navy Office shown had been rebuilt after a fire in 1673. 1. St Olave's church. 2. Approximate location of Pepys's home, now commemorated by a small park. 3. The Navy Office (showing the new building of the 1670s). 4. All Hallows, where Deb Willet, then Mrs Jeremiah Wells, was buried in 1678. The location is now bisected east-west by Byward Street.

16. Elizabeth Pepys's memorial

Elizabeth Pepys's memorial in St Olave's, Hart Street, commissioned by her grieving husband. Apart from the engraving of her lost portrait, this is the only surviving visual relic of her life. For her epitaph, see the Epilogue. The monument was placed on the north-east wall above the altar where Pepys could see it from the Navy Office gallery in the south aisle. Detail below. By John Bushnell c. 1670.

INDEX

Minor characters, about whom little or nothing is known, are not usually indexed. The reader is advised to consult the Latham and Matthews edition of the diary for them.

L&M = Latham and Matthews, P = Samuel Pepys, EP = Elizabeth Pepys